FLY FISHING OUTSIDE THE BOX

The author pointing out a nymphing fish to M. Laurent Sainsot of the International Ritz Fario Club of Paris, on the River Itchen
(Photo by Peter Lapsley)

FLY FISHING
OUTSIDE THE BOX
Emerging Heresies

PETER HAYES

Coch-y-Bonddu Books
2013

FLY FISHING OUTSIDE THE BOX
Emerging Heresies
by
Peter Hayes

First published by Coch-y-Bonddu Books, Machynlleth, 2013

ISBN 978 1 904784 56 2

Coch-y-Bonddu Books Ltd, Machynlleth, Powys SY20 8DG
01654 702837
www.anglebooks.com

Printed and bound by Gutenberg Press Ltd, Malta

Dedication

Fly Fishing Outside the Box is dedicated to Di, my wife and friend for fifty years, whose immersion in carriage driving is as deep as is mine in fly fishing (but I shall never be a World Champion).

> *'Felix, qui potuit rerum cognoscere causas'*
> (Virgil, v 490, Georgics, 29 BC)
> *Happy is he who has been able to understand how things get to be the way they are.*

A note on thinking outside the box and the 'nine dot' puzzle:

This puzzle has been used as a (not entirely reliable) gauge of lateral and creative thinking.

The goal is to join all 9 dots of the 'box' with four straight pencil lines or fewer, and you may not lift the pencil off the page or trace the same line more than once.

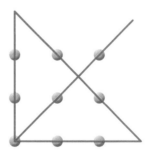

Here's one solution – to succeed you have to go outside the lines of dots, in other words, think 'outside the box' – hence the phrase.

Contents and Synopsis

CONTENTS   p 7

ACKNOWLEDGEMENTS   p 15

FOREWORD   pp 17 to 18

PREFACE   pp 19 to 23

Chapter 1   pp 25 to 33
HOW FISH SEE THE DRY FLY

Most dry flies penetrate the surface film and are taken, preferentially, by trout as emergers and not as hatched-out duns. This is the reason why the ordinary angler can hope to, and does, do well using the classic dry fly. It helps to understand what's going on – but you don't have to be either an invertebrate nerd or a religious nut to succeed. Once you do understand a bit more of what's really going on you may well feel a stronger need to move forward as a hunter of trout on your own terms, following your own ideas rather than being spoon-fed.

Chapter 2   pp 35 to 45
EMERGING HERESIES

Here we are reviewing the evidence for the orientation of natural nymphs as they rise and emerge at the surface – and finding that it is diametrically opposite to the orientation with which our upstream imitation nymphs and emergers are tied and fished. If we want to fool fish by giving them the right GISSO (General Impression of Size, Shape and Orientation), then we certainly need to use reversed nymphs, at least when presenting them upstream in the surface film, or in the last inch below it. Ditto emergers.

Chapter 3   pp 47 to 61

HATCHED FLY PRESENTATION

Our hatched dun imitations face the wrong way whenever the breeze is in an angler's face, whether they are fishing upstream or downstream. Did we really want that to happen? The good old boys had it right in their imitations of duns and also in their presentation of them. It was the angler's job to float the fly. The 'dry fly revolutionaries' wanted the fly to float itself by its modern labour-saving design but it didn't, they goofed and led the sport astray in this and other respects, and you can be among the leaders of its restoration if you enjoy a good rant and join me in this further heresy.

Chapter 4   pp 63 to 73

HOW FISH EAT

The way our tippet tethers the fly and frustrates the trout in his attempts to eat it is something that many anglers don't consider, and something that most angling writers have failed to address. Avoiding drag, generally recognised as key to not putting fish off the take and causing rejection, is also crucial, mechanically, in terms of the physics of getting the fly into the trout's mouth without it bumping out, hitting bone, or sparking ejection. Loose tippet is the answer.

Chapter 5   pp 75 to 81

CASTING EVERY WHICH WAY – BUT LOOSE

I hesitate to instruct: I'm neither qualified nor good at it. What I try to do here is to pass on my own experience for what it is worth, so that the reader can try out the casting techniques I (and others) use, and see if they work for you. All I can say is that there is a pretty solid body of conviction and practice in the sport that uses the same drag-avoiding techniques – and one which dates from at least as far back as Halford, writing in 1889.

Chapter 6   pp 83 to 87

HOW FISH SEE THE LEADER

You actively reduce your chances of hooking trout if you sink your dry fly leader. I explain how and why, and if you follow my heresy and ensure that it floats you will find I'm right and catch more fish. And we discuss ways of approaching fish without scaring them in the light of their incredibly sharp vision.

Chapter 7   pp 89 to 97
WHATEVER FLOATS YOUR FLY

This is a review of the development of fly floatants in the past and recommendations for the present. Here again, *quot homines, tot sententiae* – there are as many opinions as there are men to hold them, and everybody has their favourites. I specify three products that I use for different purposes and in different situations, each of which has its advantages. For me, keeping flies made of CdC floating without discolouring them is very important, as is keeping the leader in the surface film.

Chapter 8   pp 99 to 109
EXPERIMENTS OUTSIDE THE BOX

Other people's earlier experiments with flies and fish may be anecdotal in character and often lack the rigour of statistics – yet somehow, given that they were undertaken by very serious people searching after angling truths, one has to believe them. There are lessons in all of them for us today, and I have not flinched from drawing the conclusions. You might criticise me for this, but in my view 'you better believe it'. And they are fascinating.

Chapter 9   pp 111 to 117
FISHING IN RIVERS WHERE YOU CAN'T SEE THE FISH

If, as I mainly do, you fish rivers that keep their trout from your gaze by having a dark background or by being turbid, you can still go and learn from rivers that you can see into and draw on the help of seen fish to give you guidance on how to fish when the trout, and hence you, are 'in the dark'. There are more fish in front of you than you think. This chapter provides straightforward help with turning unknown unknowns into known unknowns.

Chapter 10 pp 119 to 125
FISHING SO THE FISH CAN'T SEE YOU

This chapter is all about how not to scare fish. It concentrates specifically on how to avoid scaring fish that are there in front of you but that you can't see. As well as examining the general principles of non-scary on-stream behaviour we look at the measures you can take to avoid rod flash and line flash, and end up addressing the finer points of how the angler can 'dress to kill'.

Chapter 11 pp 127 to 133
CAN WE GET BETTER FISHING THAN WE'VE GOT?

Most fly fishermen would agree on these three desiderata: more fishable water; more (wild) fish; and more fly life. Can they have them? The answer is yes, and in this chapter we look at how to improve the carrying capacity of a fishery both for fish and for fly. We discuss the importance of enhancing the sporting character of our fishing by concentrating where possible on wild fish, and managing our fisheries for their benefit. We look at physical river restoration, but also at the more radical idea of biological restoration.

Chapter 12 pp 135 to 155
DRY FLIES FROM OUTSIDE THE BOX

These 16 flies are the product of a fevered angling mind, and a great deal of experimentation with trout whose reactions could be seen over a period of more than 30 years. I didn't invent them – I just stole the bits. They are mainly fly designs rather than patterns – they are constructed to perform in particular ways, on and in the surface, and you can tie them in any colours and many materials to match the natural flies in the waters you fish yourself. Basic tying instructions and some hints as to their use are included, and full instructions for the 'PhD', the 'Muskrax', and the 'Hayestuck'.

Chapter 13 pp 157 to 165
TANGENTIAL THOUGHTS ABOUT NYMPHING

While I have a lot to say on the construction of dry flies I have very much less to say on nymphs and nymphing. In contrast to the dry fly, where it is my view that people have really gone a bit astray over the years, missing some good opportunities for imitating things that trout really value as food, the same is not really true of nymphs. Still, I've learned a few tricks, developed a few very successful patterns, and I'm glad to pass them on. We look at how nymphs behave in the water, and how they can be managed to fit in with the expectations and feeding habits of the fish.

Chapter 14   pp 167 to 175
THE EVENING RISE – WHAT EVENING RISE?

I thought it might be helpful to include a chapter on the kinds of strategies one can use to approach difficult situations – and the evening rise (or the lack of it) sprang to mind as one of our greatest challenges. So here we have a look at the reasons why the evening rise is so problematical and yet so important. Then we cover some practical ways of addressing them.

Chapter 15   pp 177 to 187
PUSHING THE ENVELOPE

This chapter deals with mimicking the hidden secrets of the trout's larder. It deals with the imitation of a bunch of little things that don't look very nice but which feature heavily in the diet of trout, and can in fact be tied as flies and presented to the fish successfully, given a certain amount of application on the part of the angler. Although these little critters are not always easy to imitate, the results of success can be surprising, and their use can account for some extremely big fish.

Chapter 16   pp 189 to 195
IMITATION'S LAST FRONTIER

Baetis (olives, that is) can account for as much as four-fifths of your small upwing flies, and all of them crawl beneath the surface to lay their eggs and then float up as exhausted spinners, mostly to stick to the underside of the surface film. A problem as yet only partly solved – but we review some creative innovations, each of which gets us closer to a solution.

Chapter 17   pp 197 to 203

PLAYING AND NETTING BIG TROUT

Getting to the point where you can confidently play and net big fish is a
steep learning curve with many points at which you can fall off and with
a high risk of disaster attending your efforts to learn. The stakes are high,
and the smaller your experience the scarier it is. So, no pressure then,
as they say. In this chapter we go through the logic of how best to take
away the fish's advantages and empower your own. It's the dos and don'ts
really, but it may help to add understanding in terms of the whys.

Chapter 18   pp 205 to 215

PURISM HAS GOT US FACING THE WRONG WAY

The Dry Fly Revolution was initially a technical one, but became a moral
and ethical one when Halford took it over. With his harsh judgmental
light shining on the sport, facts as well as perceptions became twisted
in favour of fishing 'perfectly dry' at the peril of not being a gentleman.
The sporting, intuitive, and imitative development of fly fishing was
kidnapped and we still need to escape from the box we got put in. Worse
still, dry flies fished upstream face the wrong way when the wind is in
our face.

Chapter 19   pp 217 to 235

READING OUTSIDE THE BOX

A fresh look at the history of fly fishing before we got put in the box.
From Berners to Halford they all fished floating flies, and fished them
as dry as they could. The past does inform the present. These Ancients
may have worn frock coats and tricorn hats but they were at least as clever
as we are, and much better fly fishermen than we have been allowed
to think. And they fished the dry fly not the wet. It was the hatched fly
they imitated. They wrote well and, if we read carefully, they tell us just
exactly how they fished the fly. With 19th century tackle 'improvements'
however, their flies got dragged below the surface, and floating your fly
got more difficult in the first half of that century.

Chapter 20   pp 237 to 243
FULL CIRCLE WITH TENKARA?

It is more than a little weird to see the modern, state-of-the-art, UK fly fishing world being led back in full circle to those only-just-lost simplicities and skills by this thing called Tenkara that comes to us from undocumented, oral-tradition Japanese practices via the highly web-documented, enthusiastic descriptions of new American aficionados. Our own, much stronger, more highly developed and copiously documented fly fishing tradition had effectively been suffocated. Nature abhors a vacuum.

Chapter 21   pp 245 to 251
A PHILOSOPHY OF FLY FISHING, FROM OUTSIDE THE BOX

Because I take up such a robust position on so many things in fly fishing, I thought it might help to understand where I am coming from if I tried to give the reader some insights into my own personal beliefs about life and fly fishing. But don't worry, I stick pretty close to fly fishing and I don't wander off into any tragedies of personal life or worries about sex, death and taxes.

Chapter 22   pp 253 to 256
CAUDAL FIN

A closing thought or two for fly fishing duffers, middle of the road anglers and experts alike.

BIBLIOGRAPHY   pp 257 to 263

ABOUT THE AUTHOR   pp 265 to 266

INDEX   pp 267 to 272

off the saddle of the cock, that are old and stiff, to withstand the motion of the water; and fine silk, both floss and tying for the bodies of the small flies, and every thing in unison, as you read in the book; handling every thing sparingly, delicately, and nicely in the fingers. There is a good deal of the "battle fought" by letting the nails grow to a pretty fair length so as to hold on grimly.

A CATECHISM OF FLY-MAKING,

By WILLIAM BLACKER.

Question.—What do you mean by Fly-making?

Answer.—I mean the artificial assimilation of those beautiful insects that appear on brooks and rivers during the summer season.

Q.—What are these artificial flies used for in general?

A.—They are principally used to afford gentlemen rural amusement and recreation, by their taking both trout and salmon with the rod, line, and fly.

Q.—Name the different materials requisite for making the Artificial Fly.

ACKNOWLEDGMENTS AND THANKS

MANY EXPERTS HAVE GIVEN me unstinting help in putting this together, both with contributory material, deep thought, and what, if they were not all of them much my superiors in knowledge and experience, I should call 'peer review'. My undying thanks are due to Tony Hayter, Paul Schullery, Andrew Herd, Timothy Benn, Charles Jardine, Don Stazicker, Stuart Crofts, Craig MacAdam, Ron Holloway, Cyril Bennett, Jon Bass, Owain Mealing, Tony Wells, Richard Ward, Paul Procter, Clive Hallam, Peter Lapsley, Chris Russell and Stephen Beville.

These include some of the greatest scholars on angling history and some of the greatest developers of advanced fly fishing, as well as some of the greatest behaviourally-inclined aquatic entomologists. In addition, through David Beazley I have been able to make reference to the work of Jack Heddon, who was a leading scholar on the development of angling history and literature.

I'm particularly grateful to Peter Lapsley, Don Stazicker, Stuart Crofts, Paul Procter, Dr Cyril Bennett, Lin Baldock, Nick Sawyer, Owain Mealing, Mark Williams and Dave Collins for allowing me to use their images (all unacknowledged photographs are ones I've taken myself).

And I am, as it were, posthumously grateful to the originators of all the historical images that I've been able to photograph and use without their permission – they being long gone to the great fishery in the sky and the images out of copyright and in the public domain (that said, I fervently hope I have not gone beyond my rights in using any image and hereby apologise unreservedly in advance if I have). And I think that, among them, William Blacker sums my general topic up nicely in the 'Catechism' shown on the left.

The Flyfishers' Club has been my retreat for some of the cogitation time and its library has been an invaluable resource, so especial thanks are due to David Beazley as Librarian and John Morgan as Curator, as well as to our Secretary, Paul Varney, for his unfailing warm welcome.

FOREWORD

THIS IMPRESSIVE BOOK is the work of one of our most observant anglers. Peter Hayes has thought in more than usual detail and depth about many of the interesting facets of fly fishing. When I first read his well-illustrated manuscript, I was intrigued with his heresies and by the evidence for them, and I consumed it quickly and avidly. At the end, an apt quotation from Virgil came into my mind: *Felix, qui potuit rerum cognoscere causas* – 'Happy is he who has been able to understand how things get to be the way they are.' I was gratified that Peter adopted it for the dedication page of the book.

For many of us some aspects of fly fishing can be bewildering and vexing, but if they are properly addressed, and understanding grows, they can be a source of delight and increasing pleasure in the sport. Anglers who are no longer on the nursery slopes and have left the basic sort of didactic manual behind will find much to ponder here. Peter places in review many of the long accepted 'truths' of fly fishing. Some of these have been laid down by figures of authority while others have evolved more slowly from the practices of much earlier times. His belief is that many of them need to be rethought and replaced with alternative ideas. Of course, many parts of former wisdom remain sound and some go back surprisingly far in time: the technique, for instance, of deliberately casting a slack line derived from Marryat and was passed on to the angling public by Halford in 1889.

Peter will feel rewarded if his readers are inspired to do a good deal of thinking. Skues had a similar approach. He got tired of reminding people not to call him an authority and urged them to do their own thinking and experimenting but the suggestive musings and hints in his writings must have given them much about which to think. As this book says: 'there is a great deal still to discover and exploit.'

Improved understanding of fly fishing tends to come in waves, and the waves never come without a groundswell that stirs up food for feeding anglers. I think this book may turn out to be a biggish wave and the feeding frenzy it gives rise to may well run and run.

The second time I read the by-then finished book, I read it slowly as if savouring a good wine. And upon arriving at the last page, I took an oath to be more observant and open-minded, and will hope in this way to become a more effective practitioner on the river.

Tony Hayter

Tony Hayter is the author of *F M Halford and the Dry Fly Revolution*, Robert Hale 2002, and the keenly awaited *G E M Skues: The Man of the Nymph*, Robert Hale 2013.

PREFACE

THE POINT OF THIS book is to engage the reader's mind about fish, fly, tackle and angler interactions, in such a way as to encourage you to think differently about them. In that rather dreadful management-speak phrase, to think 'outside the box' so as to solve the 'nine dot' puzzle. Hence the title of the book. I am not at all apologetic about the title. Why am I not?

Because I think that we fly fishermen have been rather programmed without realising it into accepting a structure of supposed truths about fishing the fly; not exactly brainwashed into it, but perhaps inertia-washed would be a better term. Into a box we find it hard to think outside.

You will probably not agree with everything, or indeed, perhaps much that I say here. But if I make you think about it, and for a moment at least evaluate things from a different angle, I shall be happy with that.

If I succeed in that, then the evidence for and against the positions that I take up in this book will present itself to you over your upcoming fishing

Getting feedback from watchable fish
(Photo by Peter Lapsley, River Itchen)

life, and you will be able to assess that evidence in the light of my heresies – and see if you want to join me in them or not. (By the way, there's not much in this book that isn't equally applicable to my second favourite fish, the grayling. I catch more grayling than I do trout.)

I shall try hard not to throw out any babies with the bathwater. Much received wisdom remains wise. Never say always, never say never.

But welcome to the world of alternative thinking – and at least some heresy.

If I achieve my objective, you will get a short read, and a long think. John Gierach said (in *Another Lousy Day in Paradise*): 'One thing I've noticed about fly-fishing writers is, the less sure they are of their subject, the fatter their books get.' By that criterion I am semi-sure of mine.

What makes me think I know anything at all is my experience of thirty years of fishing clear streams with strong populations of highly watchable wild trout and grayling: streams in which I have been able to observe the reactions of individual fish, experimentally change tactics and fly design, and follow promising avenues informed by damn good observational feedback. I have been able to pay detailed attention to *What the Trout Said* (great title, terrific book by Datus C Proper). Thirty years, that is, on the trout streams of England, chalk and limestone spring creeks, and a dozen long visits to similar spring creeks in New Zealand.

HOW TO USE THE BOOK

With each of my chapters I should like you to feel that you have been given the key to a door.

The key opens the door but does not show you all the contents. In each case there are a lot of things in the room beyond, over and above those that I talk about. What I hope is that you will be led by the things that I do talk about to discover other things for yourself. I want each chapter to encourage you to explore new approaches, and to carry out experiments of your own. To get the most from this book you will need to develop your curiosity about the insects that trout use for food, and how the insects and the trout behave – and how this behaviour can be capitalised on by your flies, tackle and presentation.

You might think that everything has been done and everything has been written on fly fishing – that everything has been enumerated and described with respect to the natural flies that everything has been created and written down with respect to artificial flies, and that trout behaviour has been thoroughly understood and described as well. You would be very far wrong. Ordinary intelligent fly fishermen still have a great deal to discover and exploit, particularly in the behavioural arena. And not all of it is in the advanced super class – quite simple lessons learnt can pay off in spades.

The iconic American author, Edward R Hewitt, wrote in *A Trout and Salmon Fisherman for Seventy Five Years* (1948): 'The Ancients wrote of the three ages of man; I propose to write of the three ages of the fisherman. When he wants to catch all the fish he can. When he strives to catch the largest fish. When he studies to catch the most difficult fish he can find, requiring the greatest skill and the most refined tackle, caring more for the sport than the fish.'

I also have tried to write this book so that it can be of benefit to fly anglers at all stages of their development. We all start from where we are now – as Spike Milligan said in that mad Goon voice, 'Everybody's got to be somewhere.' It can help to know that the skills of a brain surgeon are not required in order to move forward. It can help to know that what you thought was a pretty awful cast can in fact, with a tweak, be an extremely effective drag-avoiding one.

It can help to know that most of our flies do not succeed in representing any specific insect, so that you are not in fact required to be an entomologist before you can fish the fly effectively. It can also help to know that although we often fail to imitate with any accuracy the precise insect we thought we were imitating, we do in fact succeed in imitating the life-stage rather than the species – and that trout target particular life-stages preferentially.

So you don't need a degree in Latin and Greek; you don't need a Ph.D. in entomology; you don't need to carry 100 reference books in your car; and most of the time, one single fly box will do.

Once you have got over the perceived need to be terribly serious about everything, you can start to fish in such a way as to make it fun again instead of a kind of drudgery, attended with the fear of getting it wrong. Key to this, will be your rediscovery of how to gain hunter knowledge and hunter skills – you need to get back to being a child again. And this stuff is as important for the advanced fly fisherman as it is for the beginner.

At the same time, I have tried to write material that the advanced fly fisherman will find interesting and stimulating as well. For a long time, while (I think) I was getting on with learning to fish in a more challenging manner; more effectively; and in particular for wild fish, I had rather bypassed the history and literature of fly fishing. This was because I felt that life was too short to absorb it all (and there is one hell of a lot of it) and also if I am honest I thought that those good old boys had little to teach me in this new world of carbon fibre, fluorocarbon, and silicone.

In doing so, I fell into the common trap of those looking backwards in time, which is to allow ourselves to believe that previous generations were actually rather dim compared to ours. Nothing could be further from the truth. Because 'the Ancients' had to work with far more difficult materials and gear, they had to be pretty good at what they did. And they were every bit as observant and as capable of thinking problems through as we are, whilst being 100 miles closer to real country living and the real need for sporting skills.

As a result I have discovered that the study of angling history and literature is fascinating and useful, and although I am a mere butterfly at it, and no kind of real scholar, I have tried to bring out some of the more interesting stuff and draw some conclusions from it for the reader.

Photographic fly-sharing at the club barbecue
Two keen members capture the author's latest patterns
(Photo by kind permission of the Wilton Fly Fishing Club)

So this book has within it, intertwined, on the one hand a 'lite' scamper through some of what I think is the most interesting work of our angling precursors; and on the other, an exploration of the latest behavioural interpretations of fly and fish behaviour and their implications for our future use of flies, tackle, and techniques. I have not set out to write comprehensively about any particular aspect. As I say, I am aiming to give the reader keys to open doors with rather than a complete and detailed view of everything that lies beyond.

The fly patterns in chapters 12 and 13 are offered in the spirit of sharing, as proven deceivers of trout. Take the ones you fancy.

This book sets out to offer balm to those bruised by purists; counselling for those confused by the dry fly code; insight to those for whom the explanations of how fly fishing works have been opaque; and a way forward for thinking anglers.

Fly-tyer's view

Angler's view from above

Trout's view from below
the fly having penetrated the surface, which acts as a mirror reflecting the river bottom

HOW FISH SEE
THE DRY FLY
(Thinking outside
the box)

THE PURIST'S DRY FLY, the very imago and spinner of the fly fisher's fly, has been defined as being upright, cocked, hackled, split-wing, floating perkily on the very tips of its hackle.

> 'A fly is said to cock in dry-fly fishing when it sits perkily upon the points of the hackle and rides the surface very high.'
> (Taverner and Moore, *The Angler's Week-end Book*, 1946, p 366).

Unfortunately for the definition-obsessed law-givers of the artificial fly, but fortunately for the success rate of the average dry fly angler, the reality is very different from the theory.

Classic dry fly
Right result, wrong reason

In practice just about every so-defined dry fly that is cast more than once quickly stops being a cocked, wings-upward fly floating perkily on the very tips of its hackle with its body suspended above the surface film. The hackle penetrates the film, as confirmed by no less authorities than Ted Leeson and Jim Schollmeyer in their *Fly Tier's Benchside Reference*, Paul Schullery in *The Rise*, and Andrew Herd in *The Fly*. It becomes a semi-submerged mess.

Firstly, a full-collar hackle produces a fly that is designed to fall over because it is round and will roll like a log (see the picture 'angler's view' on the left). Secondly, the hackle will soon penetrate the surface comprehensively, producing what Oliver Edwards has described as looking nothing like the real thing – 'stupid, spiky, sticking down things are wrong'. Thirdly, the

Above:

A stuck-shuck cripple emerger
(body to left, shuck to right)
preferred trout food

Below:

The escaped dun
not so much eaten by trout

abdomen, whatever it is constructed of, will not sit on top of the surface film but penetrate it and be seen clearly and directly through the water rather than upwards through the meniscus (see 'trout's view' on the previous page). And fourthly, the school of exact imitation will have insisted upon only two or three tail whisks, and they of something soft and bendy, so these will stand no chance whatsoever of holding the abdomen up.

The result is something other than a creation that was intended only to be seen by the trout as dimples in the mirror. Instead it is visible directly through the water having made a hole in the mirror.

Luckily for the fly fisherman, this is actually a very good imitation of an emerging fly with substantial portions still beneath the surface. An emerger,

while still pulling itself out of the shuck, does have 'sticking down things' in the shape of its still half-sheathed legs.

For the trout, an emerging fly, and more especially one which stays that way as it drifts towards it, represents a win-win in its constant lookout for a positive 'benefit for effort' equation. Such artificials get eaten by trout more frequently than do perfect floating dun imitations, simply because experience has taught the trout that the dun is likely to fly away at any second, whereas the emerger will take more time and the stuck or crippled emerger is a sitting duck. More certain food + less likely effort = a better bet for growth and survival is the main algebra driving trout behaviour. Happily for us the right thing happens for the wrong reason, and the fly designer's failure spells success for the fly fisherman.

This commentary applies to the 'classical purist's dry fly' (see 'the fly-tyer's view' on p 24). This is the cocked dry fly riding high on the points of its collar hackle with paired upright feather wings. It is the fly whose invention was disputed between the Ogdens and the Fosters in the 1850s; that was made mandatory at Haddon in Derbyshire ahead of the rest of the country in 1865; that was eventually adopted two decades later in southern England by H S Hall, Dr Thomas Sanctuary and G S Marryat who originated the double split-

The author's 'Hayestuck' emerger/cripple

wing tying; and then codified by F M Halford and his disciples. These latter believed, and sought to establish for the whole fly fishing audience, that for the chalk streams and spring creeks this was the *ne plus ultra* for all time, no further development necessary or required.

Many dry fly features have been designed since, which result in better dun imitations: hackles cut away in a 'V' underneath the fly, Marinaro's thorax dun tying, parachute hackles, Swisher and Richards style no-hackle duns, and ultra-simple, ultra-light CdC duns like my own 'KmC' illustrated on page 84. These alternative dun imitations can now be combined with far superior modern floatants to allow the dry fly man to present something to a trout which actually does float above the meniscus rather than sink into it. And which very rarely rolls over.

One really important moral to draw from this is that you can make your fly float too well. It might get more trout, fished 'semi-dry' as Halford described flies fished as emergers (this in his earlier work and weaker moments). You could be constantly changing your classic dry pattern, thinking that the trout are selectively devouring some species that you are failing to imitate, when in fact they are non-selective as to species, but absolutely keyed in to emergers of any kind. Letting the first pattern half-sink would have been a better plan, had you known. When you disappointedly kill the free-rising stock fish (whose genes you don't want to invade your wild gene pool), the autopsy is likely to show many more hatching nymphs and cripples relative to hatched duns, than you are seeing on the water. Skues autopsied his kill for over half a century and also marrow-scooped released fish for over 30 years, and that is a survey base numerous enough to demand respect. These were pretty much all rising fish, whether to nymph or dun, but he consistently found masses of hatching nymphs and no, or very few, duns.

'In this year (1938) as in all since I had taken to the use of a marrow spoon to extract the contents of the stomachs of my trout, nymphs preponderated to an enormous extent over all other food.' (*Farewell to the Itchen*, Flyfishers' Club Journal, Spring 1939.) Suited his book, but the book of an honest man. And Fred Arbona in the USA based a complete analysis of trout stomach contents on 1000 fish in which nymphs and emergers dominated (75% to 83% of Baetidae, Ephemerellidae, and Ephemeridae).

Halford himself, in *Dry-Fly Fishing*, recounts his spending over an hour throwing all his key dry patterns at a surface-feeding fish, which when eventually caught on a small sedge and autopsied, had in it 'an extraordinary conglomeration of shrimps, caddis, snails, larvae, and nymphae, but not a single winged fly'. Perverse old FMH quotes this to show the difficulty of distinguishing bona fide rises to the dun versus, well, dishonest ones to nymphs that might tarnish the angler were he to cast at them.

Meanwhile, let us perhaps just note the fact in passing, that Halford's cold and unequivocal logic was correct in one central plank of his argument. If you are not fishing your fly perfectly dry ... if any part of it penetrates the surface film ... if the trout sees something directly through the water instead of seeing just silvery dimples in the mirror ... you are not imitating the hatched fly.

Another moral is that you can get too clever designing emergers as such – a half-sunk, tail-down standard dry fly does a pretty good job. One really important thing about emergers is that they are somewhere between half as long again and twice as long as the hatched-out dun. That's one reason why, when people (as they frequently do) use flies much bigger than the natural, they catch fish quite successfully and do not get the refusals you might think would result. And they can look like a total haystack from below, which I think is why over-dressed shop bought patterns often catch fish as well as my snooty, small, sparse ones.

A long and messy BWO emerger/cripple

Newly emerged olive duns are usually light in colour. We match them by tying light-coloured bodies; but again, we are helped a bit by the fallibility of our patterns and materials, which, as many commentators on the flies of the exact imitation school have pointed out, darken when wet. So the rear of our semi-wet fly is a better imitation of the darker body of the hatching nymph. Again, perhaps, the right result for the wrong reason.

This is a crucial thing about emergers: the nymphal skin they are pulling themselves out of is usually darker than the emergent fly. And that is the bit that the trout has a clear and direct view of through the water. This may well explain the success of flies that fish with their abdomens in, rather than on, the surface film and which are dark in colour, such as the Parachute Adams. The Parachute Adams is probably the most successful, worldwide, of all floating flies. Another good case in point is the traditional Gold Ribbed Hare's Ear (fished very successfully by Halford in his early years before he rejected it on the grounds that he didn't know what it imitated) which, with its gill-imitating body half sunk, and its front floated by the dubbed hairs picked out and greased, is an emerger pattern to beat all comers. And Halford did know exactly what it imitated, because in 1889, in *Dry-Fly Fishing in Theory and Practice*, before he went fully into denial, he recommended it as a specific nymph imitation for catching bulgers.

So the half-time summary here says that trout don't see the classic dry fly as a hatched dun – or only rarely – they see it as an emerger or cripple. As a result they are more, not less likely to eat it, and that is a matter of considerable cheer to the angler who just wants to fish straightforwardly with classic patterns. Anglers who followed Halford's precepts imperfectly still caught trout; otherwise the Dry Fly Revolution would have struggled to survive. This apparently illogical factor is also something that the more technical angler can learn from and build on.

Imitating emergers, cripples and wind-blown drowners is a very good plan if you want to catch fish, but it is not dry fly fishing as Halford and his disciples chose to define it. He, by ensuring his fly fished perfectly dry, ensured that he remained a relatively unsuccessful angler (as Tony Hayter observed in his definitive book, *F M Halford and the Dry Fly Revolution*). But you or I, by allowing the classic dry fly that we love to fish only semi-dry, can be really quite successful without becoming entomologically obsessed, or pharisaical about dry fly patterns. Often falling short of perfectly dry are we, well ... bothered?

In the poker game of fly fishing, in which we guess the trout's hand and draw from the deck, it can be a better strategy to run through the fly box in terms of hatch-stage (spinner – dun – cripple – emerger – inert nymph – rising nymph) rather than to run though it in terms of imitated species (Small Dark Olive – Pale Watery – Blue Winged Olive – Iron Blue – Medium Olive – Brook Dun). Stick to the same suit, go for the flush rather than the straight.

On Andrew Impey's water on the upper Itchen there are several places where big trout congregate to feed in a hatch. Over the course of some kind invitations in recent years I have had the good fortune to find a couple of them – on the right day, at the right time. One feeding lie, and in particular, one fish is etched into my memory. The current comes off the true left bank guided by a bed of water crowfoot and is set nicely in to a small archipelago of fans of starwort interspersed with other Ranunculus beds from which, when the time is ripe, the flies hatch. It all looks very smooth and cool, but the weed beds speed the water over their rising scarps, and the resultant

Overview of the Itchen feeding lies

micro-drag is frightful. The trout tend to lie and feed with their tails on the upslopes of the weed, just where your fly drags most insistently.

The dominant diner has the best table, right behind the off-setting top stand of weed where the food lane offers most reward. In the middle of August two years ago I was looking upstream at him feeding, estimating him at around 3 lbs and trying to find a position from which I could avoid lining the half dozen slightly less aldermanic fish between us. The trout was rising, his nose breaking the surface much but not all of the time. He was not porpoising, as to trapped fly or spinner, and not bulging or turning hither and thither to migrating subsurface nymphs. Duns were emerging and flying away that looked like medium olives, not having the more erect elevation in the air of the BWO.

He was offered first my 'PhD', an olive dun imitation with wings divided, and outrigger legs provided by a bent-over loop hackle. Nodded at.

Then a KmC, a very simple, sparsely tied no-hackle pattern with a tall CdC wing. Both so far treated with hydrophobic fumed silica (that white powder stuff you brush into the fly). Inspected but rejected.

Then, my 'Hayestuck', cripple-cum-emerger pattern, in the same overall colour as the previous two flies, untreated. This got a swim-over and a very close look but no final commitment. Never stopped rising.

And what did get him (actually her) in the end was a greased-up GRHE nymph with added black feather fibre wing cases on a greased tippet, right in the film imitating the inert, about-to-hatch-in-a-heartbeat larva. Black wing cases provide serious 'trout cred' in a nymph pattern. She

was 3 lbs exactly and fought like a demon, putting everything else down.

A thunderstorm exploded on the river and I went home, never happier. The experience reinforced the point that rejection is your friend not your enemy. It tells you things. Usually.

FOOTNOTE: Halford in *The Dry Fly Man's Handbook* (1913, p 126) says, 'Years and years ago Marryat and I dressed most effective patterns to represent the nymphs of duns and mayflies by tying in a few fibres of black feathers at the head ...' There then follow their reasons for discontinuing their use, (breach of ethics, and too many fish lost and rendered shy).

Fly fishing on the chalk streams is not always so clinical
Luke Kozak fishing a blizzard Grannom hatch on the Hampshire Avon in the city of Salisbury in April 2012 (Photograph by Mark Williams)

Emerging Cloeon dipterum
(Photo by Dr Cyril Bennett)

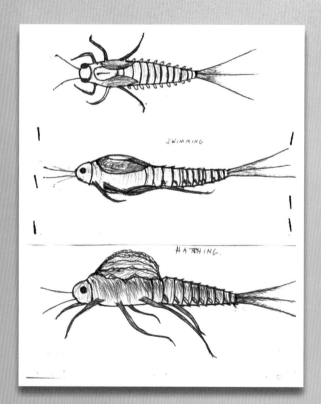

SWIMMING

HATCHING.

Frank Sawyer's drawings of resting, swimming
and hatching nymphs
(By kind permission of Nick Sawyer)

EMERGING HERESIES

WITH ALL THE STUDY of nymphs and flies over the last hundred years, there are still crucial aspects of how they live, move around, rise and hatch and return to lay eggs that arise from assumption and not observation and knowledge on our part. Are we right to present our upstream nymph with the head facing downstream? Are we right to present our dry fly ditto? Are the trout that reject us laughing at us too?

Are we sure of our orientation?

There are records of anglers, and a few naturalists, having started to watch nymphs rising to the water surface to hatch at least four hundred years ago. But for three hundred years, nymph behaviour was largely ignored and remained pretty much off the radar, not top-of-mind, for angling writers or fly designers. This remained true, even perhaps especially, when imitation of the hatched fly rose to pre-eminence over the later 1800s.

It wasn't until Mottram and Skues in the early 20th century that nymphs got really studied for imitative purposes in terms of their appearance and behaviour, although Halford had made detailed and accurate engravings of all life stages in 1889 and John Younger had suggested crude imitations as early as 1840 in

The first illustration of a modern no-hackle nymph
Mottram's 1915 hatching pattern for dimpling fish

Scotland. Every tyer of nymph imitations has tied the head of the nymph at the eye end of the hook. Most of the developers of nymph patterns have intended them to be fished upstream, and therefore the trout will see the artificial nymph coming towards it with its head downstream.

Nobody ever seems to have bothered to ask, or by observation to find out, whether the nymph in fact travels upwards to the surface head-downstream going with the flow, or tail-downstream, planing up against the flow. I have asked all my friends and scientist members of the Riverfly Partnership, and have only got a firm answer from one of them (and he self taught). Stuart Crofts (the well known Yorkshire angling teacher and guide) who knows a lot about fly behaviour as well as taxonomy, has studied enough Baetis rhodani (large dark olive) on the River Wharfe to be able to say that they make their way to the surface mainly facing downstream, going with the flow (unable to make way against it) and angled upwards to the surface – but he adds that this may not hold good for other species, or rivers. Another oasis in this desert of ignorance is Ephemera danica, our UK mayfly, the nymph of which swims actively and quickly to the surface with its head pointing as near as possible vertically upwards – albeit carried downstream by the current. At point of hatch however it faces upstream as the current swings it round. Enough of us have seen that to make it firm knowledge.

Mottram's 1915 swimming nymph pattern for bulging fish
floss silk with hackle-point wing cases

Dr Cyril Bennett (of the John Spedan Lewis Trust for the Advancement of the Natural Sciences on the River Test, and the Salisbury and District Angling Club Centre of Excellence for Aquatic Invertebrates) confesses he doesn't know, and sensibly says that the main reason is that he has only watched nymphs surfacing in slack water, because otherwise they are swept past too quickly and cannot be easily watched. It seems from what Frank Sawyer wrote that he was also concentrating on relatively slack water situations, probably again so as to be able to see the nymphs.

But I have been able to ask the question of Ron Holloway, who was the Ffennel family's keeper at Martyr Worthy on the River Itchen for a quarter of the last century. Ron, I knew, had spent time every day lying flat on their boarded footbridge watching nymphs, fly, and trout through the cracks – thousands of hours in total, millions of nymphs.

Ron tells me that in his observation nymphs swim up head-upstream during the rise to the surface, angled upwards and planing up against the current but being carried downstream at the same speed as the current, and that they maintain the head-upstream orientation on engagement with the surface film, and through the hatching process. He says that Frank Sawyer told him that he had successfully tried reverse-tied nymphs himself but he had not tried to market them (he probably thought it would be like trying to push water uphill: nymphs were bad enough juju in those days, never mind reversed ones).

Both Ron and Cyril also saw numerous nymphs simply floating upwards rather than swimming, and indeed there have been many arguments as to whether they are buoyed up by gas or oxygen secreted between the outside skin of the nymph and the already separating skin of the fly underneath (See Footnote 2 to this chapter). The many aborted rises of mature nymphs, widely reported by observers, put them at risk of being eaten prematurely, must therefore have value to the animal and may be to test buoyancy. Judging from photographs like Cyril's at the head of this chapter, from the award winning video work of Ralph Cutter of the California School of Fly Fishing, and from the 1941 paper by Kimmins of the British Museum (quoted in Footnote 2), I believe they are buoyed by gas, but it's the appearance and the action that matter to us in our attempts at imitation. Gas shines out. It's the less-than-fittest rising nymphs that drift and get preferentially eaten by trout and the fittest that survive. Dead-drifting a shiny beadhead nymph gets results. That's why. And if it is sinking when the trout sees it you might think that he'd expect it to be rising and reject it – but no, it's actually a perfect movement – to imitate the nymph that hasn't yet collected enough gas, and isn't going to make it to the surface this time. Right result, right reason.

Immature nymphs that are merely 'behaviourally drifting' (as their non-hatch-related general movement around their habitat is described) for example to find new feeding grounds, are likely to retain their head-upstream orientation when doing that. In my underwater video footage of feeding Baetis nymphs on the surface of stones, they universally face into the current. And specific nymphs, like some Heptagenids (flattened nymphs) migrate over the stream bottom, both upstream and sideways to the shallows prior to hatching. If we are to imitate behaviourally drifting

Baetis and upstream migrating Heptagenid larvae, we may again do better with a reverse-tied nymph.

These moving-times are also when nymphs are most easily available to trout feeding close to the bottom, whether in deep or shallow water. We can be sure that the trout will target these food lanes no less than they target visible (to us) food lanes at the surface, and probably more – since they can feed more in their comfort zone, in slower moving water that demands less energy, and with less exposure to possible predators. When you are able to watch trout bottom-feed in clear streams like the upper Itchen, the limestone spring creeks of Derbyshire, and in the staring clarity of many New Zealand rivers, you will often see them feed with intensity in what is clearly a concentrated sub-surface food lane.

The angler is less likely to spot such feeding behaviour than that of fish bulging, dimpling, or rising to the hatching nymph (see chapter nine). But it may be a very big opportunity missed. And when we look for (or guess at) such feeding activity and fish deep, we again need to ask ourselves whether our nymphal orientation is right.

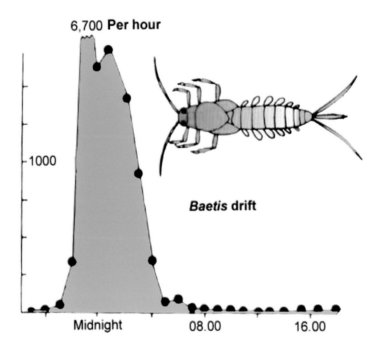

Nymphs on the midnight rampage
(Chart by kind permission of Dr Mike Ladle)

There is, importantly, one time when nymphs are particularly active in moving in terms of both drift and migration, and that is the late evening. When it is as if somebody threw the switch and the river goes dead, it is not because the trout stopped feeding, it's because they went down the water column to a new and better food lane. Note that numbers drifting, at 6700, go off the chart before midnight. (The chart shown is by Dr Mike Ladle, recently retired from the Centre for Ecology and Hydrology, a keen angler himself and the author of many illuminating papers on stream ecology that weave together the symbioses and interrelationships of the component organisms.)

Nymphing at night has been described to me as the best kept secret in fly fishing.

There is still a lot of uncertainty surrounding these thoughts. Perhaps least doubt surrounds the orientation of the nymph when it is actually in position to emerge and is the prisoner of the meniscus. At this point it is inert, as Skues maintained, except for its internal struggle to draw its fly body and legs out of the nymphal shuck. Hydrodynamics would tend to suggest that the action of the stream on the longer, lighter abdomen-cum-shuck orients, or re-orients the fish-shaped emerger into a head-upstream, tail-downstream position at this point in the process. If the nymph had been headed downstream (like Stuart Crofts' observed Baetis rhodani, large dark olive) while swimming up and before becoming inert, that head-upstream position would be swung into and established in the last inch of the rise or on contact with the surface, when active swimming ceased. Ron Holloway's lifetime observations show that on the Itchen olive nymphs face upstream as they rise, and stay facing upstream as they hatch. Dr Craig MacAdam observes (in a personal comment) that the dun, once emerged, needs to be flying upstream to make up for earlier downstream drift of both eggs and nymphs as they grow. He believes that the default emerging orientation is head-upstream – but that a fly will be turned by any wind to face into it as they emerge and take off into it, flying upstream when airborne.

If this dominance of the head-upstream orientation is correct, we should definitely switch to a reverse-tied nymph or emerger pattern when imitating the emerging insect, and we should consider using reverse ties for the rising nymph too (but weighted, if at all, at the tail).

I can see myself here falling back on the eternal mutter of the scientist, 'more research is required' (code for 'I didn't think of this when I designed my study'). The one certainty is that we shouldn't be as sure as we are of

Winged Larva

Blacker's emerger with both larval and hatching fly bodies

our nymphal orientation any more than we should be sure of our dry fly orientation.

At least some early writers knew that flies hatched from larvae that grew underwater. John Taverner in 1600, discussing the hatching of nymphs in *Certaine Experiments Concerning Fish and Fruite*, says: 'And of such young flies before they are able to fly awaie, do fish feede exceedingly.' He also, 400 years ago, noticed their repeated attempts to hatch before success was achieved.

The earliest emerger imitation I can find is the extraordinary and explicit pattern illustrated by William Blacker (*Blacker's Art of Fly Making*, 1855 edition – see above). In this, the nymph body is shown separately from, but attached to, the body of the dun. His instructions make it clear that this was a fly with two bodies and that the trout should see it as such.

My picture of a half-emerged BWO overleaf makes it clear how explicit is that appearance of two bodies in a crippled, swamped, or 'stillborn' emerger. And Blacker twice recommends it for use on windy days and says it will do best where a strong rapid stream runs into a deep pool – i.e. when and where drowned emergers will be most plentifully available to the fish. This is very early, very good observation of trout food availability, carried

mohair at the shoulder to hang over the larva body, and to flatten the end of the gut a little where you tie on the tail, which keeps it on. **Tie the larva at the side, so as it may appear like a double body to the fish in the water.** It may be made by tying on the wings first, and let them remain until the body, the larva, and the hackle, are all tied in their proper places,

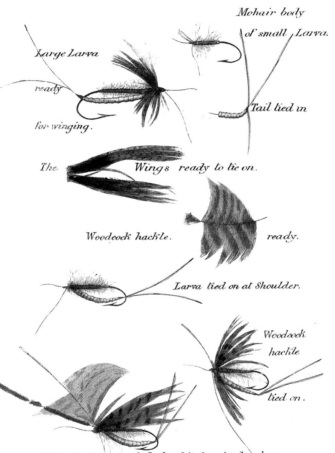

TO MAKE THE WINGED LARVA.

Page 42.

Mohair body of small Larva.

Large Larva

ready

for winging.

Tail tied in

The Wings ready to tie on.

Woodcock hackle. ready.

Larva tied on at Shoulder.

Woodcock hackle

tied on.

Wing, hackle, & harl for head tied on to show how to complete it.

BLACKER'S FLYMAKING.

Stillborn BWO
with two bodies apparent

through to fly design and to specific recommendations for presentation. Analysis of other writers in the last half of the 18th century and the first half of the 19th including Richard and Charles Bowlker, and John Younger, shows that several of them were entirely appreciative of how the dun got to be on the surface – from below, not from above. And that they also realised the imitative opportunity afforded by this, before the start of that clearly very exciting period, the second quarter of the nineteenth century – the cradle of the cocked dry fly.

Charles Bowlker may have been confused about the detailed life cycle of flies but he gave a long and fairly accurate description of the emergence, mating, and egg laying behaviour of mayflies in the early editions of *The Art of Angling*.

I'm not sure to what extent later (and indeed current) writers on the subject of the emergent fly have been cognisant of how far its imitation and use go back.

I suspect that the conspiracy of angling writer forgetfulness has indiscriminately condemned all the early boys for having thought that flies fell upon, rather than hatched from, the water.

On a cool, bright, wind-chilly September afternoon on the Welsh River Usk, Owain Mealing and I were skunked and sitting on the low gravel bank in the slight fuzz of a lunchtime glass. No fish rose, but nervous water betrayed the presence of trout in the gently shelving shallows – fish however that were cruising and that we found impossible to target in the glare. I noticed flat clinger nymphs headed consistently over and between the flat rounded stones towards the shore. First dozens, then hundreds of them. Then they started to hatch, from water too shallow for a trout to get them ... and apparently from underwater, leaving no surface shuck. Closer inspection revealed that they were hatching into the beautiful Ecdyonurus insignis, a large greenish upwing.

They were making a slow exit from the shuck on the overhung

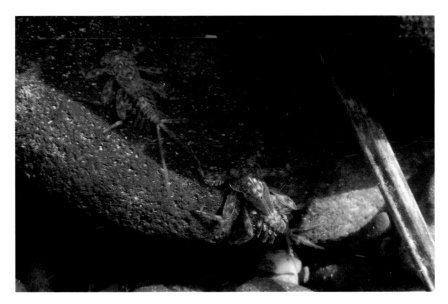

Ecdyonurus insignis nymphs migrating shorewards to hatch, River Usk

undersides of the stream-worn stones, underwater, then crawling with wings swiftly extending to the stone tops, and popping out in flight. I took a series of a dozen macro photographs of the whole process and of the migrating nymphs – not easy, because they were very shy and any shadow or movement sent them back under cover. On the migration they had dark wing cases and thoraces that were bright with gas between the nymphal integument and the fly's body underneath. Dark seen from on top, but the gas shining through seen from the side.

But at the time Owain and I had nothing with which to imitate them. We were stumped as well as skunked. (Owain is my closest fishing companion: this year, 2013, will see us fish together on the Welsh Usk, on Lough Corrib in Ireland, on the Big Laxa in Iceland, and across the rivers and

Gas clinging to the dun's body as it exits from its shuck, still under water

Ecdyonurus insignis
hatched underwater from nymph

spring creeks of South Island New Zealand. We share a rebarbative sense of humour.)

In this very shallow water, the hunting trout will be seeing them from the side rather than from on top. So the best imitation will have black, dark olive or brown wing cases, and probably a hairy dubbed translucent thorax and abdomen ribbed with thickish gold or silver wire (and that would be all the weight you'd need). A large Gold Ribbed Hare's Ear nymph with dark wing cases has subsequently been shown to be effective – there on the Usk, and also on the Mataura river in New Zealand, where big trout regularly enter the shallows on similar nymph foraging expeditions. Nothing too sophisticated in tying terms: there seems to be no need to try and make the nymph totally flat like the natural, or to tie in sideways-projecting, knotted-fibre legs like you see in fly-tying demonstrations at fly shows, which in my experience simply de-stabilise the swim of the nymph.

FOOTNOTE 1: Both Gary LaFontaine and Fred Arbona draw attention to the North American Heptagenids hatching out underwater like this. LaFontaine pointed to the Quill Gordon, Epeorus pluralis in the Beaverkill and other similar rivers, and Arbona to Rhithrogenids in the whole length of the Yellowstone River, in Michigan rivers, and in many Western rivers.

FOOTNOTE 2: The eminent British entomologist D E Kimmins responded to a paper by M E Mosely, Halford's equally eminent co-worker, with the following words (culled from his article in *The Entomologist*, August 1941) showing that the careful scientific observer of behaviour often has more to offer the fly fisherman than the scientist who specialises in taxonomy, and also adding support to those who believe that gas is an important identifier to trout, of the about-to-hatch nymph. They agreed on the air and its glint under the shuck, but Mosely, who incidentally had researched the phenomenon in the USA as well, believed that it could only be taken in at the surface and therefore could not help float the nymph up from the bottom.

> Mosely (1939) suggests that it is unlikely that the nymph would be floated up to the surface by the agency of the engulfed air. I have actually seen this happen with some nymphs of *H. lateralis* just before emergence. They were so buoyant that they could only remain at the bottom by clinging on to submerged stones. These nymphs were distinctly darker than normal, and the presence of air between the nymphal and sub-imaginal skins could be detected by their silvery appearance in certain lights. One of these nymphs, after a period of restlessness, took up a position beneath an overhanging ledge of stone and there, beneath the surface of the water, underwent its transformation to the sub-imaginal stage. The " dun," with its wings still only partly expanded, crawled up out of the water in a perfectly dry condition, and completed the
>
> ENTOM.—AUGUST, 1941. Q

> 170 THE ENTOMOLOGIST.
>
> extension of its wings on the top of the stone. The whole operation occupied only about two minutes.

FOOTNOTE 3: The word 'larva' in Blacker's Winged Larva tying instructions actually refers not to the larval body that is being imitated, but to the item that is used to imitate it – which was the shrivelled silkworm larva which came attached to the end of drawn salmon gut. A weird coincidence, but true.

Newly hatched BWO on the river Eden,
all facing into a light breath of air
(Photo by Paul Procter)

Newly hatched
BWO (Seratella
ignita) on the
River Wylye

HATCHED FLY PRESENTATION

THE WINGS ON THE hatched fly are not shaped like the tail of an aeroplane for nothing. A wind vane in the shape of the mayfly does a perfect job. The shape of its wings and the raised abdomen and tails are designed to turn it into the wind so that when it flies off the water surface it gets lift-off and doesn't get tumbled over. So in a downstream wind duns will face upstream and in an upstream wind they will face downstream. But we currently fish all our upstream dry flies facing downstream whatever the wind direction. Fifty per cent of the time they will be facing the wrong way, and our perhaps otherwise beautifully presented dry fly will stick out like a parade ground soldier turning left on a 'Right ... Turn!' command. And most of the time, knowing the wind direction, we can know it will happen, but carry on regardless. Naturally, American anglers fishing the dry fly downstream face the same issue of orientation.

Of course there are many complicating factors. There may be little or no wind in which case the natural fly will be headed in whichever direction micro-currents take it. The wind may be variable and changeable, in which case you certainly wouldn't want to keep changing between conventionally tied and reverse-tied dry flies as the gusts blow in different directions. In a laminar flow and no wind, the natural will face whichever way it was facing when it hatched – and it looks as if upstream is the 'default'.

If flies mainly do hatch facing upstream (because the current has swung the fish-shaped nymphs round that way as they stop swimming, start emerging, and become inert), then our emergers should always be tied in reverse. And our conventionally-tied fly will be a good imitation of a hatched fly, or not, depending on the wind direction. As we fish, we need to note the orientation of flies on parade that have been hatched for longer and been 'drilled' by the wind or by the current.

So maybe the fish makes an intellectual adjustment and eats it anyway in spite of it facing the wrong way compared to the naturals? Well, not really. Fish don't think about flies. The fly either fits the 'GISSO' (General Impression, Size, Shape, and Orientation – I added the O) that the trout is expecting, or it doesn't. In which latter case it is probably less likely to eat it.

As we shall discuss in chapter four, our fly is tethered by its tippet to a significant degree and it takes a pretty strong gust of wind to blow it around to the extent that it acquires the same orientation as the naturals if it starts off the wrong way round.

So all in all, it's probably worthwhile having a stock of reverse-tied dry flies which, when they alight, will face upstream into a downstream wind like the natural duns – and use them when the wind blows in our face.

You are probably thinking 'he's mad'. But now we've seen the logic, do we really want to go on with a 50/50 chance of being right, which may actually, if the wind direction is clear and constant downstream, be a 100% chance of being wrong? We rest our case, as Skues the lawyer might say. But we shall want to call witnesses. These are witnesses to the recommended use of floating hatched fly imitations from early times – for 350 years up to the time in the late 19th century when the new rule was brought in that you had to fish dry flies upstream, but tied to face downstream. (We examine their actual testimony, by means of literary archaeology, in chapter 19.) By necessary design these old-style flies faced the angler in terms of orientation, as he normally fished with the wind behind him, and hence they matched the orientation of the hatched flies that were on the water. Theirs was not a thinking orientation – it was just that reversing them would have been crazy: unnecessary.

Our main witnesses are: Leonard Mascall (1590), Gervase Markham (1614), Thomas Barker (1651), Robert Venables (1662), Charles Cotton (1676), James Chetham (1681), John Gay (1720), Richard and Charles Bowlker (1747-1826), George Scotcher (circa 1810), Thomas Best (1787 to 1846) Alfred Ronalds (1836) and William Blacker (1842). (Ten more are quoted in chapter 19 – these and all other authors referred to throughout this book are detailed in the Bibliography at the end.) They are called as witnesses because they fished hatched fly imitations; with the wind if there was one (whether upstream or down) and their flies were tied in such a way as always to have the right orientation, facing into the wind. These perceptive, inventive, and skilled angler-writers have been kicked into the long grass as successful imitators and presenters of the floating fly by the upstream dry fly supremacists who succeeded them (led in literature by J W Hills in *A History of Fly Fishing for Trout*) and dismissed as having fished downstream wet flies – when in fact they quite plainly did nothing of the sort. Instead they deserve our respect for their creative success in imitating the hatched fly. To appreciate that creativity, and to see clearly that they were representing the floating fly, take a look at this sample pair and the following sample page from Ronalds' groundbreaking, scientifically informed book *The Fly-Fisher's Entomology* (1836). (Ronalds did one really helpful thing that Halford never did, and did it 50 years earlier: he placed the natural fly next to the fly pattern in his illustrative plates).

Ronalds' Turkey Brown natural   **Ronalds' Turkey Brown artificial**

With Ronalds, the pattern is the imitation of the natural. The natural is in all cases (twenty different upwinged species in Ronalds, ten in Bowlker, plus the usual 'cast' of caddis, stoneflies and many terrestrials), the hatched fly. It is never the emerging dun, the nymph, or the rising pupa. It is as clear as the nose on your face that it was the hatched dun, caddis or stonefly they were imitating, and equally clear that they knew it rode down on the surface and not underwater. The angler's job was to present it on the surface and keep it fishing there, even if to do so he had continually to lift off.

The wings of their flies sloped backwards, not to facilitate easy entry through the surface, but in Halford pre-emptive exact imitation of the hatched fly, made to face into the wind. Their flies were cast downwind and faced into it, whether that was upstream or downstream. Their designers didn't specifically decide to make them face into the wind, of course – there just wasn't any sensible alternative. The more 'thinking'

Ronalds' naturals (above) and patterns (below) for Nemoura, Blue Dun, and Red Spinner
all are imitations of the hatched insect, he was the first to show it thus

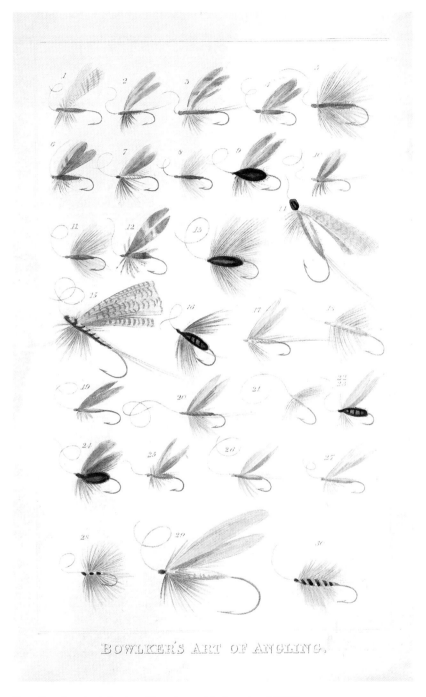

Bowlker's wind-facing flies from his book of 1839

of them (e.g. Venables, Bowlker, Salter, Stewart) recognised that it can be preferable to fish upstream since it was easier to keep out of sight of the fish, and often did so. Stewart recommended doing so; Venables preferred downstream, to avoid lining fish. So upstream fishing had its adherents over 200 years in advance of the 'Dry Fly Revolution', but it was hard to achieve against a downstream wind before silk lines became generally available in the early 19th century.

Fly fishing historian Jack Heddon pointed out thirty years ago that they could not have fished these flies under the surface even if they'd wanted to – their tackle was too light to allow it.

But why would they want to fish their flies underwater? The idea beggars belief – and yet we who learnt our fishing and read our books in the last half of the 20th century have innocently absorbed the myth of the 17th, 18th and early 19th century downstream wet fly like mother's milk sadly unattended by mother wit. Show me any fly like one of Bowlker's 1826 dry flies and my immediate (and now embarrassed) mental construct is 'downstream wet fly'. I even have a leather wallet of 'wets', dating from my early lake and river fishing days, laid away unused in a drawer for thirty years. I never did understand what trout food they were meant to imitate.

There is no arena I can think of like fly fishing for things getting discovered, published, used ... and then forgotten again and reclaimed proprietarily years later with the earlier skills and knowledge being glossed over or just bloody well denied.

I am not, by a long chalk, the first person to draw attention to these early angler-writers having fished with exact imitations of the hatched fly, tied and presented to float. A series of perceptive scholars have worked over the 17th and 18th century sources and come to the same conclusion – Jack Heddon, Conrad Voss Bark, Paul Schullery and, most recently, Andrew Herd in his comprehensively enlightening book (now a trilogy) *The Fly* (2003). Jack Heddon's work (published in the *Fly Dressers' Guild Newsletter* 1980) on the earlier writers showed categorically that from *The Treatyse of Fyshinge with an Angle* (1496) through until the latter half of the 19th century all imitation with very few exceptions was of the hatched fly (see chapter 19). In the average angler's subliminal mind, however, the misconception persists and I am glad to be able to contribute a bit more to re-instating the achievements of the 'Ancients'.

The early writers' instructions are all about concealment, observation, the imitation of the fly's behaviour as well as of its appearance, visual concentration, targeting the rising fish, and quick striking. No way was this downstream wet fly fishing. And this was not something that was changed by Halford's precepts.

It is equally clear that the fly hatches were amazing by today's standards – we are reading the work of people who didn't have to look far for a hatch, or worry too much about what to do if there wasn't one. This is what Thomas Best writes, in *A Concise Treatise on the Art of Angling* (1786) about the large dark olive and the medium olive (the brown dun and the blue dun):

> as it swims down the water, its wings stand upright upon its back, its tail is forked, and the color of its wings : it comes upon the water about eleven o'clock, and continues on till two, appearing on the water in shoals, or great quantities ; in dark gloomy days, at the approach of the least gleam of sun, it is amazing to see, in a moment's time, the surface of the water almost covered with ten thousands of these pretty little flying insects, and the fishes rising and sporting at them, insomuch that you would think the whole river was alive ; it is a pleasing sight to the angler, and affords him great diversion ; in this manner they appear on the water every successive day, till the end of their duration. The blue dun, and the brown, are both on at the same time; the blues are

Why would they not imitate the hatched fly with a floating imitation? There was no great need to think about imitating the nymph until dun numbers started to dwindle a century later with the impact of the industrial revolution.

The wind was your friend. You could not whip your fly dry by false casting, or the horsehair would break, or, later, the gut would be weakened. Paraffin was not yet thought of, nor Vaseline or petrol to dissolve it in, to treat your fly or line, and other fats are not mentioned (but may have been used). You had to keep the fly on the surface and to do so you had to keep

The lower Test valley, 1830s, no trees, enabling wind fishing
early photographs of Dovedale in Derbyshire, arguably the earlier cradle of the dry fly, show the same

it moving. So the wind was indeed your friend. And your dry fly, like the natural, faced into it.

Later, in the latter half of the 19th century when the cocked, split-winged dry fly became 'the thing', with its sharp collar hackle on the points of which it theoretically rode, the earlier flies were consigned to Room 101 and derided as wets, as part of the dry fly purists' spin.

However the great change was in actual fact not the dry fly itself – but the dry fly code and culture – the ethical, rather than the engineering innovation; the moral, rather than the presentational aspect. There was indeed a technical advance, the adoption of which upstream now did indeed trump downwind, but not necessarily for the better in all respects – as the American downstream expertise has shown.

J W Hills was not the last or the only writer on the history of trout fishing to perpetuate the myth of the universal use of the wet fly up until the Dry Fly Revolution. Arnold Gingrich wrote, in *The Fishing in Print* (1974):

'There had been frequent mentions of the taking of trout with flies 'on top of the water,' going back over nearly two centuries to the time of Col. Robert Venables. But most of these citations of surface-takes by trout were either as phenomena or desiderata, rather than to a recognized and purposive practice.'

That is just plain wrong. And another famous USA authority, Ernest Schwiebert, wrote in 1978:

'It is clear that the wet fly method reigned without challenge from the rivers of Macedonia to the Scottish highlands, until the birth of dry fly fishing in England slightly more than a century ago'.

Equally clearly: not so. Also, Leonard M Wright Jr. wrote in his excellent book *Fishing the Dry Fly as a Living Insect* (1972) that wet fly fishing held sway from the 3rd century, that the dry fly was 'not one twentieth as old' and that: 'In the beginning, and up until about a century ago, all flies were wet, incapable of floating.' American readers thrice misled, and here (and in chapter 19) I hope to help Paul Schullery and others set the record straight by describing the 350-year-old British floating fly legacy accurately.

What Hills, whose review of the literature, *A History of Fly fishing for Trout*, is excellent and well worth reading, failed to understand was that during the previous 350 years it was the angler's job to keep the fly floating – and not the job of the fly designer or the tackle. Everything in the modern world is designed and built to do the job for you and make your acquisition of skills much less necessary – but up until the middle 1800s the angler's skills were an absolute prerequisite to success in floating the fly. He was never more than two rod lengths away from it, and had a degree of control

A flotilla of duns facing the other way when the wind changed
(Photo by Paul Procter)

that by the end of that century had been traded off against the benefits of casting distance and accuracy at a distance – but this necessitated the use of flies that were newly designed to *float themselves* rather than be kept afloat by the fisherman.

These old 'wet' flies were now, well, non-U. And the new dry fly was King and Emperor. But the Emperor's birthday suit was … just that. In practice the new flies didn't, in the hands of most anglers, float any better than the old ones. Even the new 'Carshalton Dodge' (paraffin and false casting as introduced in the mid-1800s at Carshalton in South London, on the as-yet-not-terminally-polluted River Wandle) could not really overcome the tendency of 19th century innovations in tackle (gut for leaders, short rods, and silk lines plus longer casting) to sink the fly.

These new dry flies did achieve something, and perhaps rather better: when their bodies and hackle points penetrated the surface film they made very effective imitations of the emerging and of the crippled fly. Which is, as we have seen in chapter one, what trout will preferentially eat at the surface as it is less likely to fly away before they can get to it and cost them unrewarded energy expenditure. So you could fish the new trendy purist dry fly and still catch fish. Were this not the case, the dry fly code would have been dead in the water long ago. Call me cynical if you like.

But the main point of my including this historical excursion here is to provide testimony that, shepherded by the upstream dry supremacists, we have lost all touch with our imitation of the upwinged naturals' natural upwind orientation. They have led us in the wrong direction. Diametrically.

The dry fly revolution locked us into a box, fishing upstream with downstream-facing flies that are frequently wrongly oriented. Halford's precursors had actually had it right and he didn't – there was a fundamental perceptual and logical adjustment that the Revolutionaries should have made, but didn't. It's all about the shape and design of the natural, and the shape and design of the artificial, which needs to follow the former rather than 'flying in the face of it'. My own fly designs in chapter ten follow on from this, suggesting additional constructions to use when the traditional ones don't fit the circumstances.

(I'm sure the wind-facing, swept-wing earlier dun imitations sank a bit too, as the current pulled them and/or the angler got lazy, and were also taken by the trout for emergers and cripples when they did.) This orientation logic works whether you are fishing upstream or down.

Where the two fish rose on the Henry's Fork

Nigel Sturgeon and I were looking upstream (and down) over the Woods Road section of the Henry's Fork, and it was the second week of September – mahogany dun time. The river was huge, flat, and new to us and nothing moved for an hour at least. The crowds had gone, and you could see why. I was using binoculars to look for 'heads'.

On a corner a quarter of a mile upstream of me on the same true left bank was a woman fly fisher, also scanning this giant spring creek.

Between me and her, two fish began to move. One, just off a rock close to the bank, was bulging, the other, two rod lengths above it and three out from the bank, was a head and a good one.

Sadly the woman was looking downstream and aiming to fish that way, so I just stayed and watched. This girl was good, in addition to being tall, blonde, and decorative. Her reach cast made it clear why people use it. She fished into a strongish upstream breeze that will have made her presentation easily drag-free.

But the riser refused her dry fly, and then the bulger wouldn't bulge to her nymph either. Eventually she gave up and moved upstream. I waited, and both fish came back on the feed.

The bulger took my upstream nymph but thrashed and beat me, tippet clean cut by being dragged across its teeth.

The riser, head out, was eating a consistent trickle of mahogany duns and took my upstream Mahogany Dun artificial (a bivisible parachute specially tied for the trip) and stayed on for a fierce fight and a photo finish. It was a very well conditioned rainbow of 21 inches.

The girl was the better caster.

My fly was facing the same way as the naturals, hers wasn't.

FOOTNOTE 1: There is a general point of view abroad in the world of fly fishing north and west of the River Thames (and that includes the USA) that this business of dry fly purism is something that the southern English and specifically the southern chalkstream fishermen suddenly decided to invent and beat themselves up with in the late 19th century.

But they weren't the first. The first dry fly self-flagellants were not in the south – they were in Derbyshire on the Haddon Hall water of the lower Wye, in 1865. And indeed they are still there today, and have gone even further in sackcloth and ashes than the most purist adherents to the dry fly on the Test and Itchen, since they refuse to accept the Klinkhamer or any parachute hackled fly as a dry fly. When their collar-hackled dry flies sink into the surface film as far as or further than any Klinkhamer, the fly is still considered dry, no matter that it cannot be imitating the dun. No emerger patterns at all are allowed, however high-floating. Day ticket purchasers are constrained to read pages of rules before fishing.

Don't get me wrong, this is perfectly okay with me – any fishery owner letting his fishing rights of course has the right to insist on his own rules – and in this case keep the fish rested whenever they are not rising. All I want to point out is that it is not just the uptight southerners that are placing limits on their sporting freedom.

And it wasn't the southerners who picked up the rugby ball of fishing with the cocked dry fly and ran with it when it was first invented. When Alfred Ronalds published his amazing and groundbreaking book, based upon advanced entomological knowledge, and for the first time

Henry's Fork 21″ rainbow on mahogany dun
a riser to a dry fly facing the right way

accurately relating the artificial to the natural, it was the Yorkshire anglers (Pritt, Theakston, and Jackson), and the Derbyshire boys (Shipley, Ogden, and Foster) who took up the ideas and put them into practice. The southerners languished behind for another 40 or 50 years.

The story of dry fly purism on the lower Derbyshire Wye is an interesting one. James Ogden used to return to visit the Derbyshire Wye to fish for pleasure, and to test his new cocked dry fly patterns, after he had moved over to Gloucester to set up his tackle business and shop. On Monday, 5 June 1865 he was fishing at Bakewell and the locals, who used live mayflies on dapping rods, were laughing at his box of artificial mayflies. However, he caught so many fish in spite of falling in that the very next day the Haddon estate imposed the 'single artificial floating fly only on this water' rule and it has been in place ever since. The local anglers were extremely unhappy about this – and some might say that basing such a decision on one day's fishing by one man, and indeed by a day's fishing in the mayfly, was perhaps rash. Or perhaps this little story is somewhat of a parable.

FOOTNOTE 2: Skues was (as usual) wise to the reverse-tied fly. Here's what he said in a letter to the Flyfishers' Club Journal in 1939: 'I recall the publication in the Fishing Gazette in my young days of the plan of tying trout flies reversed, i.e., with the hackle and wings at the bend of the hook. But in the course of turning over my notes mentioned above, I find that Alexander Mackintosh, in The Driffield Angler, published in 1808, recommends this very plan, and not only for winged but also for hackled flies'.

Skues does not seem to have suggested the reverse-tied fly so as to match the upwind orientation of the dun however. Nor did Cosmo Barrett of Presteigne in Wales, originator of Barrett's Bane and Barrett's Professor, both reverse-tied and the latter being a prequel to the Leckford Professor. He and the Welsh author James Evans liked them because they floated better, hooked better, and the hackle stayed cleaner. Hardy stole and marketed the patterns in fact, and Barrett forced them to settle out of court.

FOOTNOTE 3: What the reader may by now be muttering, is 'If Hayes is as clever as he makes out then, and all this argument about the orientation of our dun imitations is right ... how come I'm still catching plenty of trout on floating flies that I'm fishing the wrong way round?' And it's a good question, and deserves a thinking answer. Not least, because I catch the majority of my own trout on flies tied head-towards-angler.

I think (though I don't know) that the answer is the same as the answer to the question, 'Why, if my dry fly is not perfectly dry, am I still catching fish?'

Just as trout see the classic dry fly as an emerger and not a dun, and prefer the

This real March Brown (Rhithrogena germanica) on the Usk demands a specific imitation

emerger as a target because of its higher return for effort, so they probably see the facing-the-wrong-way dun that has failed to turn into the wind as trapped, a cripple … the lame zebra that the lion targets … the trainee seal pup in the sights of the killer whale. The trout is a predator, not an epicurean. And a hatching fly that fails to make it out of its shuck completely simply cannot turn freely into the breeze like its successful brothers and sisters and it will stay the prisoner of the meniscus.

That said, if my informants are right and nymphs face upstream when locked in to the surface, the default cripple orientation will be facing the same way it faced when, as a nymph, it engaged with it. So your downstream-facing dun imitation could still be technically the wrong way round for a cripple. But cripples are to a degree subject to being blown around by the wind, because of being half emerged above the surface, and are unstable, having lost the streamlined hydrodynamic shape of the about-to-hatch nymph. The cripple will be different, your fly will be different, and a different fly is still likely to be one the more predatory trout key in on. Spookier fish will avoid it.

He may give your fly the benefit of the doubt on strict technicalities. That cripples are different is something the trout knows, not intellectually but experientially. It has seen thousands of cripples, and eaten as many as it can suck down. So, most of the time you're still in with a good chance, even with your fly facing the opposite way to the orientation of the natural hatched duns.

Thinking about what the trout will have seen in its experience is good practice in an angler. In hard-fished water, where many attempted exact imitations will have been seen, and the trout have learnt to reject them, it may make sense to offer something different, such as, for example, the same thing but tied in reverse.

Only if you need accurately to imitate the successfully hatched dun do you need to get the fly facing upstream (because the nymph hatches facing upstream) if there's no wind. It must face into the wind if there is one.

If the wind is downstream and you are fishing upstream, an accurate hatched dun imitation needs to be reverse tied. If there's no wind, ditto.

Vice versa if you are fishing downstream. If the wind is from behind you, your head-towards-the-angler fly is OK – but if it is in your face the duns will be facing away from you, and you should try a reverse-tied dry.

And there are plenty of situations in which you do need to imitate the hatched dun. As a hatch progresses, fish do come on to concentrate on the hatched fly ... and that's what you need to offer them at that time. Often it will be a specific dun that they want – a mahogany dun as in the Henry's Fork example, or in Britain a BWO, a March Brown, a Brook Dun, or an Iron Blue.

These are the times when you really do need to have your dry fly properly floating and oriented the same way as the naturals. Dry fly orientation angst is most appropriate at those times.

A rise to evening spinner, Derbyshire Wye

Focussed on a floating fly
(Photograph by Don Stazicker)

Large trout nymphing, seen from cover, New Zealand spring creek

HOW FISH EAT

THE FLY FISHERMAN'S FIRST job is to get his fly into the fish's mouth. But that's not as easy as you'd think. Even when the fish wants to eat it there's a great deal in the law of physics that frustrates easy entry. (More about getting the fish to want to eat it later – meanwhile, what stops it getting in?)

Zen and the laws of physics

Tippet tethering frustrates both angler and trout.

A serious problem in upstream dry fly fishing, it is less of a problem in upstream nymphing.

But worse in downstream wet fly and nymph fishing and often unbeknown to the angler.

The solution for the dry fly angler is to cast a looser tippet and achieve a longer drag-free drift, and/or fish downstream (see the next chapter).

Delaying the strike may help.

The solution for the downstream wet fly practitioner is to fish more across than down and avoid tethering the fly.

We would all catch more fish if half of them didn't come off. And catch even more if a lot of them didn't fail to get stuck in the first place. Although we often blame the fish for 'coming short', the failure of the

The moment of the rise, and the nose your tippet has to get round
(Photograph by Don Stazicker)

fly properly to enter their mouth is frequently more a matter of the laws of physics. First let's think about surface fly. To take a natural fly at the surface, a trout has to position his nose underneath it or just downstream, and suck the fly in. It will open its mouth and close its gills. At the same time it will expand its mouth cavity by extending it downwards, with the pleated under-chin opening like a pair of bellows. This sucks water and the fly into its mouth – which it will then close. A transient twin-lobed suction trough will form on each side.

The result may be a double whorl at the surface in the shape of the 'kidney' rise, made famous by Skues, as the fish turns down. (See the sequence of photographs on pp 70-71.) Then it will press the fly against the roof of its mouth with its tongue, close its mouth and hold the prey there whilst it opens its gills and expels the water (it only wants actually to swallow the food item, not all that water). Simultaneously it will be testing the fly for signs of inedibility, and if it finds them it will release the object with its tongue, keep its gills closed, open its mouth again and expel the fly forwards with the water – instantaneously and by instinct. A geyser of a splash can result.

If the fly is accepted as edible and the expulsion of water takes place backwards through the gills as the trout turns down, this may be another cause of a kidney-shaped surface whorl. (I had no very clear idea about the detailed actions and sequences involved until, curious about the physics, I read Paul Schullery's amazing book *The Rise* and subsequently received his generous personal help in producing the above précis, for which my own and my readers' unstinting thanks are due.)

The trout knows from experience that the suck will have to be a good strong one because it will have to overcome the resistance of the surface tension and pull the (very lightweight and hydrophobic) fly down through it. Skues says: 'I say the trout takes the fly by suction, and that without suction the fly would be missed; pushed aside by his emerging snout and carried away by the stream.' Some rises are grabs of course, but suction is probably always a part of them.

So what is the physical problem? Well, our fly is tethered. Our tippet has to bend round the nose of the trout to allow the fly into its mouth. And more than that, it has to be pulled over the skin of the trout's nose so as to allow the fly to travel to the centre of the mouth and be pressed against the roof of the mouth by the tongue. Often this doesn't happen easily, and the trout will instantly and instinctively distrust the unexpected behaviour of its hoped-for prey, and eject it. Or the

Only just hooked

hook will catch in the bony outside jaw instead of the soft interior (this is better for the trout). The angle of pull on the hook will be less favourable to the angler, and the fish will get off more easily. In the photograph on this page, the tiny spinner pattern, tethered in the surface film by a tippet strong enough to land a decent trout, only just managed to hook the fish, outside the mouth. Either the fly never made it inside, or the fish's porpoising, sipping spinner rise meant that it was pulled out as the fish moved forward, or it was ejected as suspicious.

As Fred Arbona wrote about the upstream dry fly cast in his strongly evidence-based book *Mayflies, the Angler, and the Trout*, its second disadvantage (after the potential for lining the fish) is:

'... that when the trout takes your artificial, the first thing he will encounter is the tippet, and he may 'bump' the fly right out of his mouth. For such reasons it may require more than one take to hook him. Usually he will be hooked on the upper lip.'

The solution is to cast a looser tippet and maintain a longer drag-free drift. Or fish downstream as Americans do, if that's within the rules. If your tippet lands in a mess of whirligigs, that's okay, the lack of drag will make the fish want it more, and be better able to take it. The sort of cast most instructors teach you not to make turns out to be the best one. The lighter the tippet, the less drag.

If you've been admiring the look of your cast, it has probably been setting up drag. Not that casting so as to avoid drag is easy: it's one of the most difficult things in fly fishing to achieve. Every so often I have taken a trout that surprisingly didn't fight, and I have found that the tippet, landing in whirligigs as I dump cast or bounce cast, has lassoed it round the gills on the strike. Drag gets refusals ten times more than a wiggly tippet.

Skues makes a joke of his ineptitude as a beginner, when he tied on a tapered leader he'd been given, the wrong way round:

'The first cast fell in a huge coil on the water, enough to scandalise any self-respecting trout. The trout I was casting to did not belong to that order, for he came up, picked the fly out of the middle of the coil, and when I responded with a violent strike, kept the lot, cast and all.'

But he deceived it, and later became a proponent of loose line casting (as indeed was Halford, who wrote ten pages at a time on avoiding drag). Skues said of one of only two people he knew who had given up fly fishing as a bad job:

'... in the course of development of astonishing accuracy and power of casting a long straight line the man became with every advance less and less able to catch trout – and his angling days became a long series of disappointments.'

And since in a determined, open-mouth rise the movement of the tethered fly into the trout's mouth takes a split second longer, reciting 'God Save the Queen' before striking may well help.

Skues again: 'I remember that I used to raise as many trout to my fly as I do today, but owing to my nervous haste I left far too many flies *in the noses* of indignant trout.' (my italics)

But better not to hesitate with a more cautious fish, when the chances are increased that that nanosecond instinctive rejection happens. So with fish you judge to be wired, strike like a cobra, but, if you can, softly! There aren't any rules on this, such as ... 'if this happens, then do that' – you have to rely on your own experience and judgement. And this can be tough if you have only got one rising fish to try to make a judgement about. In which case I recommend 'turn off the computer, trust in the Force'.

There's an interesting and perhaps useful footnote here. Some trout sometimes rise and take a floating fly or emerger without breaking the surface with nose or mouth. They simply suck it down by creating a vortex. This can be done, and with pinpoint accuracy, from a head's length away. You will probably have noticed that sometimes your fly simply disappears. With luck, you suddenly discover you're attached to a fish. Very likely this was because you didn't strike straight away – not trusting your eyes and still looking in vain for the fly – and as a result the trout's vortex suck had time to get it into his mouth first.

Lassoed by the leader

When we are fishing the nymph upstream to fish feeding beneath the surface, the trout does not have to make such a big suck to bring the prey into its mouth, because the current will drive it there and there is no surface tension to overcome. We still have a degree of tippet resistance, but the monofilament is more likely to slip into the scissors of the jaw and an effective hook-up is more likely. But the closer our fly is to the surface, if for example, we are fishing an unweighted nymph to a fish working immediately sub-surface, the more we are likely to have the dry fly tippet problem outlined above and a hook-up in the bony lip. I find this to be the default hooking location for light nymphs and emergers.

When we are fishing wet fly or nymph, fishing downstream does not solve the tippet-tethering problem. In fact it makes it worse. The reason is that the fly is yet more firmly tethered, with the current, generally speaking, having extended the leader so that it is taut to the fly. So when the fish goes to suck the fly in, it expects it to go into its mouth – but it stays where it is. As Marinaro says – you haven't scared the fish, you have disappointed him. Only if the fish swims forward to entrap the prey, will the fly go into its mouth. Otherwise its take may well be abortive. This is the prime cause of 'nipping' or 'bumping' takes in which the fish does not stay attached. And, indeed, many completely abortive takes are unseen by the angler in most cases. So the angler gets no feedback as to what is going on, and fishes on with admirable persistence no doubt, but no idea how close he came to catching the fish. You can see this happening frequently in underwater videos of salmon fishing. (Salmon, remember, aren't feeding fish, and the laws are different. I've never understood salmon – see Footnote 2).

The solution is to fish more across than down, to mend line appropriately, to pay out line if that makes sense – and generally to bear in mind that fish don't expect drifting prey to swoop sideways against the current – nor will feeding fish move too far out of station to get something.

Jeremy Waters (my partner for years in fishing and also in fishery management and in the Wilton Fly Fishing Club) and I once spent a whole afternoon fishing downstream from a high bridge above the Pelorus River in South Island, New Zealand, watching the reactions of the trout to our dry flies and nymphs. Sideways deviations almost always entailed rejection. It was too deep to fish upstream to these fish, but by climbing down from the bridge and wading deep enough to get your elbows wet you could fish across to them while your friend watched from above. Sideways drag was quick to set in on each drift, after which only rare takes resulted, most of them abortive. Loose casts directly up or downstream from the bridge worked much better, even with many yards of drooping line to control.

There will be exceptions. When feeling predatory, trout will pursue. Both Skues and Lord Grey, prolific and observant fishermen and writers, reported exceptional days on which sideways drag attracted fish. But as a general rule it is best avoided.

The point I'm making is that the tethering effects that keep the fly out of the fish's mouth are largely unseen when you're fishing wet and downstream – both the inability of the trout to suck the fly in and the likelihood of its being put off by sideways movement.

And for the upstream dry fly, emerger and surface nymph fisherman,

The author's drifts being monitored from the Pelorus Bridge
(Photo by Jeremy Waters)

the tighter the tippet is tethered to the fly on the take, the more likely you are to fail to hook, or to lose the fish. And the more likely is the fly to drag and get rejected. It's the physics, but not just the physics – the pull of the tippet over the lips is also a problem because they are liberally kitted out with sense organs. Many people think that drag matters less for the nymph. This may be true (and drag may be impossible to avoid) for the more deeply fished nymph. But if a nymph fished just below or in the meniscus drags, it will produce a wake, something which the natural will never do. When the natural reaches the surface, its objective is to become its prisoner – so that it can allow the force of surface tension working on its dorsal skin-split to pull the hydrophilic edges of its nymphal skin apart and let the hydrophobic dun emerge. It has to become a prisoner of the film before it can escape from it. So the hatching nymph moves entirely and exactly as that little bit of the surface moves. It may shiver in its attempt to break through (BWOs in particular do so) but it won't make waves. Any drag will be the opposite of the fish's expectations. But the moment the dun is free, it is truly free. It can skate, turn 180 degrees into the wind, be blown about by it, and fly. No surface movement can take it along if the breeze or its own wings propel it elsewhere. Your fly's tippet, however, tethers it. So you have to learn to cast it 'every which way – but loose.' (See the next chapter).

A classic rise and rise form sequence photographed by Don Stazicker on the Derbyshire Wye

note the initial binocular focus with the eyes swivelled forwards in One;

the suction trough carried past the trout's head by the current in Two;

the mouth closing after the suck in Three;

the return to station in Four;

and the gills just beginning to open to expel water in picture Five

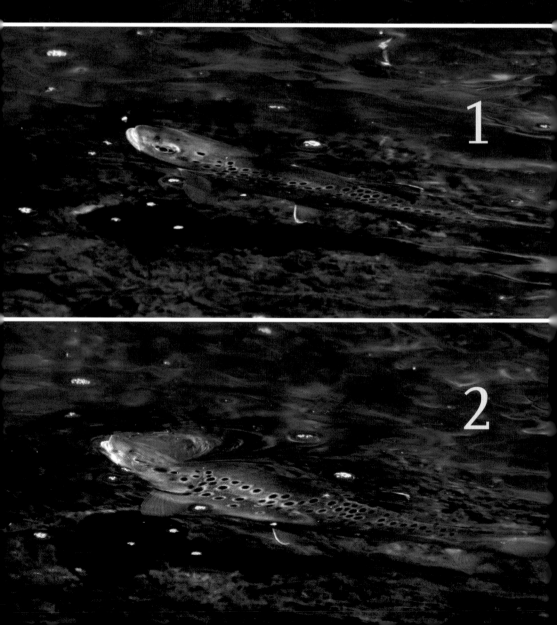

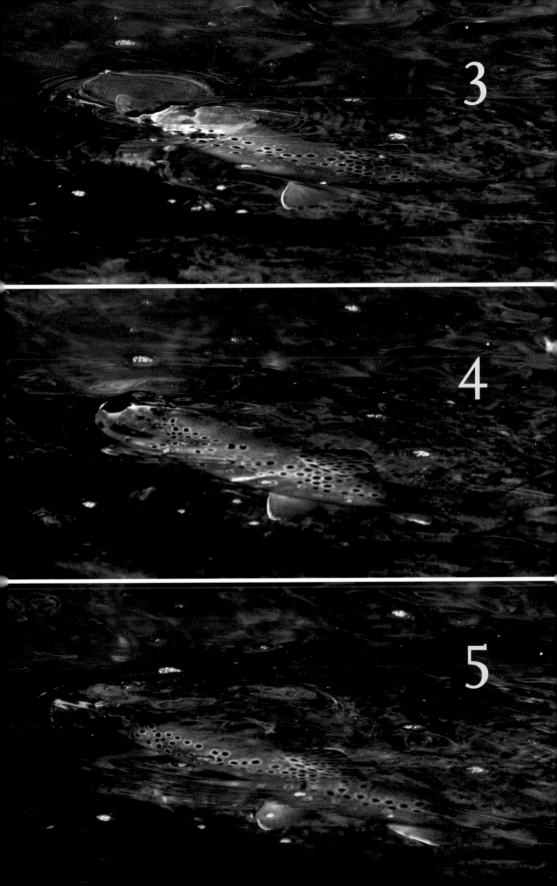

FOOTNOTE 1: There is a school of thinking that says that you can tell the species of fly that is hatching and being eaten from the rise form of the trout. When you challenge it this tends to come down to an agreement with Skues that the kidney-shaped whorl is indicative of the trout taking a hatching BWO. There is in fact a reason for this being a good guess. BWO tend to hatch in the evening (perhaps more so than any other species), so there is a good chance that the kidney-shaped rise that you see in the evening light involved the consumption of one of them. (But the more so if you happened to be able to catch one and identified it by its three tails.)

However it is my belief that the kidney-shaped rise happens most of the time when a trout eats a fly in a leisurely fashion, sticking its nose up through the surface, whatever the species of fly is involved. A trough forms behind and to each side of the trout's nose and is swept quickly downstream past the trout by the current, and the nose makes it into a kidney shape. You can see this happening in the preceding pictures. Also, there is no reason why any particular species of surface hatching upwinged fly should be eaten by trout in a different way from any other, since they all get taken into the trout's mouth in the same way, so the kidney-means-BWO theory is an inherently unsafe one. And I don't think there are any other rise forms that are associated with other particular species. Life stage yes, species no.

I might be tempted to suggest that a good splosh, with the trout coming half out of the water, indicates a chasing rise to hatching caddis, but that would not be specific to any species of caddis. A clearly defined grab with the head and mouth coming out of the water would often be associated with the trout taking mayfly (that is the big green drake of the UK) if it was in the middle of a mayfly hatch, but otherwise such a rise could be typical of any large floating prey item being taken. A porpoising head, dorsal and tail rise is often one to a spinner trapped on, in, or under the surface film, but again cannot be taken to be specific as to the species involved.

Grayling rises sometimes leave a bubble, but sadly not nearly frequently enough for the angler to be able to conclude from the absence of a bubble that the riser was a trout.

Trout can leave a bubble too. To my way of thinking, the only conclusion to be drawn from seeing a bubble in a rise-form is a logical one – the fish either sucked down air in a vortex with the food item, or took air into its open mouth at the surface. Otherwise, there is nowhere for the bubble to have come from. The conclusion is that it ate an item of surface, rather than subsurface food. Not conclusively a hatched fly, quite possibly an emergent or crippled one – but a fly which is asking to be imitated by the angler in or on the surface. This is helpful.

Tiny, sipping rises where the food item is sucked down rather than visibly taken into the mouth do tend to indicate very small prey such as smuts or black gnats or greenfly, and they are frequently taken this way because they are easy to suck down, being minimally hydrophobic and having less mass to pull down through the surface film, with less energy spent by the trout in tipping up to take them. But unless you get out your seine net to see what minimalculae are floating down, the character of the rise itself gives you virtually no clue as to what the fish are eating.

Bulging movements just under the surface, where no part of the fish shows, do normally indicate fish taking nymphs as they rise to hatch, but may equally involve sedge pupae or ascending chironomid pupae.

So, once again we find that we are much more confident with the life stage of the prey that is being consumed than we are with the exact identity of the species. Only observation or sampling will tell us what the species is, and give us the information that we need to guide precise fly selection.

In addition, avoiding drag will be more important than species imitation, providing that life stage mimicking is accurate. This is for the two reasons we have examined in this chapter – to not frighten the fish and to allow the fly easy entry into his mouth.

FOOTNOTE 2: Why do I fish for trout with enthusiasm, but not for salmon? The thing about salmon is that they have ceased to take part in the fullness of a predatory life when we fish for them in fresh water. They have opted out of their active role in the food chain and have settled for a passive one. Their minds are completely off predation and are focused instead upon procreation. All they want to do is to survive until the opportunity arrives to get up river to the redds. The salmon fisher's wits are pitted against a largely somnolent animal and that is why so very few of them are 'taking fish'.

We may annoy them into taking our fly. We may fascinate them like a snake charmer into taking our fly. We may put our fly into their parlour so that they feel compelled to remove it with the only dustpan they have – their mouth. We may threaten them, by means of our fly, with sexual competition and evince an aggressive response. We may conjure up in their mind a picture of seafood. We may, indeed, remind them nostalgically of their time as a parr when they rose to natural flies in a feeding response. An angler can be quite extraordinarily clever at achieving any of those things, and worthy of great admiration.

But we cannot insert our fly meaningfully into their niche in the food chain and fool them into taking it, as any normal, healthily adjusted predator would do. And we are nosily interfering with their spawning run at a time when they have opted out of nature, red-in-tooth-and-claw. They are not playing our game any more. So the place to fish for salmon would be in the sea, when they are still in the game – but that is largely impractical. Again, this is a decision you make for yourself. I still fish for salmon – a bit – and I still enjoy it in spite of being useless, but for choice I fish for trout.

Richard Banbury of Orvis using the dump cast on a particularly derisive Itchen trout

CASTING EVERY WHICH WAY – BUT LOOSE

AS WE HAVE SEEN in chapter four, avoiding drag, generally recognised as being the key to not putting fish off the take and causing rejection, is also crucial mechanically in terms of the physics of getting the fly into the trout's mouth without sparking ejection. Loose tippet is the answer. To avoid drag it's essential to be able to cast a loose leader and tippet – reliably, repeatedly and with dedication. Think of Schwarzenegger as in the movie End of Days he puts accurate and effective holes in successive evil people with his giant gun and comments matter-of-factly to the Devil: 'I can do this all day long.' Whatever I say about too perfect casting being drag-inducing, you absolutely do have to be or become a proficient caster, good enough at the 'automatic' level to get it out there accurately and then throw the 'poor' casts as required.

Nor is Arnie an inappropriate simile, since a muscular cast will often be a prerequisite. Let me explain:

Drag avoidance in dry fly fishing is born of three things: A fly not trapped in the surface; a leader set-up that comprises a more stiff base section and a softer tippet section; and a cast that gets curves, and even curls, into the leader.

I'm going to deal with the cast first, and then the leader.

The first thing to appreciate about an effective anti-drag cast is that it is very different from the casts that you will see demonstrated at fly fishing shows and performed by competition casters – and probably, although not certainly, different from what a casting instructor will teach you. Those will be straight line casts, and that is exactly the opposite of what you want to achieve. Fished in any direction on a river they will generate drag immediately. It does not matter how softly and thistledown-like your fly alights upon the water, if you have performed a straight line cast, it will drag.

So having rid your mind of that conceptual as-taught ideal cast, your next move should be to stop aiming your fly at the water. You want it to land on the water, of course, but you don't want it to be propelled onto the water. With these things out of the way, you are clear to think about casts that will get you a loose leader.

There are dozens of casts that you can learn: reach casts; hook casts; steeple casts; wiggle casts, etc, etc. If you have the patience, and the dexterity, it will be a good idea to learn all, or many of them. I myself am challenged in both areas and have managed to get along pretty well by concentrating on two overhead casts, plus the side cast and the roll cast. All four of these I commend to you as basics.

The two basic drag-avoiding overhead casts are the dump cast (see the opening photograph of this chapter) and the bounce-back cast. For both of these you need a fast action rod, and there is not much point in trying to make them work with a medium action or a soft one. The reason for this is not so much that you need a high line speed (although you do) but, much more importantly, because what creates each of these casts is the sharpness with which you stop the forward motion of your arm. I don't know if you ever used a whippy stick to propel a projectile of mud at your friends in childhood battles, but if you did you will know that it is the precise control of the moment when you stop the forward motion of the stick that gives you the accuracy to hit them in the most painful parts of their anatomy. It is the same control of the stop that holds the key to successful fly casting.

By the same token, if you let your wrist and rod travel forward, energy will be lost and imprecision will result. With a fast action rod, the abrupt stop of your arm brings the fast forward motion of the extended line to an abrupt stop effectively. With a medium or slow action rod, when you stop it abruptly the upper half of the rod continues forward as it bends and the extended line is not stopped sharply.

With the dump cast you aim a fast high line and a tight loop, Charles Ritz-style, several feet above the surface (and I mean 5 or 6 feet, not 2 or 3). As the line reaches its full extension, with the rod stopped at no lower than 10 o'clock, you drop your rod hand and your rod sharply downwards. The result should be a pretty fair wriggly mess in terms of the leader and tippet. There will then be long enough for the main current and micro-currents to stretch out the wiggles in the leader for you to have avoided drag for long enough to cover the fish without it yet setting in.

The bounce-back cast is performed in exactly the same way as the dump cast, except that your line control hand will additionally jerk back on the line at the precise moment of the stop. The leader and tippet then fly back towards you and land in even more of a heap together with the fly.

You use the dump cast when there is no wind, or the wind is in your face, helping you to avoid drag by blowing the leader back towards you. You use the bounce-back cast when the wind is behind you and you need additional reverse-driving energy to achieve a collapsing leader. If the wind is strong enough not even a bounce-back cast will achieve that and if the rules allowed, you would do better by turning around and fishing into the wind. And incidentally, if I had a luncheon voucher for every time I have heard somebody say how nice and helpful it is to have the wind behind you I would never

A fish is much more likely to eat this fly than a dragging one, in spite of the apparently horrifying mess of floating tippet

starve. But the fact is, having the wind behind you more or less guarantees your fly will drag.

The side cast is something that should be a standard part of your repertoire, if only to allow you to fish under overhanging branches. However it will also make it possible for you to cut casts in under the wind. Practice and confidence are the essential enablers of successful side casting. And if you can achieve enough control of the stop, which is equally required in the side cast as in the overhead cast, you will be able to achieve a positive hook cast as well. And if you let the energy of a side cast die, you can sometimes achieve a reverse hook cast. At which point, you can certainly allow yourself some self-congratulation.

The roll cast is the thing to use when you don't have room for a back cast of course, but it is also the technique of choice when you want to deliver a fly without drag perpendicularly across the current to a feeding fish. To be successful in it, you have to let the recovered line come back smoothly towards you until it forms a 'D' behind you and then roll it smoothly upwards and outwards in the direction of the fish. But you will probably know that. One thing that you might not know however is that the roll cast is not at its best when it also tries to change direction – in other words if the line has progressed downstream at perhaps a 45° angle and you wish to recast at a 90° angle across the stream, you are going to have to get it out in front of you again before making the delivery cast – as my instructor and friend, Simon Gawesworth of Rio, says: 'The delivery cast must be as parallel as railway tracks to the recovery.'

I have to admit I can't find success with those casts like the reach cast and the wiggle cast, in which the line is intentionally moved in a certain way during delivery. I don't have the lightness of touch to move the fly line but not also to straighten the leader, and thus get straight back into the drag I wanted to avoid. Others can do it well, but I stick to my four basic casts.

What is really important is leader construction. It is too complicated a subject to go into all the detail here, but in principle you need a leader constructed with something stiff for the butt portion and something soft for the front portion and tippet. These curve-prone leaders were originated by George W Harvey who taught fly fishing skills at Pennsylvania State University to 35,000 students over several decades, and popularised even more by Joe Humphreys, notably in his book *Trout Tactics* published in 1980. You tie them yourself using typically four sections of hard monofilament (Mason or Maxima) for the butt, tapering for a 10 foot 4 inch leader as follows: 10 in @ .015 in; 20 in @ .013 in; 20 in @ .011 in; and 12in @ .009 in. To this you knot soft mono of your choice, which can be nylon, copolymer, or fluorocarbon as follows: 14 in @ 3x or .008 in; 18 in @ 4x or .007 in; and 30 in @ 5x (.006 in) or 30 in @ 6x (.005 in). This, the home made way to do it, really does work.

However, following a tip in Joseph A Kissane's book *Drag Free Drift*, I tried using Airflo polyleaders for the butt section and have never looked back except for using furled leaders for very close contact work in small and bushy streams. Polyleaders transmit energy well, float better than any monofilament, form 'S' curves well, and don't spray water at the fish too much. I usually use a leader twice as long as my rod in total, based on a 5ft polyleader in the 12 lb breaking strain size, and appropriate lengths of 12.5 lb, 9.5 lb, 7.5 lb, 4.75 lb and if necessary 3.5 lb fluorocarbon tippet material. Sometimes the leader gets made much longer: accuracy suffers, but rejections are fewer when you do get the fly to the trout.

Can the trout see the knots? Yes, emphatically. Do they care? No. Not unless they are hungry enough to want to eat them.

I cast a very high, fast line. When I sent the third replacement fly line back to my old friend Jim Teeny (the well known originator of the Teeny Nymph for Pacific salmon and inventor and manufacturer of specialist fly lines) complaining that it had cracked up in less than a season, he politely declined my further business, casting aspersions on my casting, but sent me a fifth one anyway. Pot calling the kettle black – you should see Jim cast! Schwarzenegger isn't in with a chance.

FOOTNOTE: The best book to help you understand this stuff and improve (understandable by duffers too) is John Judy's *Slack Line Strategies for Fly-fishing* (1994). Well, it has helped me. And Halford said in *Dry-Fly Fishing In Theory and Practice* (1889):

'... the meaning to be attached to the expression throwing a slack line is, that the force to be used should be a trifle more than is needed to put the line out straight, and in making this cast the hand must be checked slightly, so that, as before, the fly and last yard of the gut are extended, while the upper part of the cast and a portion of the reel-line lie in curves or loosely on the water.'

(I did say he wrote usefully much of the time.)

Halford had perfected his casting by watching Marryat, and indeed his illustrations of casting in *Dry-Fly Fishing* use Marryat, with his characteristic Tam 'O Shanter hat, as the illustrative casting expert (*facile princeps* – by far the best). You can learn a great deal from watching other people casting; and I have learnt a great deal myself from watching experts fishing.

Taking video of an expert casting to a lie or to a rising fish can be extremely helpful, and it is easy enough to do now that pocket waterproof cameras are available that take good video. Then you can take it home and look at it on the big screen, and see what it is that the expert does that is different and better. It will teach you more than casting skills. It can show you how to approach fish, how to get the best angle on them, how to ensure you stay hidden and yet present the fly effectively.

Consensually filmed of course. I have really useful video footage of Oliver Edwards, Paul Procter, Stuart Crofts, Tony Hayter, and Tony Wells, to name but a few. From each I have learned different things. For example, Tony Wells, who leads the Services Dry Fly Fishing Association (where Frank Sawyer was for so many years the keeper), has been addressing difficult fish for well over half a century, and I am frequently astonished at his ability to put a fly over a fish that I would have abandoned as impossible. Sometimes I can emulate his skill. Tony Hayter showed me that no fish is too difficult to try for, and that you earn success with failures. Paul Procter is the ultimate practitioner in the low profile creep-up and drag-free drift. Stuart Crofts' skills are legion but what I have learned from him is the intuitive identification, and intensive coverage of lies and fish. Watching Ollie Edwards spotting and covering big wild fish in Iceland made me realise how much I was, if I'm honest with myself, unnecessarily fiddling about before addressing a fish – he would have landed it before I had made a cast. Paul, Stuart, and Oliver, all from the North of England are, through their highly perceptive and prolific writing and their generous teaching, leading contributors to the growth of what you might call the Third Age of British Fly Fishing.

I think I would offer only two other pieces of advice:

Tony Hayter attached to a 17 in trout taking a rare upwing in the nascent River Till by the main arterial A303

The first would be: always and continually ask yourself whether you could not get a better angle on a fish, so as to avoid crosscurrents and drag, by changing your position. Getting your person across the river is better than getting your line across the current.

And the second would be: do not cast a line a foot further than you need to. The closer you are to the fish the better you can see him. The closer you are to your fly the better you can see it. The longer length of fly line between you and the fly the more it will drag. So keep it short. And think outside the conventional casting box.

When Charles Cotton advised his readers to fish 'fine and far off' it was good advice, but we need to remember that in his time two rod lengths from your feet was about the practical distance limit. Tenkara (see chapter 20) is bringing us back round full circle to that precept.

Double vision from below

HOW FISH SEE
THE LEADER

I HAVE ALWAYS BEEN curious to know how the fish sees your fly as it approaches it from underwater, and the advent of small digital underwater cameras has meant that I can satisfy my curiosity. This picture of my KmC (Kiss my Cul) shows the fly floating in the surface film from underwater, with the (supposedly invisible fluorocarbon) tippet submerged. To the trout, and to the camera, the fly is in the mirror, which is where it will be when the trout initiates its rise. Note that the fish will see two hooks and two tippets in each case, one seen directly through the water and one reflected in the mirror.

Every book, every guide, every fishing instructor tells you to grease your dry fly but de-grease your tippet. Then, they say, your tippet will be less visible to the fish. I am afraid this is a terrible mistake and a ghastly piece of misinformation that has been foisted upon us as anglers for decades by the supposed authorities. And acted upon by us. We can't easily get over the fish seeing two hooks, but we can make sure that it only sees one leader, by greasing it so that it stays in the surface film and does not sink. By doing so we will also ensure that this fish does not have to push the tippet aside with its nose in order to engulf the fly.

Is it in the mirror that the fish first sees the fly? Vincent Marinaro was clear that it is, and he probably spent more time and effort working out the angles of approach, studying and photographing rising trout than anyone before or since. But actually it doesn't matter whether the trout sees the artificial fly that you cast at it in the mirror or in the window. Either way, if you sink the leader, the trout will still have a completely clear view of it, and it will still have to push past it in order to take the fly. And it runs counter to reason to suppose that that is a good thing.

The inescapable fact is that the tippet is considerably less visible and

The KmC from above
tippet floating

... and the same KmC
in the surface from below, in the trout's window, tippet floating: single vision

massively less obstructive to the fish if it is floating. Here are two more photographs of the fly pictured on the previous page, this time taken from above and below, but with the tippet floating rather than sunk. It is hard to imagine that the tippet could ever be less visible to the trout if it were sunk.

I am in favour of keeping your leader and tippet clean, as that will usually be enough to float it in clear water. I use a folded blade of grass, now that Paul Procter has vouchsafed that excellent 'dodge.' (Paul is a colleague in the Wild Trout Trust, a well known British writer in fly fishing magazines, an international angler and an Orvis guide.) If it sinks, I will use one of the less off-washable fly floatants to make sure it stays in the surface film (see chapter seven). The grass trick will give you a tippet that distorts the meniscus less than a greased tippet, and so if that will float it, don't grease it.

Proponents of tippet sinking (almost everybody) argue that the leader casts a bigger shadow on the stream bed if it is floating rather than sunk. This is true, but angler-centric. Worry about what the trout definitely sees as it approaches the fly with its excellent binocular vision focused on it, rather than what it might possibly see with peripheral vision on the bottom of the stream below it.

This doesn't mean you can 'line' your fish with the leader with impunity, of course. Floating or sunk, your leader stands a good chance of putting a fish on the alert and reducing its likelihood to take if it lands on its head or very close to it. However, whether it lands and sinks, or lands and floats, is not likely to alter the degree to which it spooks the trout by the act of landing close to it. If anything it must be less spookworthy if it doesn't enter the trout's medium and 'personal space'. In fact fish that have seen a lot of flies, leaders and anglers are quite likely to be spooked by the leader whilst it is still in the air and unrolling flashily towards them.

1859 cartoon of the Hurstbourne Water (the iconic Hampshire Bourne)

'Saw thousands of fish – and they saw me.'

Lining a fish with a drifting line is a hell of a lot better than lining a fish by landing the line on him.

So it is worth our while to find a method of getting the fly to the fish from one side or the other; and landing the fly well upstream of the fish if we are fishing upstream, so that the leader is as far away from the eye of the trout as possible. As usual it is a trade-off, and the further upstream we land the fly the less noticeable will be its landing, but greater the chance of drag setting in – and the more obtuse the angle it comes in at from the side, the less the likelihood of spooking the trout, but the greater the chance of the fly being dragged sideways.

Many wading anglers forge unstoppably upstream without considering the possibility of a perpendicular cast across-flow from the opposite bank to the fish, whether wading, or kneeling. If a slack-line cast is achieved at 90 degrees to a rising fish, the chances of spooking it with the leader are minimised and you don't have to land the fly so far upstream of it. In addition, the chances of a hook-up in the scissors are maximised. Roll casts work well here, especially if they are as aesthetically unimpressive as mine.

There is another reason for not sinking your leader when fishing the dry fly. If your leader is sunk, when you lift off to recast you pull the fly down through the surface and it rips through the water making a loud zipping sound. This sound can be heard by your target fish and also by others. If they are already sensitised to anglers in general, or to the presence of your good self, this will put them in a heightened state of alert and that will severely damage your chances with subsequent casts. So float your tippet.

Some say trout have a blind spot above their heads and behind. I believe that this has been shown to be a fallacy by Eric Horsfall-Turner in his contribution to C F Walker's book *The Complete Flyfisher,* and by Paul Schullery in his terrific book, *The Rise.* It may be true that a fish which has its eyes focused and oriented forwards towards approaching food will be less likely to see something directly behind it – a fact which we frequently exploit – but if it is alerted by something falling onto the surface there is no doubt that it can swivel its eyes in their sockets enough to see something directly above, or even behind its head. If this is right, then casting directly up behind your fish with the tippet landing immediately over its head is no advantage – and I don't know about you, but my casting is never that accurate; my cast will always be sufficiently to one side or the other (feet, not inches) as to ensure he can see it without swivelling his eyes.

Also relevant is the fact that feeding fish that are addressing nymphs, emergers and duns will be orienting their eyes sideways to look at prey items and assess whether they are worth a move to intercept them. Feeding fish will also be moving their bodies from side-to-side to take a better sight of individual items of food. When eyes swivel and/or bodies bend, their peripheral vision to the rear changes to a more direct angle, and you, your leader, and your line are in the frame. If you have the presence of mind, it is worth freezing your movement when your target fish makes a sideways move. Mid-cast, this takes willpower. The moral is: keep low, keep off the skyline, wear dark clothes, and move slowly.

FOOTNOTE 1: The term 'mirror' means that when it looks up at the surface the trout can only see, because of refraction, a reflection of the bottom, or weeds, in a rather jiggly mirror formed by the surface. He can only see through it in a circular hole, varying in size with his depth, immediately above his head.

FOOTNOTE 2: Trout see incredibly well, much better than we do. Ralph Cutter, in hundreds of dives, has watched them 'prick their ears' at food items the size of punctuation dots from several feet away, seconds before he could make them out himself – and sometimes so small that he never saw what they ate.

FOOTNOTE 3: It's honestly unclear as to whether the thickness of your tippet really matters. There are many examples in this book indicating that it doesn't. These include Skues tying a leader on the wrong way round in chapter four; the experiments of both George Harvey and Ralph Cutter referenced in chapter eight; the heavily fished for Icelandic trout 'Harald' taking a size 20 chironomid pupa tied to 7.5 lb tippet in chapter 15. I could adduce many others, including my friend Jeremy Waters taking a New Zealand six-pounder, that I had lost in the willows the day before and briefed him up on, on a size 18 dry fly tied to 12 lb nylon. Probably the answer is that trout will forgive and ignore thick tippets if they are hungry and feeding and focussed on the food items themselves. Otherwise, spooky trout that aren't feeding hard can be expected to be spooky, but it'll be drag that'll spook them ten times before leader thickness will.

The author fishing the Hampshire Bourne
'... saw thousands of fish – and they saw me.' (Photo Stephen Beville)

I use the thinnest material I can consistent with not losing fish. This means, where I fish, never tying on a tippet under 3.5 lbs breaking strain. Never say never – but I don't carry a spool of thinner stuff. 4.75 lbs is my UK standard and default: 7.5 lbs in Iceland and New Zealand. I use the best fluorocarbon, and it's very thin for its breaking strain. Am I concerned about tippet-tethering? Only in the very much thicker sizes such as 9 lbs and over, and where additionally the fly is small.

FOOTNOTE 4: This business of sinking the tippet with which I so disagree has been handed down for decades, but actually only for a few of them. Skues, writing in *The Way of a Trout with a Fly* in 1921 (p 41) referring to what he had learned from looking up through the sunken window of Dr Francis Ward's experimental pond, said that when thrown on the surface dry, the gut was not noticeable from underneath except in the window, and not very noticeable then. Sunken gut he says 'became obvious', and goes on to say that 'the insistence of the dry fly angler on ... absolute dryness of gut and fly seems ... to be thoroughly justified.' So not only did Skues see the same as my camera, but he is clear that keeping your tippet floating was de rigueur up to the 1920s at least. Who was it that led us astray?

Kiss my Cul from above

Kiss my Cul from below

WHATEVER
FLOATS YOUR FLY

IT HAS BEEN CALCULATED that an artificial weighs, at minimum, three or four times as much as the same-sized natural (Datus C Proper), so it starts at a huge disadvantage if complete floatation is the objective.

In fact it is pretty damned hard to float any dry fly for longer than a cast or three. This chapter is about floatation. Making flies float better has been an understandable priority for fly fishers, and although as we have seen that semi-dryness is not disastrous, the angler certainly needs the best tools at his disposal.

Whatever floats your fly
Historical and current practicalities

What floated your fly back in the 1500s, 1600s, 1700s and 1800s was the structure and materials used, together with your own skill in keeping it 'swimming'. These materials included the water-repelling feathers of waterfowl and ducks, as well as poultry hackles, long guard hairs in dubbings and water-resistant hair like that of pigs. The coming of the cocked dry fly and the development of 'spreading' (circular or figure-of-eight false casting), and of

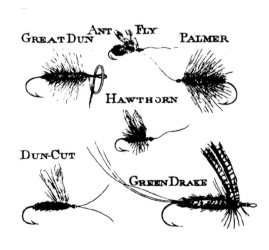

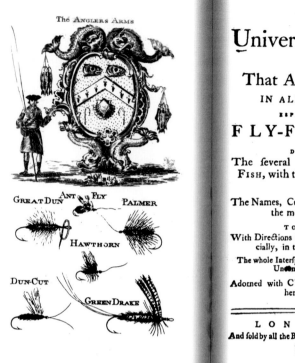

Thé ANGLERS ARMS

GREAT DUN ANT FLY PALMER

HAWTHORN

DUN-CUT

GREEN DRAKE

THE
Univerſal Angler;
O R,
That ART Improved,
IN ALL ITS PARTS,
ESPECIALLY IN
FLY-FISHING:
DESCRIBING
The ſeveral Sorts of Freſh-water
FISH, with their propereſt BAITS.
ALSO
The Names, Colours, and Seaſons of all
the moſt uſeful Flies
TOGETHER
With Directions for making each FLY Artifi-
cially, in the moſt exact Manner.
The whole Interſperſed with many Curious and
Uncommon Obſervations.
Adorned with CUTS of the ſeveral FISH
herein treated on.

LONDON Printed ;
And ſold by all the Bookſellers in Town and Country.
MDCCLXVI.

Frontispiece of the Richard Bowlker book of 1766

floatants, didn't substantially alter the fact that materials and construction were, and are, the main things that make your flies float. Silk lines and gut casts made things worse, not better.

Only advanced floatants and different fly designs, as we shall see in this chapter, changed things radically, but not until the latter half of the 20th century. Mind you, the softer hackles of the pre-cocked-dry-fly anglers will have bent more on the meniscus, and pierced it less – and in my guess, did so by design. That's why they typically faced slightly backwards and away from the direction of tethering. Cocked flies needed the newly available floatants to help stop their stiffer, perpendicular hackle points piercing the film.

On the following page the two example of Halford's recommended patterns for the standard basic Olive Dun and Olive Spinner show how much he relied on what we, nowadays, would call drastic over-hackling.

No. 8

OLIVE DUN

FEMALE

And as we shall see, the introduction of silk lines, and of gut casts that sank much more readily than horsehair did, meant that the fly had much more of a downward pull to overcome to stay afloat – and for longer. The heavy, fully-wound hackle was part of the solution, but also made the fly fall over.

The solutions to this, the innovations that made the classic dry fly possible, were false-casting and the use, first of paraffin, and then of Vaseline diluted in petrol. Both were used to pre-waterproof flies, and the former to treat them in use as well. Other oils, such as gun oil, had also been used as early as 1857 – mentioned by Hi-Regan (J J Dunne) in *How and Where to Fish in Ireland* (1904). The flavours didn't seem to put the trout off any more than did Ronalds' experimentally pepper and mustard-coated flies (see next chapter) although non-smelly paraffin was developed in case it did.

Purified red deer fat was used to make your silk line float, as were numerous other treatment regimes that involved patience and hard work – lines had to be dried, shellacked, powdered and polished, or rubbed down with Vaseline and beeswax. The fact was, dry fly fishing had become hard work, and several writers recommended it only for trophy fish.

More and more sophisticated floatants came with the progress of the last century, no doubt aided by spin-offs from the boiler house scientific development generated by two world wars – I dare say many a military 'techie' was also a fly fisherman. The most used of these spin-offs was Mucilin, first as a paste floatant for lines, and later as a liquid treatment for flies. The red tin version was the traditional formula dating back to the

No. 12

OLIVE SPINNER, FEMALE

early years of the century, whilst the green tin version came much later and contained silicones. A veritable explosion of floatants has burst forth since the 1960s, instant sprays with silicones, pastes of ever more refined materials, dry hydrophilic (water-absorbent) shakes, hydrophobic (water-repellent) powders, silicone drops, pre-proofing morning-after liquids ... if it can be conceived of, we have it available to us now.

Personally I have, after a fishing lifetime of trial and experiment, lit upon a small shortlist that I always carry and use as alternatives. As you will know by now I like to float my leader and tippet as well as my line. For all three I use a clear paste floatant called Dave's Bug Flote. It makes them float really quite well, lubricates the line for casting and doesn't wash off too quickly. Used on the fly, it coats it and will make it float well in the rain. It's also very good to coat a nymph with so as to make it float in the surface and give it the impression of a nymphal skin ... this is a particularly good trick. Bug Flote is much the same as the ever-popular Gink, but I think it is better. Neither is much good for CdC, however – too much clogging of the little frondy bits.

For CdC I used to (and still sometimes do) use hydrophobic fumed silica – that's the white superfine powder that you brush into your fly. It does discolour the fly, making it lighter and whiter but it is supremely effective. It's sold in little bottles under a fancified name at what must be one hundred times the manufacturing cost, so I cannot bring myself to recommend it by brand name. As a retired marketing man I do know about the costs of selling and wholesale and retail mark-ups ... but really! Go and Google hydrophobic fumed silica and buy it in industrial quantities is my advice ... but don't breathe it in when you get it, and use it downwind of your nose and eyes.

As a great believer in the iron blue, our tiny olivey-black Baetis that likes to hatch in bad weather, but which trout seem to prefer above others, I was troubled by the whitening of the fly by this powder, and looked for a super-floatant that didn't discolour the fly. Until recently, there wasn't a liquified paste floatant that did a first class job on CdC without clagging it up – but there is now, in the shape of Tiemco Dry Magic. It, too, is immorally expensive, especially in the UK and Europe – but it is so good it's worth an amount for which you can buy a good meal. Go without the meal, lose weight, and buy a tube of it.

With these very much better floatants you can now expect to make almost any fly float high, even, and indeed particularly, no-hackle flies

Hydrophobic duckling showing the silvering effect of air
(Note you don't have to be proud of the surface to be dry and floating. No proofed fly ever fails to dent or bend the meniscus around it. But sharp, unbending hackles would sink him)

like the KmC. Such simple sparse dun imitations really do get fewer last minute refusals. Dry Magic and Bug Flote are so good that in anointing just the front end of an emerger, you need to be careful only to use a tiny amount, otherwise the force exerted by your cast will make the floatant migrate through the whole of the fly and the shuck-imitating rear end will float as well, when you don't want it to. Of course, if you have followed my advice and tied your upstream emerger in reverse that problem doesn't arise as the emerging head end will be at the back – but you will want to degrease and perhaps apply a sinkant to the last few inches of your tippet. A tiny split shot can also help in achieving the correct angle.

All these preparations can be removed from flies with any proprietary spray can of brake and clutch cleaner from your local automotive store. Then offering flies up to the steam from a kettle will re-prink the hackle and other fibres before re-proofing. Worth doing if your fly isn't in a tree like mine, and you want to offer it again tomorrow using a 'morning after' treatment like 'Watershed', the effects of which last longer (although not all morning I find). And I usually climb trees to get my flies back, since I am a slow tyer and of part Scottish ancestry. And if like me you forgot to avoid drying your treated flies on your piece of amadou, and your amadou no longer absorbs water so well, give that a squirt of the brake and clutch cleaner too. It's the only way the Nanny State will now allow us to access carbon tetrachloride; that's not the only solvent it contains, by the way, and an extra advantage is that it will take lunchtime grease spots off your shirtfront if you go out to dine later.

Fuller's earth powder (sold by online health product stores), made into a paste with washed-out scouring-powder residue (powdered pumice), will sink leaders well for nymphing. It will also take the flash off them prior to applying floatant, and this can be a big help in avoiding rejections.

Jeremy Waters and I took a midday break from habitat restoration work on the South Newton Reach of the Wylye and went into the Bell Inn for a pint. Taff Stephens, long time head river watcher for our Wilton Fly Fishing Club was there, accepted his usual half, and plunged into heavily Welsh-accented conversation with us. We talked about the flies that were hatching and imitative patterns, with me listening hard, Taff being no mean fly-dresser and the trainer of the Welsh fly fishing team.

The Great Anusol Disaster of 2005

'Look you, Peter,' he says 'you know the very best fly floatant don't you?'

'You're going to tell me something I don't know, aren't you, Taff?'

'Yes, well,' he says, 'here it is, then ... Anusol'.

'How did you find that out?' I say.

'By accident. You want to try it!'

Well the next few times I went into a chemist there were pretty young things serving, so it wasn't until months later that, in the Amesbury Boots I found an assistant of whom I didn't care if they thought I had piles. The picture on p 60 shows the result. One untreated PhD is happily floating on the surface of a beer glass full of water. The other – treated with Anusol – is pinkish white all over and has sunk like a stone to the bottom. You can't see this of course, but it also smells quite pleasant, with a perfume no doubt designed to mask others. Anusol is an emulsion, effective for troubled fundaments, but not for flies. I had been had.

FOOTNOTE 1: I had often wondered what on earth possessed dry fly designers to specify, and fly-tyers and anglers to use, the up-eyed hook. It puts exactly the wrong angle of pull on the point in trying to achieve good hooking. If you try it out by attaching an up-eyed hook to a length of tippet and pulling it across your thumb nail in the time-honoured test of hookability, you'll find it drags every time and the point can't easily get a purchase. I now realise that the up-eyed hook does not make any sense at all unless the fly is attached using a Turle knot. The Turle knot was invented around the time (1879) that H S Hall was creating the designs and setting up the manufacturing of his eyed hooks. It was invented by, and named after, Major W G Turle, a neighbour of G S Marryat with whom Halford and Hall were cooperating. With the Turle knot, the fine drawn gut was led directly through the upturned eye and then fastened around the shank behind it with a slip knot loop, space having been left in the tying so as to achieve this. It resulted in the fly lying horizontally along the line of the hook shank, relative to the surface of the water. It is not now much in use for small dry flies (although used for salmon flies still). However the tradition of using up-eyed hooks for dry flies has survived the virtual extinction of the Turle knot – to the detriment of hooking ability. They really should be outlawed now. On the following page is a representative collection of chalk stream flies from the early part of the last century given to me by the well-known chalk stream fisherman and biographer of Frank Sawyer, the late Sidney Vines. They are nearly all on up-eyed hooks, and although depredated sadly by moth, can be seen to be small and very dark dun in colour relative to the average of current dry flies.

Sidney Vines' old chalk stream flies

FOOTNOTE 2: Tony Hayter, on p 56 of his book, *F M Halford and the Dry Fly Revolution*, drew attention to the first known use in this country of duck preen gland oil to waterproof the fly by Dr Thomas Sanctuary in 1867 on the Dorset Frome. Sanctuary wrote to the *Fishing Gazette* about this successful experiment 57 years later in 1924. He makes it clear that on the Itchen at Winchester in the late 1860s dry fly fishing was only just coming in and no floatants were used, only false casting to dry the fly. His gillie had suggested it: 'Pity, Zur, that you can't oil the fly like a duck oils his feathers, then her wud float surely.' It worked, but the oil gland he had surgically removed became somewhat 'whiffy' in his pocket so he 'was obliged to discard it' and apparently didn't pass on the idea to others (or seize the notion of using the CdC feathers themselves in fly-dressing – if he had we might have leapt forward a hundred or so years in one bound).

There's another reason for us to be cross with Sanctuary. When the grayling record was established by a River Test fish of 4 lbs 8 oz, he went back and falsified his diary to show that he had caught a 4 lb 9 oz grayling (actually 1 lb 9 oz) at Bemerton on the River Nadder (actually on the Wilton FFC waters on the Wylye) but did not change the date. The *Diary of an All-round Angler* (1949) of Patrick Smythe records the details of their fishing day together at Great Wishford on the Wylye

GRAYLING. 4 lbs 9 ozs.

Postcard dated by stamps to 1953
the record fish attributed to Sanctuary on the reverse

on 24 October 1883 and keys precisely to the altered details in Sanctuary's own diary for that date – a 66-year posthumous conviction for the angler's lie. You can see it's been altered.

Tony Hayter is the person who discovered this, and he tells me that Sanctuary's weasel-claim was made in *The Fishing Gazette* 26 July 1913. In referring to the Wiltshire Avon he wrote, 'In the latter stream, or rather in one of its tributaries, I once caught with a small dry fly a perfectly shaped and conditoned fish which weighed just over 4 1/2 lbs.' The claim was accepted, and the above picture postcard shows that the lie persisted even after Smythe's book was published.

FOOTNOTE 3: Very recently my research has turned up the possibility of even more dramatic improvements in floatation (actually waterproofing) products for application to fibres (initially outdoor clothing), created by nano-technology. Tested briefly and totally insufficiently on CdC flies on a very cold and fishless river session, the results were encouraging – still floating high after the rubbed-in spit test. I think we shall see more of this nanotec stuff before too long. I've also been looking at nano-filament tippet material from the coarse fishing world. It is amazingly fine and light for its breaking strain, but opaque. (It can be coloured with marker pen however). If you think like me, that drag will put trout off more than seeing the tippet, it may have its uses – but it is so light that it may not have enough weight to collapse the tippet loosely on the surface, and instead get blown out too straight by any breath of a breeze. Exciting stuff though for the inveterate experimenter.

waiting trout below. As the drifting duns approached, Mr. Kell began to pick them off the water and, holding them as delicately as possible, severed the wings from the bodies; he then carefully replaced them upon the identical line of drift and sent them to the waiting trout downstream, all of them still alive and able to assume the characteristic pose with body and stylets pointing skyward. Time after time this operation was repeated. Sometimes several wingless bodies were placed to encircle a winged natural and sometimes these were placed in a long breach between the winged naturals. In all, 37 wingless bodies were sent down over the same feeding trout *and not a single one of them was taken!* The winged insect, even when surrounded by the wingless bodies, was always chosen to the entire exclusion of the latter.

Now that is an earth-shaking experiment for the flyfisherman and it contains many implications which cannot be idly dismissed but must be properly examined in order to form an accurate estimate of their worth.

73

Trout and Visibility of Gut.

We have the following note from Mr. Percy Laming.

I have seen a great many articles lately with regard to trout taking the fly and there are many reasons put forward as to why they either do or they don't.

"A good many years ago I was standing on the bridge on the River Itchen at Marketworthy with the late Mr. Halford. There was quite a good rise of fly and fish rising well, but we could not do anything with them. I suggested that the only possible reason was that the fish could see too much gut. He rather pooh-poohed this and said we had not got the right fly. However, I thought I was right so I suggested dropping a few flies into the river to see if they would be taken. We dropped about a dozen, nearly all different patterns, and every one that went over a rising fish was taken, no matter what the pattern was. I think nothing could more clearly demonstrate that the reason for fish not taking the artificial fly is the presence of gut, and I have often noticed that they see more on a cloudy day. There is always hope of a fish in very bright sun."

Top:
Vincent Marinaro, *A Modern Dry Fly Code* (1950), p 73

Above:
***Salmon and Trout* magazine**
(October 1925)

EXPERIMENTS OUTSIDE THE BOX – A lot of which are still relevant to us today

EXPERIMENTALLY-MINDED ANGLERS HAVE, over the last century or more, tested the trout's predilections and aversions by setting up, either by design or by accident, numerous trials. These experiments vary from the simply anecdotal to several that were more carefully designed, and although none of them have been subjected to the rigour of statistics, one or two of them are robust enough to make you think. Even the little test conducted by Percy Laming (a celebrated salmon fisherman of the day) and shown opposite (bottom left) was enough to call in question the pattern-centric statement of Halford. And those addressing the importance of wings on a dry fly have certainly influenced my own designs.

I find these experiments quite fascinating and I wish I could find more of them. Perhaps readers will oblige?

Vincent Marinaro was certainly fascinated by such experiments, and so were his successors Datus C Proper (*What the Trout Said*) and Gary LaFontaine in his book *The Dry Fly*. Marinaro mentions, without detail, records of numerous experiments showing that any artificial dropped to the waiting trout without a leader would be taken; and others, however, in which the trout would accept only one of many patterns floated down to them without leaders.

He tells the story of an argument in the London Flyfishers' Club which was brought to a demoralised end by one of the members relating an experience in which he had the entire contents of his fly box, twelve dozen flies, snatched by the wind and distributed helter-skelter on the water below the bridge he stood on. 'His dismay was overpowering, since the flies represented a costly investment, but imagine his amazement when there came a sudden and tremendous rise of trout to the manna of leaderless artificials.'

He immediately tied on a succession of flies from his remaining stock but could not get a single rise. He concluded that the fish had consumed the best and most tempting flies that he had from his first box, but sadly for the life of him could not remember what was in it.

He might however have come equally logically to the alternative conclusion, the same one as Mr Percy Laming, that it was the gut that was putting the fish off when he started fishing, rather than an unhappy choice of pattern – or it was the drag?

Yet gut, or nylon, or fluorocarbon, is not itself the cause of rejection. Here is a quotation from George Harvey's *Techniques of Trout Fishing and Fly Tying* (revised edition, pages 20-21):

'I made my way to the head of a flat pool I knew held a good population of trout. I sat down upon the bank and started a chum line of [Japanese] beetles. It wasn't long until I had about a dozen trout taking every beetle that floated down. Now I took twenty-inch pieces of hard nylon of all sizes I had with me and inserted the end of the nylon into some of the beetles and sent them down the chum line. Since there was no drag on the nylon, the browns picked off most all of the beetles that were attached to the nylon.

This was not my idea. I had read of a similar experiment conducted by John Crowe and I wanted to check it for myself. Let me tell you, I was really impressed. Most of what we read today and what most fly fishermen believe is that the fine terminal part of the leader is more invisible and that this is the reason for using fine tippets. In fact many articles have been written that recommend that the size of the terminal tippet should be determined by the size of the fly one is using. This experiment blasts that theory because the stream-bred browns did not refuse a live beetle on the free-floating and drag-free pieces of nylon is sizes up to .015in.'

And Ralph Cutter (on his website) wrote:

'On Fall River and Fort Creek I've glued foot long pieces of 15 pound Maxima to Hexagenia mayflies and grasshoppers. These notoriously selective fish rose to the bugs without hesitation, yet they turned away from the same fly attached to 5X tippet connected somewhere upstream to a fly rod.'

So don't worry too much about the thickness of your tippet. If it is wiggly, you're still in with a chance, so lengthen it before going thinner if the fish are big.

It's the drag that puts fish off, not the tippet – attach your tippet to a fly line and cast it, and your tippet tethers the fly (as we have seen in chapter five), with the inevitable result that drag, whether micro-drag, or mega-drag sets in before very long and results in refusal. So we need to learn to cast our fly without drag.

Really quite a long time ago, in the 1830s, whilst preparing for his groundbreaking book *The Fly-fisher's Entomology*, Alfred Ronalds built an octagonal observation chamber overlooking his beat on the River Blythe. The chamber was a few feet above the water and carefully designed so that the occupant could observe trout in the river below without disturbing their activities. From this he made notes that constitute one of the first systematic surveys of trout behaviour (as Andrew Herd notes, in his book *The Fly*).

Amongst Ronalds' many conclusions was the crucial one that 'one-fly men' are mistaken in their approach, and that trout do distinguish and have preferences between one insect and another. So success in imitating preferred prey flies by GISSO (General Impression of Shape Size and Orientation), is a worthwhile objective to pursue.

In fact, most if not all of the thinking, experimental, and observational angling writers over the last century have addressed the issue of how successful it is to concentrate entirely on presentation – with the pattern being immaterial – or alternatively to concentrate entirely on pattern rather than presentation: and have come to the conclusion that both these extreme strategies reduce the angler's effectiveness. Whilst sometimes pattern can be paramount, and sometimes presentation, the outcome of their deliberations is that you really have to pay attention to both. None of Ronalds, Halford, Mottram, Skues, Marinaro, Proper, LaFontaine, Cutter, Schullery or Herd would disagree. So don't listen to the siren voices of those who tell you that a 'little brown job' is all you need. It may work some of the time but you will fail to maximise your chances. But it will, of course, almost always work for stockies, being pellet-colour. Do you want to go and catch stockies using a pellet approximation? If so, you are failing to get as much real sportingness into your fishing as you could, and also reading the wrong book. This book could yet be your Road to Damascus, though, if you've got this far into it.

Fred Arbona (the tireless surveyor of trout behaviour) perhaps put it best in his book *Mayflies, the Angler and the Trout*:

'The correct placing and drift or action of an artificial is the most important factor involved in getting the interest of a trout; the selection of an exact imitation in conjunction with proper delivery is the key to make him take it. The two fly fishing principles go hand in hand and are not meant to be divorced from each other.'

So work on your presentation as well as being fussy about your patterns.

Ronalds also concluded from his observation room that, since trout assess the edibility of items using their tongues, softness in the construction of an artificial fly is an advantage, and that hard bodies may be risen to and taken well, but lead to greater levels of rejection:

'The bodies of these delicate insects are sometimes beautifully imitated by stained hair and gut; but a fly should be made as soft as silk, and softer, if it is to be retained in the mouth of a fish many seconds. This is the chief reason why wings stiffened with varnish and gut bodies cannot supplant the old-fashioned furs and feathers.'

Again Arbona agrees with this finding – soft bodies are better. So tie, or buy, hairy and feathery flies that are a little bit squishy; or be sure to strike quickly when using hard flies.

Experiments concerning wings seem to me to provide crucial input to successful dry fly design.

Many writers have conducted experiments using tanks and ponds with windows to evaluate how the trout sees the fly. The most thorough and comprehensive experimenters were perhaps E W Harding in the UK, and Vincent Marinaro in America, and they explained everything with drawings of great clarity.

They came to the conclusion that the trout will always see a hatched fly first by the dimples made by its feet in the mirror. Next, the trout will see the tips of its wings appearing over the edge of the mirror and into the window. So the wings are the confirmation that the thing that made the dimples is a dun. (To the trout, this is experiential knowledge, not intellectual knowledge).

But, as they rise to investigate the fly they will normally keep it at the edge of their window. Only if they feel they need to get a really good look at it, if something is suspect, will they let it come right into the window, and, if an even longer look is necessary, drift downstream under it. To do so, however, makes the issue of whether to eat it or not into more of a cliffhanger for the trout, since every inch downstream will cost the fish unrewarded energy (expended to get back up to its feeding station) if it doesn't take the fly.

So wing experiments are important. See the photographic clipping (at top left) on the first page of this chapter. The full story is as follows (from Marinaro *A Modern Dry Fly Code* p 73):

'Moved by a powerful curiosity to discover more about the relative importance of the window and mirror, Mr James Kell of our fly-fishers company devised and finally engineered a plan during the height of the Hendrickson hatch on the Yellow Breeches a few years ago.*

An opportune time and place were discovered where a fair-sized trout was feeding with clock-like regularity on the drifting duns. The trout's position was located in a narrow line of drift where he was able to intercept any or all that he pleased. After noting that the feeding trout allowed very few of the Hendricksons to pass, Mr Kell began to pick them off the water and, holding them as delicately as possible, severed the wings from the bodies; he then carefully placed them upon the identical line of drift and sent them to the waiting trout downstream, all of them still alive and able to assume the characteristic pose with the body and stylets pointing skyward. Time after time this operation was repeated. Sometimes several wingless bodies were placed to encircle a winged natural and sometimes these were placed in a long breach between the winged naturals. In all, 37 wingless bodies were sent down over the same feeding trout and not a single one of them was taken! The winged insect, even when surrounded by the wingless bodies, was always chosen to the entire exclusion of the latter. Now that is an earth-shaking experiment for the fly fisherman.'

*The Hendrickson is an Ephemerella, the same family as the British BWO. In the States however the name BWO indicates a Baetis. Two cultures separated by the same language.

Both Datus Proper and Gary LaFontaine calculated that in order for the wings on an angler's artificial (which sits lower down in the water than

Skues' high-wing dun patterns

the three-to-four times lighter natural) to end up being seen as the same
height as those of the natural by the trout ... they need to be half as long
again. LaFontaine says: 'A size 18 with wings the size of a size 14' is his
go-to recipe. And Skues' dun patterns, as illustrated in the Frontispiece
to *Minor Tactics of the Chalk Stream*, had wings of exaggerated length
relative to Halford's. So my dry fly patterns in chapter ten have over-long
wings. I didn't invent them, by the way, I stole the bits. So your flies'
wings should not be stinted as to length either.

Gary LaFontaine built upon Kell's experiment as follows:

'For the fun of it, my friends and I devised an offshoot of this
experiment. Painting the wings of mayflies odd colours with
marking pens, we expected absolutely no results – there was no
theory preceding these tests. What happened? The sampling wasn't
large enough to be reliable, only 242 mayflies! (*my exclamation
mark*). But the trout showed some interesting biases. Chartreuse
wings worked slightly better at noon than red ones, but in the
evening this preference was reversed. Also, brilliant white wings

attracted a lot of attention all the time, and metallic coatings of silver and gold failed on the trout. What did all this prove? That we had a lot to learn about colour.'

All I can say is that if the brilliant white wing attracted a lot of attention all the time, then that tends to add yet another reason why the Parachute Adams is, worldwide, the dry fly that demonstrates most attractiveness to trout. And a reason why the non-imitative Royal Wulff, with two white wings, is a worldwide go-to as well. So make sure you always have some Para Adams in your box, in different sizes down to 20.

Although the details of his experiments are not recorded, William Stewart in *The Practical Angler* (1857) was able to say that 'a fly with the exposed part of the hook taken off will raise more trout than a fly with the same left on', and my friend Clive Hallam was able to confirm this after becoming a Buddhist and cutting the points off all his flies so as not to cause pain to an animal.

Perhaps this is not a very helpful finding, since, as Paul Schullery observes on this, why should we care as long as the trout takes the fly anyway? But it does tend to lend support to one's having available, for difficult fish, some flies tied in the upside down mode. (Which was not, incidentally, invented by Goddard and Clarke as they mistakenly claimed in their book *The Trout and the Fly*, but by Robert Venables in 1662). So always have a few USD flies in your box too. Neil Patterson's Funneldun works well, though naturally I prefer my own USD, PhD.

Gary LaFontaine, and more recently Ralph Cutter (author of *Fish Food*), have spent thousands of hours diving and snorkelling to watch fly and fish behaviour. They both talk about the sparks of light, like little jewels, that nymphs and flies present themselves as – underwater and in making their journey to the surface.

Paul Schullery and John Gierach disdain beadheads and, since their dislike is aesthetic, they have every right to, but at the same time there is every reason to believe that beads imitate these phenomena and that trout are attracted to nymphs incorporating beads that flash – and for an imitative reason rather than because of a more visceral aggressive or chasing reaction. So carry and use some bead heads.

In one particular study, LaFontaine's diving group cast a great deal of light on the trout's rejection of natural insects. They watched trout breaking off a rise because of some odd action by a natural. The conclusion

The wrecked PhD at the end of the rainy day on the River Wye
effectively an emerger

they came to, after snorkelling downstream on their backs and studying emerging duns (a brilliant idea and an observation you can't achieve from a fixed point because they are swept away from you too fast) was that fish mainly abort a rise when the wind pushes the dun across the current. So they then sampled the stomach contents of fish they caught on both calm and windy days, and discovered a difference in their feeding pattern. Whilst on calm days emergent nymphs constituted 56% of stomach contents and duns 44%, on windy days emergent nymphs shot up to 73%, and duns fell to 27%. The moral they drew, which increased their success rate under windy conditions, was to use a damp emerger instead of a dry fly. So go for emergers on windy days.

I have experienced the same phenomenon. Last year I was fishing up the Monsal Dale stretch of the Derbyshire Wye in a storm of wind and heavy prolonged rain. Duns were hatching prolifically and being blown away by the wind very quickly. I tried to imitate them with my PhD but the rain waterlogged it in spite of all attempts with the best floatants to make it sit up. However the fish took it avidly all afternoon and I never had reason to change the fly.

Trout will swim over to eat the (tiny) iron blue
I think they like its flavour

One experiment that I love is that carried out by Ronalds on taste and smell in trout:

'I once threw upon the water, from my hut (by blowing them through a tin tube), successively, ten dead houseflies, towards a trout known to me by a white mark upon the nose (occasioned by the wound of a hook), all of which he took.

Thirty more with cayenne pepper and mustard plastered on the least conspicuous parts of them, where then administered in the same manner. These he also seized, twenty of them at the instant they touched the water, and not allowing time for the dressing to be dispersed; but the other ten remained a second or two upon the surface before he swallowed them, and a small portion of the dressing parted and sank.

The next morning several exactly similar doses were taken by the same fish, who probably remembered the previous day's repast, and seemed to enjoy them heartily. From these and similar experiments, such as getting trout to take flies dipped in honey, oil, vinegar, etc,

I concluded that if the animal has taste, his palate is not peculiarly sensitive.'

Perhaps a conclusion that the trout's palate is not sensitive to the same stimuli as ours would have been safer. Or, like the angler eating curry, Scarface might have suffered a bit in the morning ablutions ... but been able to ignore that later discomfort in favour of a repeat of the first and more favourable, eating experience. Ronalds' underlying assumption was that trout would not like pepper and spice. The good scientist doesn't make assumptions! *Musca domestica* vindaloo (hot housefly curry) might have worked an even more powerful mojo.

FOOTNOTE 1: Anthropomorphising trout isn't always wrong. Nor is the reverse procedure (piscimorphising men). Men, like trout, are driven by their needs for cover, good food in return for least effort and, at the appropriate time, sex. I am reminded

The Gary Loomis sponsored American-British-Russian Kola Peninsula Northern Rivers Exploratory Group 1990
(from left) Eric Redman, Dave Griswold; Nigel Sturgeon; Herb Good; Jerry Melcher; the author; Andrej Velikanov (living with animals) (Kent Hansen took the picture)

of what our Russian guide Andrej Velikanov said in 1991 when asked on camera what it had been like to live for ten days with five Americans and two Brits. Accentedly he growled: 'Am biologeest. Am used to leeving with animals.'

FOOTNOTE 2: Skues in the 1920s went and spent some time viewing natural and artificial flies through the window of Dr Francis Ward's underground observation chamber beside his pond. In addition to being fascinated by the trout's 'window' and impressed by the brilliant lighting of the naturals seen in it, he also noted that with a dry mayfly pattern the gut was not very noticeable: but that with a wet pattern the gut stood out like a sore thumb (Andrew Herd, *The Fly* 1st edition, p 352). This is the same conclusion that my underwater photograph illustrates at the start of chapter two.

FOOTNOTE 3: Many experimenters, including Ronalds, have concluded that trout cannot hear underwater. My waterproof digital camera can hear and record the sound of me and my friends talking, when held a foot beneath the surface. A better hypothesis might be that trout don't always react with fright or flight to airborne noise. But my belief is that they can hear it, and can therefore become sensitised to noises they come to associate with danger. Just as carp have been shown to become sensitised to a gong and associate it with food in that other well known experiment. So best to 'study to be quiet'.

I am conscious that there is already 'too much information' in this chapter, and too many small pokes at great writers whom I admire, so I shall leave the hole now before digging any deeper. Or, as Skues put it signing off a letter to the *Flyfishers' Club Journal* in 1937: 'I think, perhaps, you will be grateful if I end my observations here'.

Fifty Shades of Green
a previously unseen trout rises for the second time on the River Wylye

FISHING IN RIVERS WHERE YOU CAN'T SEE THE FISH

IN THE PREFACE, I rather made it sound as if I always fish rivers in which you can see the fish most of the time. But, although that is my preference, I actually spend three-quarters of my fishing days on rivers where you can't see the fish. This is the normal situation for most fly fishermen everywhere. You have to learn how to deal with it. Mostly you do with it by sitting down, keeping a low profile, and waiting for a trout to give itself away.

If the river is in good heart, the water temperature is not too cold or too hot for the trout's metabolism, and they are in a mood to feed, one or more of them will give themselves away within half an hour and often sooner. Having the patience to wait and the concentration to watch for that period will give you a much better chance of a much better fish than would an immediate frontal attack on the water.

Luckily for us the trout is omnivorous, and luckily for us there is usually some form of food floating down on the surface, however infrequently. This means that there is really quite a good chance that a trout that is getting 95% of its food below the surface will come up for the one in twenty item that floats down above its head. But infrequently.

So learn to wait and watch.

This is what happened in the photo opposite, and a wild trout of two pounds came to my floating mayfly on the first cast following the taking of the photograph. (I had resolved, for once, to take photographs of rises on the Wylye before I cast to them rather than as usual taking a snapshot of the place I caught a fish in, afterwards).

On the River Wylye in Wiltshire, where I have fished for 30 years now, the invisibility problem is not normally caused by a lack of clarity in the water. It is a proper chalkstream fed by purified and clarified water from

Glare and the angle of the evening sun make fish spotting impossible here

the chalk aquifers. But the water is so fertile that weeds grow in profusion, and the gravel substrate is covered in green and brown algae. Whilst this is terrific food for nymphs and larvae of all kinds, it invests your whole view of what is in front of you with 'Fifty Shades of Green', and that makes it usually impossible to see a fish until it is too late, and the fish has seen you. And the glare by itself can blind you entirely to activity under the surface.

The same factors create invisibility for trout on the other rivers that I fish – on the Derbyshire Wye, on the Welsh Usk, and on the Big Laxa in Iceland where the bottom is black volcanic sand. Clear waters in all cases; the trout can see you though you can't see them because of the dark bottom and general background.

One of the prime tricks in learning how to deal with trout that you can't see in rivers where your visibility is compromised, is to go and somehow get access to rivers in which you can see the trout. Of course, when you can see them, you can see, evaluate, and learn from their reactions to your fly and to your presentation. That in itself is a major learning opportunity, the lessons from which you can carry back to your home river and act upon.

But the main thing you learn from fishing for trout in rivers where you can see the fish is that on your home river, if the fish are on the feed and have come out of their resting and shelter holts, there are going to be plenty of them in front of you. On your obscured-vision home river they would be within your sight if you could see them. Ask yourself; why should it be any different when you are looking at a river where you cannot see the fish? They are there.

If you would hesitate to move forward on the sighted-fish river for fear of scaring them, why should you behave any differently on the unsighted-fish river? You have to assume that they are there if there are signs of fish feeding at all, and put a fly over them or among them.

The most important thing you learn from rivers with visible fish, is that there are just as many fish in front of you in rivers with non-visible fish. Does that sound like Irish logic? Just learn to behave as if they are there.

Another thing that fishing a sight-fishing river will teach you will be to see the almost invisible, evanescent surface disturbance associated with a refusal. You will have seen this on the river where you can see the trout, so you will recognise it, when all you can see is that tiny surface blooming, on the river where you can't. That will tell you that there is a trout there, but he didn't want your fly, although he did rise in the water to look at it. It gives you the opportunity to change your presentation or your fly or both, and to rest the fish for five minutes until he has 'come unscared'.

Shadow and a dark river bottom obscure vision of a big trout's holt on the Derbyshire Wye

Terry Ellmore, a 'good keen man' and expert of many years' standing on the Hampshire Avon and Dorset Frome and Piddle, tells me that Dick Walker, fly and coarse fishing guru and specimen hunter, used to say that 'trout come unscared at about twenty minutes to the pound' and that is a useful ready reckoner. So it is worth giving a refuser time, and worth not reinforcing his sense of unease with a further cast until he has had a chance to relax again. This should be our default precautionary assumption when a fish has rejected our offering. And probably change the fly while you are waiting.

So learn to 'rest' your fish, and to change the fly after a refusal.

The next tactic, the one you learn to move on to if no fish shows itself to your patient watch, is to work out the feeding lies in which fish are likely to be, and place a fly that they are likely to be used to eating (or an attractor fly) just there. Naturally this can be a dry fly or a nymph depending on your assessment of the conditions. And if a small one doesn't bring a response, a big one may. Or a combination of dry fly and nymph in the New Zealand-style may do the trick.

The best way of knowing where the fish are likely to be is to get to know the particular stretch of river really well. The second best way is to ask somebody who fishes it regularly, or the river keeper if there is one. I reckon that if you can acquire both knowledge of your own and information from a second pair of eyes as well, that is ideal, and better than either input taken separately.

So do both – learn the river, and ask too.

Reading books helps a bit, sometimes. (You know – the sort where the author produces drawings of wiggly river stretches with stylised fish showing where they may lie in respect of curves and rocks.) But to be frank, there is no substitute for learning about the particular stretch of the particular river that you are setting out to fish. 'Time spent in reconnaissance is seldom wasted.' I actually draw my own maps of the key stretches of the rivers I fish, and as the seasons progress I mark in the precise sites where I have seen or caught fish. That way I build up a useful database of places to go, and lies and fish to look for, in the rivers where I can't see the trout.

Keep a low profile; keep vegetation behind you; keep off the skyline; use shadows to give your polarised eyes the chance to see into the water. Wade if you can. I took a picture of my fishing partner Chris Patrick on the Wylye doing all those things, and casting a lovely loose line too. He

Chris Patrick, fishing the Wylye, has used tree shadow to spot a fish in a known lie

caught a beauty of a grayling that lived there, was visible but wasn't rising, on a Yellow Humpy that, well – attracted it.

Returning the favour of the amazing trip to the Itchen last year (related at the end of chapter one) I took Andrew Impey, the owner of the best chalk stream beat in the world, to the Wylye. With me spotting for him off the high banks like is done in New Zealand, we addressed half a dozen major trout, most of which could not be seen (though I knew where they lived), or could be seen only by me on the bank. Only one of them could we hook, though a few rises were forthcoming. Andrew is a damn fine angler and did everything right. He was kind enough to say how much he enjoyed the day, and he meant it. I relished it too. At least one essential ingredient of his enjoyment was his knowing the known unknowns – the fish were there. Without that, on a river where you can't see the fish, it is easy for disappointment and frustration to be the main product of such a day.

So fish with a friend whenever you can, and help each other to spot trout that one lone angler cannot. And learn to temper your expectations of rising fish.

Andrew Impey into a fish on the Wylye

As Ted Leeson put it (in *Inventing Montana*, 2009 – and nobody to my mind has ever put it better):

'Much of the technical fly-fishing literature at which anglers have suckled for over a century possesses acutely hallucinogenic properties. Ingesting it produces weird distortions, and never more so than in the matter of hatching insects and rising fish, which generations of recreational users have been induced to believe are the default condition of the average trout stream and a routine component of the ordinary angler's experience in fishing. While never nakedly advanced, this gravity-defying assumption hovers so invisibly in the background that it verges on a form of corruption.

In these instructional texts for which so many trees have given their beautiful lives, the expert always arrives stream side to meet with hatching flies and feeding trout as though by appointment.'

... and:

'The angler who regularly steps into a river at the recommended hour and sees neither a single insect nor a solitary rise feels not so much disappointed as personally inadequate, like a man who finds himself incapable of appreciating French cinema. The experts, he feels, would not have this problem. Something in the system has let him down. He pities his small patch of water, then discreetly sniffs himself and smells failure.'

... and:

'Nothing bespeaks both hope and the perils of optimism more than the thought of rising trout.'

These observations were made in relation to the Madison, a river fabled worldwide for its hatches.

Our forebears enjoyed, in the centuries through until the twentieth, very much better and more regular hatches than we generally do. But already, a hundred years ago, Lunn, Skues, Hills and others were reporting the lack of expected fly – sometimes whole species and for whole seasons. So it's living without fly hatches that's the given (See my own work on the National Fly Abundance Survey, referenced in chapter 14). There's no point in letting the lack of rising fish eat away at your enthusiasm; you have to get used to it and move on. Fishing in rivers where you can't see the fish, the title of this chapter, is what you have to get good at.

Owain Mealing fishing unseen by fish

For the Chub and Trout.

See where another hides himselfe as slye,
As did Acteon or the fearfull deere;
Behind a withy, and with a watchfull eye,
Attends the bit within the water cleare,
And on the top thereof doth move his flye,
With skilfull hand as if he living were. *
    Lo how the chub, the roch, the dace, and trout,
    To catch thereat do gaze and swim about.

His rod or cane made darke for being seen,
The lesse to feare the wary fish withall,
His line well twisted is, and wrought so cleane,
That being strong, yet doth it shew but small.
His hook not great, nor little, but between,†
That light upon the watry brim may fall.

From John Dennys' 'Secrets of Angling'

FISHING SO THE FISH CAN'T SEE YOU

IN THE PICTURE, OWAIN has positioned himself in the shade, under a withy with thick bush behind him so that he is not skylined, in a position from which he can see into shaded water, and is wearing dark, willow-coloured clothing and a lovely dark hat that I made him wear in preference to his habitual light-coloured one.

In the poem, dating from 1652, the poetic angling author, John Dennys, describes just that situation. He says that the hunter of trout hides himself as slyly as did Actaeon (the mythical hunter who saw the hunting goddess Diana in the altogether and had his hounds set upon him by her) as slyly as the timorous deer hides itself – behind a withy – and looks through the bit of the water he can see through. His rod is stained dark so that it cannot be seen by the fish, his line is thin, and his hook is as small and light as it can be. The basics of our sport, unchanged for at least the half-millennium since the printed word started to reinforce what may well have been a strong antecedent oral tradition.

There is a very big downside for many fly fishermen, a blight on their success, which results purely and simply from their fishing in rivers where they cannot see the fish. As we have seen in the previous chapter, the pessimistic assumption that there are no fish in front of you is the common and frequent consequence of not being able to see any fish.

This insidious belief that if you can't see them, then either they are not there or if they are there, they can't see you, leads inevitably to your doing things that scare them. And because you don't see them being scared, you don't get the feedback on your actions and you fail to modify them appropriately. The solution is always to act as if there is a whacking great big trout in plain view in front of you and looking straight at you.

If that was the situation, and there was such a trout, there are a whole bunch of things that you simply would not dream of doing – but which you probably do quite commonly when you cannot see into the water.

You would not stand up on the bank in full view against the sky. You would not walk up the bank. Instead, you would walk some way back from the bank, struggling if necessary through the uncut herbage and would look for signs of fish feeding either from that behind-the-scenes position, or try from a kneeling or seated position closer to the water.

You would not wear light-coloured clothing, especially not a light-coloured hat or shirt.

You would not make any sudden or fast movements – or indeed any movements at all that you did not absolutely have to make. You would wait for anything up to thirty minutes in any new spot, to

See how far your shadow falls when you can see it
but you don't see it in a dark river!

give any feeding fish present a reasonable chance to give itself away.

None of that would be a problem if the water was crystal clear and there were trout in front of you that you could see. But it is surprisingly difficult to remember to behave in that precautionary fashion when it isn't, and there aren't. The trout are however just as effectively scared – and will be shooting away upstream and scaring others that you yourself had not yet succeeded in scaring directly.

Am I getting my point across? I hope so.

We, as poor unreliable individuals, have a hard time remembering the necessary precautionary behaviours. That is normal, and for individuals it is a matter of what you might call conscience, a matter of whether you really care about being an effective hunter of trout. If you fail in this and don't catch as many trout as you might, many people would find it easy to understand and forgive. Behaving in such a way as to catch the maximum number of fish is not after all a moral imperative – it is a choice.

What is not easily understandable, and certainly not forgivable, is the way in which fly fishing tackle manufacturers conspire to provide us with rods, lines and other appurtenances which are guaranteed to scare fish unnecessarily. And the way in which they do not give us a choice.

If you want to buy one of the top performing rods, it will almost certainly be necessary for you to buy it coated in varnish that will flash like a heliograph both across the river and up and down it. In the wilder and more open river valleys of New Zealand, where you can be easily separated from your companions by a mile or more, I have often relied on rod flash to rendezvous with absent friends. (But they cannot rely on my flashing rod to locate me, because I have de-flashed all my rods). Worse still, these manufacturers, if you rub down the flash-producing varnish with fine grade wire wool, will insist that you have invalidated the guarantee.

From the trout's point of view, which you may remember we looked at in chapter six and found that they could easily see behind them, the flash generated by a rod with which the angler is casting starts at the butt and travels up the rod to the tip with incredible speed as the rod's power is released. It shoots towards the fish like a missile. Not one angler in twenty does anything to prevent this happening, and it is a very rare rod manufacturer that doesn't prioritise flash to catch the angler over flash that will scare the fish rigid. Brian Clarke and John Goddard drew clear attention to this in *The Trout and the Fly* 25 years ago, but virtually nothing has been done.

So de-flashing rods is essential, and if you do not want to invalidate your rod guarantee, I recommend the use of artist's removable matt varnish. This can be removed with white spirit should you need to claim against your guarantee, and is effective as long as it is sprayed in

Removable matt varnish and its effect on a rod

warm, dust free conditions and allowed to dry fully. Mask the rod rings with masking tape before spraying on the matt varnish, or your line will fail to shoot as well as you would like.

Line colour is also crucial, as was shown again with clear photographic illustrations by Clarke and Goddard a quarter of a century ago. They showed that in the trout's mirror, which is where most trout are likely to see the line most of the time, light-coloured lines are much more visible and dark ones blend into the reflection of the river bottom in the mirror. In the trout's window, which is where you would hope the trout would not see the line as you would be lining him if he did, lines of all colours are equally obvious. So the conclusion was, and remains, to use a dark coloured fly line – darkish olive or brown.

Good line colours for disguise against the river bottom reflected in the trout's mirror

Since fly line manufacturers persisted for decades in their lunatic devotion to producing bright coloured lines (pink, fluorescent orange, fluorescent chartreuse, bright white – anything as long as it would scare fish as its loop unrolled scarily towards them) I had myself for the last twenty years bought whatever line had the right tapers for me, and dyed it dark with olive, brown, or black fabric dye. This is still an option if you have a favourite line with a taper that suits your casting but it only comes in some insane colour.

However, in the last very few years we have been offered olive coloured lines. This would not have happened if there had not been thousands of people going to New Zealand to fish, a place where everybody knows that you should use a dark coloured line if catching fish rather than scaring them is an important part of your sport. There was actually enough demand for dark-coloured lines for the manufacturers to respond at last.

There is still a tendency however for line makers to take the view that it will be a paramount need for the stealthy angler to lay out a long straight, light line. Therefore, they have tended to offer dark-coloured lines with long thin front tapers. However as I pointed out in chapter five, it is far more important to be able to cast high and fast, achieving high line speed, and stopping and or dropping the rod at the end of the cast to achieve either a dump cast or a bounce-back cast, and a loose leader. Long thin front tapers are not what you want for this.

Mainly the manufacturers are still wedded to the idea of offering quick-loading, short-front taper lines in fluoro shades, much to everybody's disgust. In fact Richard Ward, of Bakewell on the Derbyshire Wye, has had to design and get manufactured his own dark-coloured short front taper line. Two of the few that are available are the olive-coloured Sage line that is designed to suit their fast action rods, and the dark green Jim Teeny 'Gary LaFontaine' line – both do the job beautifully. However neither is distributed in the UK because 'There's no call for it, Sir'.

What you want is a fast-loading short-front taper line in a dark colour that shoots really well (because it will be your sudden stopping of the fast shoot that will project a loose leader and tippet) and a long leader and tippet that will land in loose curves. The front of taper of the fly line should not attempt to be a leader as it cannot succeed in being one. You need a long leader, and putting a long leader on the front of a long thin fly line taper is de trop and will mess up your presentation as well as preventing you casting into the wind.

The line I use myself is the Airflo Ridge line, an experimental version of which they made in dark olive as opposed to the one they currently offer in light olive. I think I bought most of the surplus stock when they decided against it. But it delivers energy very well, stands up to lassoing flies out of trees, and shoots like a bullet. When I have used them all up I will buy the as-marketed light olive version and dye it.

The fact is I modify most of my kit so as to achieve effective camouflage and avoid scaring fish. Zingers on my waistcoat are either black or olive, or if I can only get the one I want in spooky chrome plate I paint it with green stained-glass-window paint from the craft shop. This has the advantage

Pete Tyjas, well-known guide, demonstrating rod and reel flash

of being extremely hard-wearing. I bought a lovely little Torrentis sampling net from Stuart Crofts; it was white, and I dyed it black, which actually improves it for taking photographs of duns to show their colour. I carry a little white plastic cup in which to photograph nymphs, and the outside of it is painted green. My reels – the ones that I use that is – are all grey, black or green. Bright shiny reels send flash to the fish as you cast.

My beaten-up old seagrass summer hat is painted with green shed paint – a fantastic marriage of base material and decoration which has lasted for ten years now without needing a repaint (I'm wearing it in the photograph in the Preface). Other hats are brown, green, or camouflage. Totally regardless of style, my fishing shirts are green, brown, or camouflage also. Waders I don't bother about as in my case they are mainly underwater and, where potentially seen by trout, seen against the open water column. But I guess I could get creative in that department as well if I thought it would spook fewer fish. I might try to source some broken background camouflage waders if I fished downstream a lot, in, say, the United States, and knew the trout would be facing me.

I have frequently been embarrassed by, perforce, listening in to the conversations of walkers who have not noticed that I'm there. Surprising how frank these can be.

As so frequently happens, the best lessons about hunting fish without being seen by them can be learnt from Mother Nature. It was the last day of our autumn trip to fish the Henry's Fork and Yellowstone, and the river was high following a day's continuous rain and sleet. Nigel and I had spent the previous day researching and taking photographs of all the creative American flies offered for sale in Trout Hunter Lodge and across the road at Mike Lawson's; talking to René Harrop upstairs at Trout Hunter about the crawl-down under water egg laying habit of Baetis; and tying flies. We drove from Last Chance to West Yellowstone, and we hit the fall close-out sales in every fly fishing store we could find, buying stuff that costs twice as much at home in the UK.

But today, come hell or high water, we needed to get back to fishing. The skies were clearing fitfully, although sleet showers were still sweeping in. I asked René Harrop where we should go to fish, and he said to go just a little upstream to where there were some rocks just by a large sign – and that if a fish was going to rise anywhere in the vicinity that would be the spot. So we got wadered and booted up in the sleet, pulled our hoods down, gritted our teeth and started creeping up towards the rocks. Sure enough, the head of a big fish started coming up, and it seemed from a distance that the fish was taking nymphs since we could not see any hatching fly. We tossed for the first cast and I won.

At that moment two things happened. First, the sun came out briefly with the sky clearing over us. And then, as I readied myself for an upstream approach with an un-weighted nymph, a dark shadow swooped over us from behind. The osprey glided swiftly in on the trout at zero feet and was unseen by it until too late. That was the only fish in evidence. I did at least have the presence of mind to reach for my camera. It is not a very good shot being taken at some distance, but it does show the decent size of the fish. No doubt the osprey frightened every other trout in the vicinity and certainly nothing showed over the next half hour, so when the sleet set in again we called it a day and went back to the lodge for hot coffee and commiseration. I suppose you can't really begrudge a fish to an osprey, and I guess that in reality we did finish the trip on a high note. If there were lessons to be learned, they were about concealment and about the importance of getting the first approach to the fish exactly right.

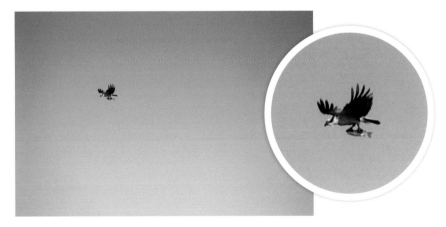

Nature teaches the fly fisher
the first shot has to be unseen by the fish and deadly accurate

Re-energising the river
the author directs operations (Photo by kind permission of the Wilton Fly Fishing Club)

Jamie Windebank and Adrian Simmons, river keeper on the Wylye, weaving living willow current deflectors

CAN WE GET
BETTER FISHING
THAN WE'VE GOT?

MOST FLY FISHERMEN WOULD agree on these three desiderata: more fishable water; more (wild) fish; and more fly. Can they have them? With appropriate investment on their own part (mainly an investment in time, partly only an investment in money) they certainly can – and within medium term planning horizons. Others will help, with grants for example and with advice, but getting the work done will be largely down to anglers getting themselves self-started, and following projects through.

Most of our rivers are still in a mess whatever spin the Environment Agency puts out. There isn't a stretch of river anywhere that could not carry more fish if it were in better condition – and that doesn't just go for the UK, it holds good right around the fly fishing world. So the idea of producing more fishable water, how to get a quart out of a pint pot, is a good place to start. These words are aimed at fishery managers, but fishery managers need to be pushed or else the things that need to be done won't get to be done until it's too late for you to see the benefits in your lifetime. I should know; I used to be one. So push your fishery manager. It's not that they are indolent or supine, far from it, it's just that fishery management is the same as all business nowadays – life is too full and too complicated and too taken up with administration, form filling and other debilitating rubbish.

Taking the unchangeableness of water quality and water quantity as givens for all practical purposes, there is still a hell of a lot that can be done to make a stretch of river hold more fish. You just need to start with the clear knowledge of the trout's needs: to be spawned and born; to grow without check; not to be eaten; to have places to shelter; to have places to feed; and to have places to spawn themselves. Just check out your river carefully with respect to each of those criteria. You can always find ways to provide better spawning gravels and better access to them and protection from predators for spawning fish and also for swim-up fry. You can always and easily provide better habitat for fry and parr to grow in, for example, simply by throwing stones into the river. You can always do more to inhibit predation. The provision of cover with rocks and large woody debris is not difficult. Wild trout will always find food, but if you can concentrate food lanes you will concentrate taking fish. You may be able to increase the number of invertebrates. And something as simple as walking the river in December and January will tell you where your trout are spawning and give you the chance to take steps to reinforce their productivity. Get the Wild Trout Trust in – they are real experts with their knowledge founded on an appropriate mix of science and practical experience. The WTT provides *The Wild Trout Survival Guide*, free advisory visits, with full reports, and free practical (working) visits too and can source funding for projects.

It's good that fly fishermen everywhere are increasingly valuing, and demanding, wild fish. It may be a lot of fun to catch farm-bred fish that have been reared selectively for early maturation and high growth in concrete ponds, habituated to human company, fed copious amounts of floating food and taught to look up to the surface for it – fish that have never had to worry about their security or their safety from predators (and especially not from humans). By the time people get to fish for them, these innocents have been turned out into a river without frequent meals and where there is an energy-sapping current to swim against and any floating confection is worth grabbing. It may be fun, and it can be a nice focus for socialising, networking even, but nobody could call it sporting. That's not a damnation, by the way, (and, as a minor captain of industry, I used to organise and enjoy such hospitality days), and neither is it heresy; it is just a truth.

The whole thing that makes fly fishing for trout more sporting is when the fish you are trying to catch is a wild one. It is more sporting, more interesting, and more rewarding to fish for (not necessarily even to catch) a wild fish that is completely equipped to sense your presence as a predator, to ignore you, evade you, and if hooked, to escape you. Any amount by which the trout's ability to be on the qui vive, to spot you, evade you or rumble your deceit is reduced, other than by your success in hunting him, reduces the sportingness of what you are doing. No, stocking is not the answer to our getting more fish to go for. It is hard to visualise a successful corporate day without the availability of easy-to-catch large fish (unless perhaps it were fixed up for a group of reasonably capable fishermen on a wild trout water, for sport and with catch-and-release the rule). Equally, if you want to take somebody fishing to give them a treat, to say thank you for a favour granted, or to bend their ear or seek their advice (as you might give them a game of golf) – and they could fish but weren't much good at it – you'd want to take them somewhere where they had a reasonable chance of catching something. There will always be a need for stocked fishing to exist and a demand for it, with the price elasticity of that demand being high.

However, I don't see why it has to be on a river. On a river, the not-so-skilled fly fisher is at a distinct disadvantage by not being able to do a good job of gathering in line and staying in touch with the fly; and as a result they find it frustrating and this tends to interfere with their enjoyment. I recently took two experienced anglers fishing on the Wylye who bought a day with me in a Wild Trout Trust auction: but if the truth be known, they had little or no experience of fishing upstream and their day was spoiled. Much better for them to have had the fun they deserved on a stillwater. And stillwaters can be stocked with no danger of genetic introgression, by mixed breeding between farmed fish and wild fish, screwing up the gene pool. If I were the Minister for the Environment, I would set a course towards banning the artificial stocking of rivers and confining it to stillwaters.

I would do that in the knowledge that there are very significant and vibrant populations of wild fish underlying the lumbering giants of stock fish in every river that is stocked currently. (I know that to be true because when I visit such fisheries and fish appropriately I keep catching them.) But also in the knowledge that the wild fish are bullied, inhibited, their growth limited, and their preparedness to rise to the fly repressed by bigger stocked fish taught to look upwards for pellets. It would follow that those who in future were to enjoy hospitality on rivers would need to attain a degree of skill in fly fishing first, or else be prepared to put up with a degree of frustration, less chance of catching fish, and few or none to take home.

Iconic spring creeks and chalk streams, that we ought to love, foster, and be proud of, would then stand a chance of being the drop dead gorgeous wild trout fisheries that they deserve to be. The River Test is a disgrace in this respect; however the upper Itchen in the next valley is a fabulous wild fishery with every size of trout including big ones (see the

A Wylye giant, 7 lbs 5 oz to my mayfly spinner in June 2008

closing paragraphs of chapters one and 14). Yet it is very hard to get onto the latter, whilst sufficient money will always get you onto the Test. But if there were lots of wild trout fishing available on the Test, access to the upper Itchen would no doubt ease. The Test and Itchen may loom large by repute, but 98% of the total UK angler spend of £170m on non-migratory trout fishing lies elsewhere. The priorities, looked at as trout numbers and angler numbers, for making wild trout happier and giving fly fishermen a more sporting opportunity, lie away from the big name enclave; itself only a minor part of the British chalk stream fishery. But the Test is crying out for healing.

Can we have more wild fish? Emphatically yes, and not just by removing the inhibiting effects of stocking with farm-reared trout. I used to think that the numbers of wild fish could be usefully increased by supportive stocking with swim-up fry, fresh out of gravel boxes in which the eggs of wild fish can be successfully hatched at the rate of 95% and more. On the lower Wylye, with in-river spawning hamstrung by heavily silted and concreted gravels, we at the Wilton Club put in 100,000 swim-up fry from farm bred eggs every year for almost a decade, believing that the few survivors would be the fittest for the river and would survive, and possibly interbreed usefully and harmlessly. However, when we finally got some DNA analysis done we found that there was only one of these fish in our extensive sampling, and no fish at all of mixed breed. During the latter part of this period we also put a lot of resources into a series of wild brood stock schemes which would have allowed us to replace the farm bred swim up fry with wild ones – but these all failed for various complicated reasons and I cannot recommend going down that route.

Luckily, by then we had physically restored almost the whole seven mile stretch of the river, thereby improving spawning gravels, and the numbers of small wild-bred fish increased by a factor of three. During the same period a change in club ethos which led to 97% catch and release, helped very much to increase (actually doubled) the catch of wild trout of over eleven inches. And a few giants turned up too.

The moral of this short history is that you can get fantastic results if you simply enable the river to heal itself – and that is the entire principle that lies behind the work of the Wild Trout Trust.

The business of enabling the river to heal itself is however not simply a matter of physical, structural changes aimed at re-energising its flow and providing habitat both for growing and for adult trout. It is possible (although it has not much been attempted) to restore a river biologically as well as physically.

Introduced coir matting
habitat for freshwater shrimp on the iconic, but fragile, Hampshire Bourne

In my view, this idea offers huge and as yet unexplored potential for the building of higher fish populations, faster fish growth, cleaner and less turbid rivers, cleaner gravels with the organic fractions of the interstitial silt removed, more light getting to the weed (and hence more weed), and more shelter habitat and algae grazing areas for a much increased invertebrate population.

The answer lies in the (easy) identification of the creatures that make most contribution to the well-being of the river, and encouraging the numbers, growth, and health of those that can practically be helped, through biomanipulation. Suitable cases for treatment include the reed smut (Simulium), the angler's olives especially BWO (Seratella), the shrimp (Gammarus), the river midges (Chironomidae), and the mayfly (Ephemeridae). And to those targets for help we can add river weeds too, especially Ranunculus; but whatever weed species favour invertebrates and can grow successfully in good conditions in the river in question.

With all of these they can be supportively stocked or restocked where necessary, and steps can be taken to enhance and optimise their habitat and their food sources, both naturally and artificially.

In chapter 14 we'll have a look at the successful re-introductions and supportive re-stockings of fly by Dr Cyril Bennett. When you get to chapter 15 ('Mimicking the hidden secrets of the trout's larder') you'll find me talking about the equally exciting, equally unexploited, potential for better imitating some of these food items and catching big trout on them.

But I want to make it clear that fly fishermen really can have their three main wants (more fishable water, more [wild] fish, and more fly). To get them they will need to get active themselves; the authorities will not deliver the angler's desiderata within his lifetime – or, probably, ever.

In saying that, I am speaking as a leader of a campaign against unsustainable, exported-from-catchment aquifer abstractions, and other issues such as diffuse pollution and fly declines for over twenty years. The past five of which, email archaeology tells me, I've sent a total of 635 communications to officers of the Environment Agency alone (and received in return 457 – not bad, EA). We have had some small wins, eventually, and I may well be past my fishing years before the benefits are delivered.

As I write, The Salmon and Trout Association has lodged a formal legal complaint with the European Union against the UK Government's and its Agencies' failure to protect the designated species of the southern chalk stream special areas of conservation and sites of special scientific interest. This is an initiative I've been involved in, and it's a marker thrown down to show them how we mean to proceed. The other way will be ... virally.

A FOOTNOTE ON FLY ABUNDANCE: It is clear that anglers on many rivers should simply not put up with the pathetically sparse and infrequent hatches they are getting. On the fabled chalk streams, as a particular case in point, not only did my National Fly Abundance Study (see chapter 14) show there had been huge declines since the 1970s, but it is possible to compare nymph numbers currently encountered by trained Angler Monitoring Initiative operators, with other rivers elsewhere. In Derbyshire and Yorkshire, in Kent and in Surrey, there are rivers where a three minute 'kick-sweep' sample commonly yields 1000 or 1500 Baetis, whereas in Wiltshire and most of the Hampshire rivers, over 100 would get you dancing a jig. And now Gordon Mackie has confirmed, in his chapter in the recently published book *Chalk Stream Fly Fishing*, 2012 (available through the Salisbury and District Angling Club website), that 30 years ago things were very different. He calculates that during a hatch on the Itchen in 1976, three million duns floated past him in thirty minutes, and says that until the 1980s it was relatively common to see 10 duns per square foot on the chalk streams generally. On one evening on a bridge on the Wylye, he calculated that 15,000 mayflies and 220,000 blue winged olives flew past him going upstream to lay in just ten minutes. 'Fly fishermen are always complaining about not enough fly,' says the Environment Agency.

Anglers should get more and more vocal, because they are right.

The making of the paraloop hackle on the PhD

DRY FLIES FROM OUTSIDE THE BOX

THESE FLIES ARE THE product of a fevered angling mind and a great deal of experimentation with trout whose reactions could be seen, over a period of more than thirty years. I didn't invent them – I just stole the bits. I owe a debt, you could say, to Nicolai Ivanovich Lobachevsky.

The Great Lobachevsky, as those of you who remember the songs of Tom Lehrer (find the lyrics online or better still buy the CD) will know, taught us to move onward and upward by copying other people's work. He exhorted us to 'plagiarise, plagiarise, plagiarise', urging us to let no-one else's work 'evade your eyes', but to be sure, always, to call it 'research'.

Well, when it comes to creating effective new fly patterns, I believe in following Lobachevsky's dictum. Start with research, find patterns that work, and make them better. Discover what has been doing the trick; emphasise that, and replace other less effective features with better ones. Or find the elements within the fly which trigger a response from the trout, and steal them for incorporation in 'new' patterns.

My own new patterns look and behave nothing like the old ones that I stole the bits from. But there's something in the bits that helps to make them work. What I have added is newer fly-tying methodologies, many of these also unashamedly borrowed. My patterns may look new, but I am more their thief and synthesiser than their inventor.

So let's begin by doing the research and pick some patterns known to work. Some of the most interesting of all are those which work really well – but for no strong apparent reason – usually because they don't seem to the eye to imitate the natural. Examples would be the Royal Wulff, the Half Stone, the Kite's Imperial, the Tups Indispensable, the Greenwell's Glory, the Grey Duster, the Orange Quill, the Wickham's Fancy, and the Adams.

The success of these is based in what Gary LaFontaine called the empirical approach. These were patterns that were invented and evolved (not without great creativity) over long periods of time, and were widely used simply because they worked – they fooled trout when presented well with tackle which was not a patch on ours today, and still work now. (Gary LaFontaine, sadly now dead, was one of the most brilliant interpretative analysers of why flies work, with many of his conclusions based upon long underwater diving observations of trout behaviour in response to fly presentation. His book *The Dry Fly: New Angles* is riveting.)

Each of the flies listed above has one or more elements that are crucial to the attraction of trout, and in each case these elements imitate something that the trout sees in the hatching or newly hatched dun, or in the spinner. Here is my short list of them (the reader may disagree but I did not get where I am today, nor can I fish successfully, without confidence).

The Royal Wulff has distinctive forward-pointing bright white wings that appear quickly in the trout's window, and is cocked up by a bushy hackle, forcing its heavily-dressed tail down into the meniscus where, together with its peacock ruff, it successfully imitates the whole, legs-included shuck of an emerging insect. It doesn't look much like your average Ephemera danica, but it's an excellent fly to represent the hatching mayfly.

The Half Stone's body would appear to be too light in colour relative to the blue dun of its thorax and hackle to be successful as a general olive imitation (if it was light all over, it might imitate a pale watery) but Clive Hallam tells me that the abdomen of the newly-emerged olive is quite extraordinarily light in colour for the first minute or two. And the same is true of the large dark olive – dark it isn't, not to start with, not underneath!

The Kite's Imperial is of decidedly weird coloration – no quarrel with the heron herl but deep purple silk and honey dun hackle? (Yet the iron blue has a purplish body and honey dun coloured legs.) But again there is a tremendously important element, in this case in the fattened and humped thorax, which Kite was, I think, the first to incorporate in a dry fly. That alone has been enough to ensure consistent success for this pattern relative to the generality of un-humped patterns.

Many writers on flies have drawn attention to the translucency of the abdomen of the newly hatched dun, especially the female, with her eggs already developed inside her often providing an orange tinge. There is no doubt that the extraordinary historic success of the Tups Indispensible owes much to this factor. Reject any flat-pink or opaque ones you may be offered. Go for the proper Tups thorax mix and the yellow silk (yes, silk) body.

The magic combination of yellow silk and wax in the body of the Greenwell's is also an unbeatable medium olive and BWO abdomen, and the Greenwell hackle with its dark centre suggests a thorax. The Grey Duster, tied without a tail as is proper so that it capsizes and rests body downwards on a hackle that becomes a parachute, brilliantly and simply represents the hatching olive. The Orange Quill seems to conjure the sunset into the evening-hatching BWO.

The Wickham's Fancy is the only fly to capture the metallic brightness that results when the body of the dun with its hydrophobic surface detaches from the inside of the translucent nymphal shuck at the point of eclosion – and it also has the general mess of shuck legs and emerged legs caught brilliantly by its palmered hackle. (I am again indebted to Clive Hallam, who has spent thousands of hours observing and filming insects hatching, for this insight.)

And lastly, the Adams, possibly the most successful general imitation of a newly hatched dun worldwide, has hackle point wings inclined forward to appear quickly in the trout's window and trigger the start of his rise, a distinct thorax suggested by the density of brown and grizzle hackles, and the wonderful aura contributed to the body by the use of waterproof muskrat fur. Once the rise is initiated this is one the trout will not easily turn away from. Why? Because LaFontaine's observational work identified a kind of aura in the meniscus-break surrounding the hatching fly, and showed that this aura is critical to trout maintaining their suspension of disbelief – and Hallam confirms this. The Parachute Adams is even better than the standard version.

Well then, here is the challenge – pick the bits out of that lot!

The way forward lies somewhere between Lobachevsky's visionary precursor to the World Wide Web; T Texas Tyler's 'The Soldier's Deck of Cards'; and Johnny Cash's 'I Built It One Piece at a Time'. There are constant themes running through the design and the success of these traditional patterns. Understand the themes, and hence the aspects of the natural fly and its behaviour that these themes succeed in imitating, and you are halfway there. The rest does require patience, experimentation, a knowledge of modern fly-dressing methodologies, and perhaps just a little creativity.

Here is a fly to be going on with, something to tie a dozen of, as a stock olive dun for the new season.

Basically, what you do is to take the yellow silk from the Tups/Half Stone/Greenwell and add the finest dubbing of greyish-dun muskrat fur from the Adams – and you have a translucent olive body with an aura. Then you take the distinct humped thorax from the Imperial, and the flat-in-the-film hackle from the Grey Duster and Parachute Adams to put the hydrophobic body in the surface film. Add the exaggerated forward-pointing wings of the Wulff and the Adams, and you have a combination of trigger factors which add up to a strong caricature-style dry fly which will not only stimulate a rise but also imitate the newly hatched olive dun well enough at close quarters to minimise the number of last second refusals.

The only modern materials incorporated are microfibbets for tails, and their stumps used for the parachute post; and the only novel technique is to bend over the parachute hackle and post to divide the wings and keep them in a separated 'V' that gets a right-way-up landing out of most casts. Fully treated with the best floatant to float in the film but without being part of it, this fly will float for hundreds of casts; and in terms of structural strength will last until tree or trout remove it from your leader.

What's it called? Well, since 'research' it was that gave rise to it, it is aptly named the PhD. That also happens to stand for the 'Peter Hayes Dun'.

Trout's eye view of the PhD

PHD (PETER HAYES DUN)

This, the PhD, was the first fly I designed, and that was thirty years ago. I know that because I came across an early example the other day and the wings were made with distinctive hackle points from a cockerel my brother Bob had then. I designed it by stealing the bits from other successful flies. The overall build uses a light dun grizzly paraloop hackle bent over to split the long, forward-facing, mallard flank wings. This method of tying is different from the classic parachute hackle in that it forces the hackle points downwards and sideways at an angle so that they support the fly-like outriggers and tend to bend rather than pierce the surface. The body, which is muskrat fur dubbed on primrose silk over primrose silk, and ribbed with primrose thread, gets held somewhat higher in the surface than happens with a normal parachute hackle. The tails are microfibbets, the butts of which are carried forward to form the post for the paraloop hackle.

Here are the full pattern and tying instructions, and plates to clarify:

How to tie the PhD

Hook:	*Fine wire, round bend, down or straight eye #16-20 (I now use Tiemco 102y with the barb filed down. It's more of a Limerick bend, but I've got better at tying it on the shorter shank. I'd advise starting with a round bend hook).*
Thread:	*Uni-Thread # 8/0, Light Cahill (i.e. primrose) as the basic tying-in thread and the over-rib, and Pearsall's primrose silk as the abdomen winding and thorax base.*
Tails:	*Olive microfibbets, splayed and lifted by a ball of thread.*
Abdomen:	*Muskrat fur sparsely dubbed on and over*

primrose silk (this is real silk, Pearsall's Gossamer Primrose; tying thread is not translucent), ribbed with twisted tying thread for trout tooth protection.

Thorax: *Dubbed muskrat, fat.*

Hackle: *Genetic grizzle cock's, dyed light dun – wound as a parachute hackle on the microfibbets base as a post, then bent over forwards to divide the wings and tied in at the head.*

Wings: *Mallard flank feather fibres, bunched, angled forward and divided.*

PhD method

You want a reasonably long-shanked hook to maximise the length of the body relative to the hook point, so as to be able to cock up the tails at the extreme end of the shank. Also, with the parachute post being bent forward and tied down at the eye, you need, if you're anything like me, to avoid running out of space.

Start your tying thread, not at the eye, but at the very top of the bend. Spin the bobbin (so the thread doesn't spread) before you build a tiny ball and then pinch and loop the microfibbets hard up against the ball, straight down onto the bare shank, and bind them down 60% of the way towards the eye. The tails should be no longer than the body, and preferably shorter. Cock the long bases of the microfibbets up about 60% along the shank with a couple of turns in front and bind in primrose silk on a second bobbin, and wind the thread and then the silk back to the tails. Splay the tails with your specially developed fly-tying index fingernail and leave the tying thread bobbin hanging or carry it back to a spring holder. Take your primrose silk and wind a tapered body between the tails and the parachute post, finishing back at the tails.

Dub the silk, very sparingly indeed, with the tiniest fuzz of muskrat fur (Plate 1 shows this stage) and wind it so that the fur appears almost absent

at the rear end of the abdomen and thickens as it progresses up the body. Take a couple of turns to secure the silk in front of the post, and then spin the other bobbin to twist the tying thread and rib it forwards over the dubbed abdomen, carrying the tying thread beyond the hanging silk, up to the eye and back to the tune of 10% of the shank length, to where you are now going to tie in the wings.

Take a healthy bunch of mallard flank feather fibres and, rolling them between finger and thumb to mix their curvature and avoid fly spin, tie them on top of the shank at this point in a single bunch facing forward. Let the bunch be tied in good and long, so that the wings will eventually form an exaggerated feature of the fly. LaFontaine's work shows how important this is, and the extra millimetre or two of length will help your fly to land right way up.

Tie in a good quality dun-dyed grizzle hackle at the hackle post and carry the tying thread forward towards the eye, securing with a couple of turns in front of the wing. Let it hang. Now go back to the primrose silk hanging from the parachute post, dub it relatively thickly and tightly with muskrat fur (Plate 2 shows this stage), and wind a substantial thorax starting with the first turn behind the parachute post and finishing with the last turn in front of the wing. Whip-finish the silk and cut it off.

Now wind the parachute hackle around the microfibbet stumps as a post, holding the post up with the right hand and winding with hackle pliers in the left hand. On each turn, you will have to catch the hackle pliers in the other fingers of your right hand – or you could use a gallows tool. Wind up the post to the distance that will bring the top of the hackle immediately behind the wing when the post is bent forward. Then wind the hackle back down again through the upwards windings to the base of the post (Plate 3 shows this stage,

with the para hackle wound on the microfibbetts base fibres as a post). It's easy to end up over-hackled, so space the turns a bit …

Pull the hackle post forward between the already-separated wings, tying it down with the tying thread behind the eye and whip finish (Plate 4

shows this stage, with the microfibbett stumps being pulled down between, and splitting, the wing fibres prior to being tied down).

You have to pull it down tight, and tie it down tight. This is not an easy operation and takes some practice but you will get there in the end, and the result is a very sexy impression of the newly-hatched upwinged fly. Cut off the micro fibbett bases very closely, and then the end of the hackle less closely so that it will stay in place and not unwind. The parachute hackle tips are forced sideways and downwards to look more like legs and make the fly ride higher. The wings are forced into a distinct 'V' and kept there.

And now you have a PhD! You're a wannabeologist, just like me …

USD PHD

Here is the USD PhD. Same basic design and technique, but with the hook upside down. It is a fly which, like the standard PhD, will land the correct way up virtually all the time. With this version that means upside-down with the hook point out of the water. This is achieved by the angling up of the wings and tails – it is basically a question of shuttlecock aerodynamics. I particularly like using this fly, in size

14 or even 12, in the early stages of the British mayfly hatch (Ephemera danica) when the trout haven't quite got onto the fly and are distrustful of more accurate imitations. Both its smaller size than the natural and its

concealed hook, or rather its hook up design, seem to lull the suspicions of the fish and reduce rejections. But in smaller sizes it is a very good general representation of the usual range of upwing flies, and makes a great alternative to switch to from a conventionally-tied fly when addressing a difficult fish. Bitch to tie, though.

REVERSED PHD

This is simply the Reversed PhD. Unlike the USD PhD it is quite easy to tie, easier even than the standard tying of the fly. This is a good fly to use in an olive hatch when the wind is in your face and the duns are facing into it and away from you. Just like the original fly, it is a design and a construction without specific requirements for materials and their colours, which you are free to change so as to match the hatch. For example, the abdomen could be gold-ribbed hare's ear instead of primrose-ribbed muskrat, or mahogany seals fur ribbed with tan silk. The colour of the microfibbets, which are essential to the construction as they form the post for the paraloop, can also be varied; and a very nice pair of darker wings can be made by splitting a roll of bronze mallard instead of splitting a roll of light mallard flank. If you were convinced that the fish were taking emergers you would cut off the tails and let the abdomen sink a little – but still grease the leader.

MUSKRAX

This is the Muskrax (or muskrat thorax). It builds on the work of Marinaro and of Datus Proper. Tied on a bronze hook, the abdomen is formed of primrose tying silk soaked in liquid wax. It will retain its translucent quality for the life of the fly. Again it utilises microfibbets, but in this design they are bent down on either side of the hook at the forward end of the abdomen and formed into a bunch below the hook. Then the wings are tied-in by splitting a bunch of mallard flank fibres and figure-of-eighting them. Then you take the silk back to the front of

the abdomen, tying in a dun-coloured grizzle hackle as you go. Then dub the thorax area generously with muskrat and wind the hackle forward through it to just behind the wings, where you tie it off. Then bring the sticking-down bunch of microfibbet butts forward so as to splay the hackles sideways and tie it in at the head – thus forming a thorax breastplate and non-meniscus-piercing outrigger hackles.

How to tie the Muskrax

Hook:	*Fine wire, round bend, down or straight eye #16-20.*
Thread:	*Pearsall's Gossamer Primrose.*
Tail:	*Olive microfibbets.*
Abdomen:	*Pearsall's Gossamer Primrose.*
Thorax:	*Dubbed darkish blue dun muskrat underfur.*
'Breastplate':	*Microfibbet butts.*
Hackle:	*Genetic grizzle cock's, dyed light dun.*
Wings:	*Mallard flank feather fibres.*

Muskrax method

I like to get the maximum body length out of a hook: that's why I use a round bend hook, so that the tails will sit up nicely at the rear end of the body and not be forced forward by one of those slopey bends you get on the model perfect. The old-style square bend hooks are even better if you can get them. I always have a tendency to run out of space at the head and, for that reason and also so that I can see to tie

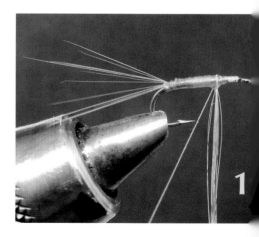

it on, I like to use hooks with outsize eyes like the Orvis Big-eye.

Form a small ball of thread at the start of the bend and tie in the fibbets, cocking and splaying them up over it. Wind a tapered body and at the forward end of it pull the fibbet butts down to 90° and secure them in that position with a few turns of the silk in front. Anoint the body with liquid wax and let it soak in. Light brown varnish is a more durable alternative.

Tie in the wing bunch just behind the eye and separate it into two, angled forward with the thread in a figure-of-eight. Trout lock on to wings as they appear at the edge of their window, so I like them to be slightly over-long. And 'V' wings may not be accurate but they'll land your fly right way up.

Tie in the hackle in front of the body. Dub muskrat underfur between body and wings (including the guard hairs does no harm) thickly to form the thorax.

Wind just three or four turns of hackle through the muskrat, and tie it off with two turns of whip-finish in front of the wings and behind the eye.

Finally, rotating the fly to upside-down if your vice allows you, pull the microfibbet butts forward to form the breastplate and splay the hackles sideways, tying them down firmly under the fly's chin – whip-finish twice and cement. Trim off any errant hackle fibres. Treat with overnight type floatant.

Fish with confidence.

The Muskrax (construction sequence) –
1: Muskrax ready to tie in wings, hackle, and dub dubbing
2: Muskrax ready to dub thorax and wind hackle
3: Finished Muskrax with microfibbet butts brought up to splay hackle sideways

HAYESTUCK

The next emerger imitation is aptly named the Hayestuck for two reasons – it looks like a haystack and it successfully imitates the half-emerged dun stuck in the surface film. You will see that, just like the natural cripple pictured on page 26 in chapter one, it is half as long again as the hatched fly will be if it gets out OK. The abdomen and tails of the shuck are imitated by light brown tying thread, teased out with a tiny dab of superglue on its rear tip to stop it splaying out on the water surface, and to help it to sink so that it can be seen directly through the water by the trout. At the front end of that, on the bend of the hook, the thorax and legs of the shuck are imitated with a bunch of dubbed brown natural fur with a dyed brown grizzle hackle wound through it and clipped on the top. The emerging abdomen of the fly is primrose silk dubbed with muskrat and ribbed with primrose silk; a dun-dyed grizzle hackle is underclipped for the legs and for floatation; and the wings are two looped CdC plumes.

How to tie the Hayestuck

Hook:	*Your favourite down-eye dry fly hook #16-20.*
Thread:	*Pearsall's Gossamer Primrose silk.*
Shuck:	*Thick brown tying thread, teased out.*
Shuck legs:	*Brown grizzle neck hackle, short points.*
Abdomen:	*Muskrat fur, darkish dun (the mayfly/greendrake version has white snowshoe hare's foot fur, ribbed with dark brown flexifloss).*
Rib:	*Pearsall's Gossamer Primrose silk.*
Thorax:	*Dubbed muskrat (or for the greendrake pattern, hare back fur).*
Front Hackle:	*Genetic grizzle cock saddle, dyed light dun (or for the greendrake version, honey dun with a dark centre).*
Wing:	*CdC loop.*

Hayestuck method

Start at the bend. Fold two strands of thick brown tying thread and tie them on in the middle just below the bend. Leave a three-inch tail of silk hanging in a forward direction to use for the abdomen rib (or, for the greendrake emerger, use brown flexifloss). Use a dubbing brush or something similar to tease all the shuck fibres out, apply a very small drop of superglue at a point about the length of the body again from the bend, and make a finishing cut across it. This is to make the shuck sink instead of splaying and floating. The shuck should basically stick out rearwards and not be angled at any great degree downwards – shucks stay pretty much horizontal as the insect levers itself out of them against the pull of the meniscus. Now wind the neck hackle to represent the shuck legs, secure it and cut off the upward facing points. Wind the silk forward to a point two-thirds of the way up the shank, and back again, building a tapered base for the abdomen. Dub the silk sparsely with the fur and wind forward to form the abdomen, then wind the rib and secure.

Next, tie in the CdC loop to imitate the half-extended wings of an emerging insect, and then a good quality saddle hackle. Dub the silk again and wind a generous fur thorax up to where the head will be formed. Wind the saddle hackle through the thorax fur with some turns behind and some in front of the CdC loop wing. Turn the fly over and clip a 'V' out of the underside of the front hackle. That's it. Multiple

The Hayestuck
1: Ready for body dubbing and rib
2: Ready for thorax dubbing and hackle
Opposite: Finished, hackle clipped underneath

procedures but a simple sequence. If it looks a bit messy and crowded (a bit like a haystack), well, so does the hatching insect.

KISS MY CUL

This extremely successful hatched dun now has many claimed sources and names. I published it as the 'KmC' (Kiss my Cul) in an article in *Fly Fishing & Fly Tying* magazine (September 2006), without claiming to have invented it and acknowledging that Clive Hallam had sent it to me as an unnamed prototype. I now know that Stuart Crofts and other England Team members brought it back from Eastern Europe and it became a favourite of the Derbyshire/Yorkshire fly fishing cognoscenti, although I think not many of us fish with it in the South. Microfibbets tails, Fly-rite body, both in whatever colour matches the hatch, and unless it's on a very small hook, two cul de canard tips as wings. It lands right way up, defies gravity, and in spite of having no hackle sits up on the surface beautifully when treated with either hydrophobic fumed silica dust or a really good paste floatant. My most successful dry fly for ten years now – in black, makes a superb iron blue.

REVERSED KISS MY CUL

This is the Reversed Kiss my Cul, for fishing into a downstream wind. Does this work? You bet it does. It works because (I choose to believe) it faces the same way as the hatched naturals. On hard-fished water, it also has the distinct advantage that the fish will not have seen many tied that way round. It is tied the same way as the traditionally-oriented pattern, with two small differences. The stubs of the

CdC wings are prinked up in front of them at the hook bend so that they do not get bent the wrong way in casting, relative to the aircraft tailplane arrangement of the wings on the natural facing into the wind. And the

second difference is that I like to use something other than nylon for the tails, for example muskrat guard hairs which will splay out sideways somewhat with the force of casting. With the traditional orientation I use microfibbets because I can splay them by tying them tight behind a ball of tying silk, and they will, being stiff, retain that splay in spite of the force of casting.

SPINNERMALIST

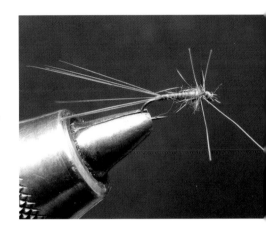

This is probably my second most successful dry fly pattern. Like most fly-tyers I had futzed around for years with spinner imitations. What I mainly experimented with was wings of different materials. I tried hackle stalk loops, CdC clumps, wound hackles clipped top and bottom, organza – you name it, I tried it. Most of them worked, but none of them worked better than the traditional patterns for Little Red Spinner and Lunn's Particular. I ended up looping the butts

No. 12
OLIVE SPINNER, FEMALE

of microfibbets that I used for the tails. This was a neat design which looked good in the hand but didn't work terribly well in the water, because the loops tended to twist out of the horizontal and as a result they bent the meniscus too much. You could only afford to have one loop on each side or they stuck up above the water and got refusals. So I tried cutting the loops and that proved to be the right answer. Just two butts sticking out on each side, with a bunch of thinly-dubbed brown rat hair for legs. Body of tying silk. It's called the 'Spinnermalist'. Unlike Halford's over-hackled fly in contrast (see inset).

BLACK-CADDER

I tied this first in New Zealand on a size 18 hook to match a little caddis that was hatching sparsely but being eaten every time it appeared on the surface. It had wings of blotchy black and gold, and a very dark brown,

almost black, abdomen with slightly lighter legs. I'm not even sure that there was just the one species – some were very black and some were lighter, almost golden bronze. But the size was the same – 18. Somewhere between micro caddis and the smaller sedges; in UK terms, the size of a small Grannom. The Black-cadder was a huge success on the spring creeks of South Island, and of course I tried it at home. It works particularly well on the Derbyshire Wye when caddis of that size are about. The wing is of gold 'present-tying' ribbon darkened with black permanent marker and folded into a tent shape down the middle. The body is very dark brown condor herl, but any good furry herl will do; and the hackle is furnace and of the extreme genetic variety.

COOT.COM

A gleam came into my eye one day ten years ago as I was watching a family of baby coots running about over the water in the margins of the Wiltshire Wylye, where I do most of my fishing. They were actually running over the water and the weeds without getting wet even when they fell in, which was frequently. Covered in black fur, they seemed to be completely hydrophobic. Later I found one that had got separated from its family and died of cold overnight. I dried it on the cooker at home and cut all the fur off it to make a dubbing. I thought it would go nicely on a very tiny hook with a starling neck hackle to imitate any or all of those small, black, not-easily-matchable, nothings that fish frequently start eating just to annoy you. And so it proved. This was the time of the dot-com boom, and there was a floatation that caught a lot of people called Scoot.com: so I named this fly, Coot.com.

MAYFLY

Here is the Mayfly (Ephemera danica i.e. greendrake) version of the Hayestuck. It differs only in the size and materials from the small fly emerger/cripple version detailed on a previous page. Tied on a long shank size 12 hook, it has the same tying thread, brown fur and brown hackle shuck imitation at the back – just larger. The abdomen is white snowshoe hare ribbed with dark brown twisted silk floss or Flexifloss. The emergent wings are formed from a couple of CdC feathers tied in a loop, and the honey dun hackle is wound through a thorax of more white snowshoe hare dubbing and clipped underneath. This fly, fished to a sighted BIG fish rising in an evening mayfly hatch on the River Anton in Hampshire, got me a fish of 11 lbs. 4 oz.; the largest brown trout ever to my rod, which actually passed all the tests for being a wild fish. Crucially, its pectoral fins were well over 15% of body length. It also broke my landing net and trashed some rather fine weed beds. Lindsay Masters, whose water it was, was prime witness (Lindsay has left us now, which is a shame).

'OOKEY RAT

This, another fly I would not be without, is the 'Ookey Rat. Of similar design to the Once and Away, it is a fly of Welsh origin which Owain Mealing proffered after I had spent over an hour with at least a dozen different patterns trying to deceive a consistent riser on the Usk. The fish had it first chuck, and was a fat two-pounder. He said it had not got a name and on being told what the dubbed thorax was I suggested 'Ookey Rat, because it was tied on a bent hook using rat fur. The body is tying thread, very slightly tapered. This fly successfully imitates a hatching river chironomid, and most of them are small so it is best tied on a size 18 hook or smaller. It also does very well in a hatch of olives if the body is any colour in a range from brown to light olive. Never mind olive emerger bodies are straight and not bent; the bent hook simply forces it through the film (same principle as the Klinkhamer). And it has done amazing execution in a very small size with a bright green body in falls of greenfly. ('ookey = bent = stolen)

CDC WING GRHE

This is my version of the traditional Gold Ribbed Hare's Ear dry fly. All I have done is to add CdC wings in line with the tenets of Marinaro and Proper to the effect that tall wings are a key trigger of the rise. The gold wire ribbing tends to make the abdomen sink below the surface in accurate imitation of the emerger's body still in its shuck; and the escaping hare's ear fibres suggest the gills at the sides of the nymphal abdomen. The picked-out hare's ear fibres of the thorax form a better imitation of the legs of the dun because, in comparison to a sharp hackle, they bend rather than pierce the surface, and thus create a more foot-like indentation in the fish's mirror – the underside of the surface film. It is one of the very greatest dry flies of all time, but is successful because it is an exceptional emerger imitation. You treat the front half of it only with floatant, and it is better not to use one of the more gooey ones (e.g. Dave's Bug Flote) or it will quickly migrate to the bit you want to sink.

SUSPENDER GRHE NYMPH

These suspender versions of the GRHE nymph are included in this collection of dry flies because effectively they are fished no less dry than many of the others listed here. Again, you treat with non-gooey floatant only the thorax/emergent wing end of the fly. The white suspender bundle is created by dubbing white CdC onto the tying silk and then forcing it down into a bobble á la Arbona. It sits between the two wings of a 'V' shape made of black razor foam. These imitate the parting sides of the emergent nymph's thorax (the shuck it is leaving) and simultaneously aid floatation of the front end of the fly. The gold wire ribbing helps the abdomen to sink below the surface. The reverse tie has not, if I am honest, yet had enough of a trial to show clearly

whether it catches more fish. If it does, it will be because most nymphs at the point of eclosion are, I believe, facing upstream and not down. I already know enough to say that it works, and works extremely well.

BLACK WING CASE GRHE NYMPH

And this is the standard Gold Ribbed Hare's Ear nymph with black pheasant tail fibre wing cases added to supercharge its trout 'cred'. Although this fly works well subsurface and that is the main presentation with which it has been used traditionally, I use it increasingly, thoroughly greased up, with the tippet also greased, to imitate the 'hatch-in-a-heartbeat' nymph. The coating of floatant on the nymph itself

makes it look, underwater, as if it has a nymphal skin still shrouding it. Logically, it needs to be tied in reverse for this particular presentation method. I admit I have only recently used it in a reverse tying, and it has worked very well. Mind you, it has caught me enough big fish tied the 'wrong' way round (including the big one on the Itchen mentioned in chapter one) for me not to have worried about its orientation until now. The next production batch I tie will be reversed.

DEVI-ANT

This last is my 'when all else fails'
pattern. It's a personal belief that's
been confirmed so many times
by trout that it must be right, that
the image of an ant is genetically
wired into the brain of every trout.
It's not a hard imitation to achieve,
and pretty much any pattern will
deceive. However ants fish best when
hanging in the film, and this and their

blackness makes them hard for the angler to see – just when he needs
to. Hence the addition of a tuft of DV fluorescent pink yarn, giving rise
to the name, 'Devi-ant'. This has a body cut from the 2mm thickness of
black razor foam in a square-section strip and looped front and back –
and I have a variant that sometimes works better being less high-floating,
in which a fat abdomen is dubbed round the bend of the hook so as to be
forced under the surface (on the right in the picture). It's not proprietary;
many people use a similar tufted ant.

All these are fly designs rather than patterns – they are constructed to
perform in particular ways on and in the surface, and you can tie them in
any colours and many materials to match the natural.

As we have seen in chapter one, in the poker game of fly fishing, in
which we guess the trout's hand and draw from the deck, it can be a better
strategy to run through the fly box in terms of hatch stage (spinner, dun,
cripple, emerger, inert nymph, rising nymph) as much as, and often more,
than to run though it in terms of imitated species (small dark olive, pale
watery, blue winged olive, iron blue, medium olive, brook dun). Stick to
the same suit, go for the flush rather than the straight. And ... we need to
get our orientation right.

FOOTNOTE 1: Here's a picture of the big wild trout that came to the Hayestuck Mayfly Emerger. I miscast, four feet to her left, and she swam calmly over, opened that enormous pink mouth, and ate it. Then trashed the entire fishery, and the landing net.

27" x 17" girth, Hayestuck Mayfly, River Anton, May 2005

FOOTNOTE 2: Although his patterns didn't specifically derive from ideas about the orientation of the natural, Roy Christie of Sexyloops (and other fame) has perfected some terrific reversed patterns, USD patterns, and reversed USD patterns, that are well worth looking up on the Internet.

Frank Sawyer and his Pheasant Tail Nymph
based on a display by Nick Sawyer
(By kind permission of Nick Sawyer)

TANGENTIAL THOUGHTS ABOUT NYMPHING

WHILST I HAVE A lot to say on the construction of dry flies I have very much less to say on nymphs and nymphing. In contrast to the dry fly, where it's my view that people have really gone a bit wrong over the years, the same is not really true of nymphs. Still, I've learned a few tricks and I'm glad to pass them on.

You can't really structure nymphs to behave in the water as creatively and effectively as you can dry flies upon it – the same possibilities aren't there because they don't possess the same degrees of freedom and they only have the one element to work in. I mean nymphs are going to be in the water column and only in that, as opposed to dry flies which have the water, the air, and the intermediary slippery-but-sticky surface film, the current, and the breeze. You can still create better visual imitations of course.

In what I write here, the term nymph embraces imitations of all insect larvae, including pupae, and the like of shrimps and scuds.

Huge amounts of creative thought have gone successfully into the design of nymphs. Voluminous books have been written about their design and by now almost all possibilities must have been covered, both in terms of the insects whose larval stage can be imitated, and in terms of the design of the flies themselves. It is definitely my view that paying careful attention to nymph design and presentation can massively improve your catches, and the quality of fish you succeed in deceiving, but there is plenty of great writing and Internet content out there to help you, and there are only a few small things that I feel I can usefully add to the corpus of existing work.

The first one is of course that of the orientation of nymphs relative to the flow of the river and hence to the fish, a subject which I have already covered, if not done to death. Hatching nymphs locking in to the meniscus will be facing upstream and your conventionally-tied nymph, with its head facing you as an upstream fisherman, will be out of line, not what the trout is expecting.

Nymphs that become available to the trout close to the river bed will generally have become available because they have got dislodged. In that case it may well be advantageous for their intended imitations to be tied classically, with their head facing downstream and towards the upstream-fishing angler. The angler's imitation will always be, like the dislodged larva or pupa, in free fall or swimming as fast as they can for cover in the water column rather than, like sheltering or feeding larvae, clinging on to a stone, gravel, timber or weed. No particular orientation is likely to be a right one.

When nymphs are rising through mid-water to the surface to emerge, the question of which way they face, upstream or down, is a bit vexed – we're honestly not sure. Except that they do swim, and swim head first, and you can be sure they are facing upwards.

Now generally, the upwards drag of your leader, with its friction at the surface film point of entry and water resistance below that slowing its descent, will ensure that your artificial nymph will indeed stay facing upwards like the risers. For most of its journey back downstream towards you from the point you cast it to, however, your nymph will be sinking or (having achieved equilibrium between its own weight and the tethering effect of your leader) travelling at a constant depth. As we have seen, ephemerid nymphs commonly make several sorties towards the surface before their last and hopefully successful one. So trout are used to nymphs sinking downwards and may even target these as being, for the moment at any rate, the weaker ones – those less fully prepared for emergence.

I will frequently use a long thick leader with only a short fine tippet when nymphing, to achieve two things: firstly, to tether the nymph higher in the water than it would otherwise sink (fat leader plus grease equals limited sinking depth) and secondly, to achieve better sighting of take indications without potentially scaring fish with a close-to-nymph sight indicator. I usually attach the short fine tippet with a loop-to-loop join so as to exaggerate both of these useful effects. Loop-to-loop is also the safest way of joining light tippet to any leader point of above 20% greater diameter, I find, so don't be shy of it just because it looks a bit messy and stares at you from the surface. This falls within the same logic as trout not being bothered by wiggly tippets as long as they avoid drag.

The current version of the BBWON

The larvae of many ephemerid species, worldwide, cock their abdomens and tails up like a scorpion when at rest, and between bursts of swimming. It has always seemed worthwhile to me to cock up the tails on nymphs that you tie to swim hook point-down – and also to tie nymphs with weighted bodies that curve round the bend of the hook, so as to fish 'upside down' to imitate this feature. This is a particularly strong characteristic of Ephemerella and Seratella species (in the UK, the BWO). They swim poorly, with many kicks and rests, rather than with an animated continuous wriggle as do, for example, Baetis nymphs. It has the added advantage of you being able to fish the fly close to the riverbed with fewer hitch-ups on rocks and weed. My 'BBWON' (Better Blue Winged Olive Nymph) pattern is now tied to achieve these results. Again, I didn't originate this design; it was a feature of some large, heavy nymphs sent to me as examples to copy prior to some visits to the fast rivers of Austria in the late 1970s by the celebrated angler and artist, Wolfgang Tambour, of Vienna. It forms the basic structure of my 'MCJ' too; the Midriff Copper John. Interestingly, many of the PTNs tied by Frank Sawyer were tied more than somewhat round the bend, and depending on the amount of copper armature wire used, may have fished upside-down and mimicked the BWO nymph rather well. The example at the start of the chapter is from a display of Frank's original work.

Where, in my view, you need to have some reverse-tied nymphs tied up and ready, as I have said, is in the top inch of the water, and in the

Reverse tying of GRHE with black wing covers

surface film itself (as long, that is, you are fishing upstream). I have been giving pretty extensive trials over the 2012 season to light, unweighted or wire-only-weighted reversed patterns, greased up, and I have been delighted by the results when trout are rising but not taking the hatched fly. Since most nymphs that hatch at the surface have distinctly dark wing-buds, it is definitely worth tying your reverse nymph with such. As for the rest of the pattern, tie it like all of my constructions, to match the natural. How do you know what the natural looks like? Get a Torrentis seine net and a fish-friendly stomach pump from Stuart Crofts. The seine will get you a better sample of about-to-hatch nymphs, but with the pump you'll know which ones are being eaten. If tying in advance, go for Gold Ribbed Hare's Ear, and Pheasant Tail.

For a basic, drifting mid-water nymph, there's nothing to beat what I call the 'Itchen Nymph'. It's quite heavy, with a tapered body of fine lead wire under the feather fibre abdomen, and a bead head made of brass or tungsten depending on how fast and far you want it to sink. Hence it gets

down well in small sizes. Small nymphs are disproportionately useful to the angler because trout will mainly have seen large artificials. They are more likely to take small ones for real ones, and less likely to be spooked.

The flue of the feather fibre is as sticky-out as possible to exaggerate the impression of gills (condor is the best for this if you can get it, vulture or eagle tail is good, and pheasant tail is fine in very small sizes). The Itchen

Itchen nymph, green version

Nymph has proved itself all over the world. A version tied with a dull copper bead, a thorax of Hends No. 45 dubbing or Orvis Peacock Ice Dub (the reddish variety), a pheasant tail abdomen ribbed with proper reddish copper wire and a brown squirrel tail has been very successful for friends on European rivers, and for me on the Derbyshire rivers and in New Zealand's Southland spring creeks like the Mataura.

Copperknob, Hends 45 version

As I mentioned in chapter two, it is worthwhile using the flash provided by gold beads and/or, gold wire, to represent the subcutaneous gas (air, that is – it's not something weird like argon) that shines out of the nymphs when they are ready to hatch. But bear in mind that on heavily fished rivers, trout will have seen a huge number of goldheads, and learned to associate them with danger. Even on a remote West Coast South Island spring creek, the entry of a goldhead into the head of what we call the Banana Pool has been known to clear it of a dozen, until-then happily feeding, big trout. Use black, or gunmetal, or dull copper – or paint your bright beads with olive stained-glass-window paint from the craft shop.

I don't think it's useful to try and tie faithful likenesses, although I admire Oliver Edwards' brilliant imitations and I know they catch fish. Mind you, a brick on a hook would catch fish in Ollie's hands. You don't need anything too sophisticated in tying terms; there seems to be no need to try and make the nymph totally flat like the natural, or to tie in sideways-projecting, knotted fibre legs, which in my experience simply destabilise the swim of the nymph.

When you want to fish really deep in fast water, Czech nymphs or the Peeping Caddis are the thing, and you may need to fish Czech-style to fish these most effectively. It's not something I've done a lot, except in the Tongariro and similar rivers in New Zealand and Patagonia – hard work, but effective.

Heavy shrimp (Gammarus pulex) and water louse patterns are a good way of getting down to where fish are feeding and offering them something nutritious that they like to eat. Colour and translucency are important. The naturals are usually olive, but with a gesture towards eau-de-nil. In limestone rivers, in the Welsh Usk, and in the Cumbrian Eden catchment, I've often found them to have a Prussian blue tinge and blueish patterns have worked some magic. My own pattern is the 'Gam 'R Us', which utilises a mix of dark olive and white seal's fur with hare body

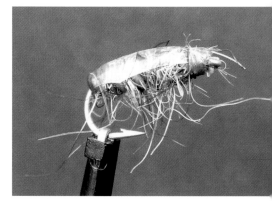

The Gam 'R Us, standard version

fur dubbed over thick lead wire that has been strapped to the top of the hook shank to make it fish upside-down, ribbed with primrose silk floss, and shell-backed (over the rib so water can get in and make it translucent) with plastic strip in light olive.

Variants with a red spot (as originated by Neil Patterson to imitate the Pomporhyncus parasite), and orange shrimps to imitate dead ones, are very effective alternatives. The parasite makes the shrimp swim randomly which gets it preferentially eaten by ducks, which themselves are the parasite's next animal host in the chain, or trout.

Otherwise shrimps are fantastically good at avoiding being eaten by trout, the approach of which they can smell even from upstream (as Swedish scientists have shown). Shrimps actually swim stretched out straight, by the way, not bent round in a curve: and that's the way a trout will expect to see them at close quarters when they are swimming fast to get away. Use straight hooks.

Can you, or rather should you, use strike indicators? Silly question: of course you should. Why would you want to miss fish by not seeing the take?

Should you use the same one inch child's toy balloon indicator on an English chalk stream that you would use on the Fifty Mile

The MCJ

Riffle of the Madison? No – because it's always going to be (and look) a bit silly to use an indicator that is any bigger than you absolutely need to use. And it's always a good idea to try and avoid winding other anglers up unnecessarily. Indicators may be banned. Nymphs may be banned. You may be banned.

If I use one at all here in the UK, it's often just a tuft of wool or polypropylene fibre, dark or bright to suit sighting conditions. I'm going to be trying the trick given me by David Lambroughton, the famous fishing photographer – using short strands of that white foam, duty-free bottle protector net they give you in airports – you clove hitch or through-loop it into the leader and when you tighten on a fish the leader cuts through it and it's gone without a knot remaining.

In fast water with intervening currents, however, a super-buoyant indicator will enable you to mend your line right up to it without deranging the drift of your fly – and thus avoid sideways drag setting in and getting you unseen rejections. John Judy shows and tells how, in *Slack Line Strategies for Fly Fishing*.

It's amazing how many dry fly anglers there are who've never seriously tried nymphing. Perhaps some of the writers make it sound too difficult. But it isn't – and it's a crucial enabler of better catches in these days of depleted daytime fly hatches. Also very tolerant of bungling dufferdom while you learn.

And it's amazing how many people who nymph, only ever use nymphs of size 14 or bigger. The fact is that there are always going to be a thousand times more naturals available to fish of size 20 than there will be of size 14. Maybe ten thousand times more. Why? Because virtually all of the larger ones have either been eaten already or have hatched – it's a pyramid, size 14 at the top, size 20 in the middle, and the rest of the gazillions of them too small to imitate (but not too small to eat).

So it's worth going small. Pictured here is a size 20 nymph I use when tiny Baetis are hatching, to get down on waters where only one fly is allowed and I don't want

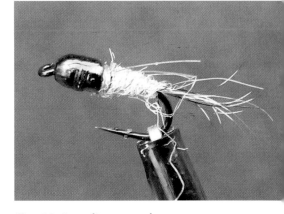

Size 20 tiny olive nymph

to use split shot, with two tiny 1.5 mm tungsten beads for weight and to mimic dark wing covers. And the fish will probably not have been frightened by many artificials that small, so your likelihood of getting a spook reaction is much reduced, and of getting a take, much increased.

FOOTNOTE 1: An exception to there being no particular right orientation for the dislodged larva could well lie in a peeping caddis that you might tie to imitate the Brachycentrus (Grannom) family. There are a lot of visual witnesses in the United States to this cased larva drifting, dislodged or 'behaviourally', with its head down. Some Troutnut.com forum contributors say they have found that a reverse-tied

peeping caddis with weight and peeping head at the bend of the hook is more effective. It would certainly make sense for a cased caddis to drift with its head down, so as to be better able to grab the next piece of stream bottom structure it gets swept past. Worth an experimental tying, I would think. Here is mine, with the new head-down peeper on the left and the traditional tying on the right. The new pattern could perhaps be named 'The Monorchid' (the medical term for a male with only one testicle – you can see why).

The new 'Monorchid' (left) and the old-style Peeping Caddis

FOOTNOTE 2: For many people the best knot for joining two leader lengths of greater than 20% difference is the water knot with 3 or 4 turns – they swear by it. But I find myself that it's unreliable when the thinner length is 5X or smaller – I think because the thinner material can too easily slip within the knot and burn out when it is placed under sudden strain. For differentials of between 20% and 35%, if I don't want to use a loop-to-loop join, I follow Gary Borger's recommendation in his book *Presentation*, and use a blood knot with five turns on the thick material end and seven on the thin. Or a tucked double grinner is very strong and safe. I tie all my knots very carefully, lubricate with saliva, nurse them up together, tighten them fully, and if I have any doubts at all I re-tie them. Fish can see all knots, remember, so there's no point in trying to make them vanishingly small.

FOOTNOTE 3: Nymphing didn't start on the chalk streams, any more than dry fly fishing did. John Younger, in *River Angling for Salmon and Trout*, published in Kelso in Scotland in 1840, wrote:

> 'When the flies come quickly on the surface and no trout takes them ... then for a trial of skill mutilate the wings of your flies by picking them off about half middle (not cutting them); or rather by tying down the top of the wings to near the tail of the fly which makes them appear something like the maggot released from its first case on the bottom stone and on its ascent to the surface. Then as much as you can let them sink low in the water, altogether below those flies on the surface, and you will most likely succeed in getting a few trouts.'

Even earlier, the unknown author of *The North Country Angler* (1786) said he believed that an intentionally sunk point fly catches fish because the flies that fish eat are bred under stones on the bottom and rise up through the water to hatch. So here was perhaps the first nymph angler recorded in literature.

Even if we discount the northern English and Scottish spider fishing (which some would say is close to nymphing) we can still place the start of larval imitation hundreds of miles away from the southern chalk streams, and a hundred years before the early, slightly shifty and soon-to-be-abandoned experiments of Marryat and Halford, and sixty years before Mottram's and Skues' conviction that it was a good idea.

We southerners may have flagellated ourselves with nymphing for 120 years, but we didn't invent it – that took observant and creative anglers from the north. As is all too normal in fly fishing, the original inventors were forgotten, and it was re-discovered later on.

Evening caddis swarming
on the River Usk in Wales
(Photo by Dave Collins)

THE EVENING RISE –
WHAT EVENING RISE?

THE EVENING RISE IS perhaps the biggest consistent disappointment for today's fly anglers, and that perhaps makes a look at it worthwhile.

What has caused its decline, and how can the angler fight back?

Timothy Benn, the celebrated angling publisher, asked in a magazine recently why we often don't see a spinner fall and evening rise even when the hatches during the day have been good. And he also asked why we seem to be getting as good hatches after the trout season (October, November) as we get during it – some people on the Test say even better.

In fact, a chorus of 'whatever happened to the evening rise?' quite frequently goes up (from anglers old enough to remember what such a thing was once like). The most relevant questions are: is this vanishing rise real; what are the reasons for it; can anything be done to bring it back; and in the meantime, are there strategies the fly fisher can usefully employ?

The work done by Dr Allan Frake (the fish-and-fisherman-friendliest person in the Environment Agency, now retired) and myself on the National Fly Abundance Survey, conducted over the first decade of this century but looking back over the last half of the 20th century as well, showed that total small fly abundance had fallen drastically to about one-third of previous levels before stabilising at the lower levels. So

An old drawing thought to be by Joseph Crawhall, 1864
The Fankled Angler, Night Coming On

one should expect poorer evening as well as daytime rises. But there is a suggestion by many anecdotal reporters that the evening rise has declined more. And now that many anglers are monitoring nymph numbers on a regular basis under the Angler Monitoring Initiative, they report that these latter are in fact quite abundant relative to hatching fly and to the number of egg layers seen.

With less than one in twenty nymphs making it through to emergence and less than one in twenty hatched flies making it through to egg laying, you would indeed expect to see plenty of nymphs relative to spinners. However, many of these commentators are experts, and I think we can conclude that something is indeed going on.

One reason is that trout won't rise unless there is an adequate banquet of surface fly to eat – in other words, as evening hatches and spinner falls have declined in line with total fly populations, they are going to have dropped below a critical threshold in this respect. There's just not enough to come up for.

And as we have seen from the graph of Baetis nymphal drift in chapter two, there is a huge competing food source down below to keep the fish away from the surface; one which multiplies logarithmically in late summer evenings. Here's the graph again to spare you searching. Note the drift numbers go off the scale.

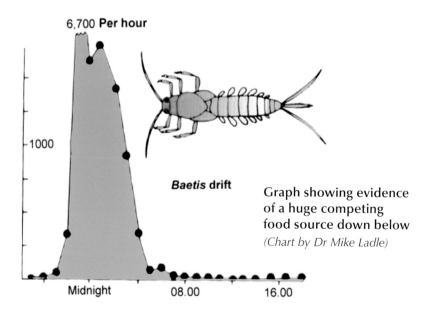

6,700 **Per hour**

1000

Baetis drift

Midnight   08.00   16.00

Graph showing evidence
of a huge competing
food source down below
(Chart by Dr Mike Ladle)

Prime hatching time for BWO on an English chalk stream

A second major reason for an apparent (but mistaken) absence of egg laying spinners in the evening is that most of the hatching fly on the average river in the southern part of the country (from which the complaints emanate) are Baetis of one species or another. And they don't dip or drop their eggs – they crawl down underwater to lay them on structure – and they don't (mainly) come back. Even the males also follow the females, perhaps as sacrificial fish fodder to help more females escape predation until egg laying is completed.

I also think, for what it is worth as an un-evidenced theory, that as fly populations decline each year the numbers of their predators don't immediately follow suit, so that the impact of predation (predominantly a daytime phenomenon) on the sloping shoulders of declining populations is disproportionately damaging. We get this picture with signal crayfish preying on caddis; the crayfish population decline trails that of the insect, with the predator remaining in the ascendant, and an accelerating vortex of prey destruction the natural result.

Fly Abundance
Fly in General - All Rivers

Mean Scores (Base: Number Answering for river in year)

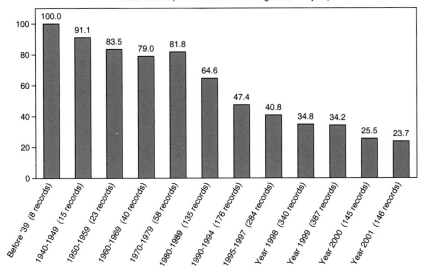

Falling fly hatches from pre-1939 to 2001 shown by the Millennium Fly
Abundance Survey

What started out as safety in numbers ends up being few enough for
every fly to be picked off by a hungry chaffinch. I know – I watch them
doing it with increasing despair. Then, by natural selection, the originally
relatively small numbers of post-dusk hatchers and egg layers in each
declining species will have survived and bred in greater numbers than
the over-predated daytime hatchers, exploiting as well the below-surface
nymphal feeding and growth opportunities freed up by the latter's decline.

Many fly species have multiple generations each year, so it will not
have taken long for the balance between the daytime and the night-time
hatchers, and daytime and night-time egg layers, to be reversed. Anglers
don't see the night-time hatches or the night-time egg laying that goes on
(unless they are Stuart Crofts, whose torchlit witness of their profusion
is very much congruent with this theory). In other words, the nymphs
are still present in the day as at all times, easily found and counted by the
AMI surveyors, but there has been a shift in their hatching, and in the
spinners' egg laying activities, away from the daytime and into the night.

This is the single greatest likely cause of the mismatch between a couple
of hundred fly fisher and river manager observers in my Fly Abundance

Survey reporting drastic hatch declines ... and the Environment Agency reporting much less great (though directionally identical) falls in nymph numbers.

Coming back to the seasonal change that is being reported: in actual fact there have always been quite substantial hatches, particularly of BWO and large dark olives, in the winter months.

J W Hills in *River Keeper* reports in tabular form the observations of William Lunn on the Houghton stretch of the Test over two winters, a century ago. These flies hatched in winter back then too, and in measurable quantities. It is the numerical balance, once again, that has changed between the seasons just as between day and night, and once again the logical finger of suspicion points at natural selection over multiple generations, driven by predation on falling summertime populations. The predators are dominantly summertime actors, just as they operate mainly during the day and not at night. So we get fewer summer fly, and relatively more winter fly.

So what can be done about the population falls, and what can the angler do in terms of changed strategy?

The answer to the first question is easy. Following the recent work of Dr Cyril Bennett on the Surrey Wey, the Derbyshire Wye, and the Hampshire Avon (following closely that of William Lunn on the Test, but a hundred years afterwards), supportive restocking of appropriate and responsive species is now a practical proposition. In particular, the blue winged olive, the British fly fisherman's sheet anchor, whose numbers have always fluctuated scarily but which manages to combine locally disastrous declines with amazing abundances close-by, turns out to be a very fit subject for restocking. But it will be a long process. Converting your aquarium to bouillabaisse is easy, but reversing the procedure takes longer, as the Environment Agency has discovered in its approach to the Water Framework Directive.

How can the angler fight back? That is more difficult. Here are a small number of strategies that work:

The first is to be in the right place – precisely – at the right time.

There is almost always some evening rise activity somewhere on any given reach at some time in the evening. A good bet is to look for a hatch of BWO, often sparse but sustained, coming off weeds or rocks close the surface in fast water. It will happen on most summer nights and a number of fish will know about it and be there, though in the fast water the rises to hatch-in-a-moment nymphs will not be easy to spot. Trying nymph, emerger and dry fly, in that order, would be my recipe.

Small chironomids will typically also hatch in the late evening in glassy glides, and they too will be very hard to spot and to identify the rise to. It is a largely unseen hatch but they are extremely numerous in rivers as well as in stillwaters, and there are over 400 species, many of them tiny. Nor are they easy to imitate except with an emerger with the right orientation – hanging straight down in and from the surface film. Something like the Sawyer Bow-tie Buzzer or the 'Ookey Rat in a size 20. Timothy Benn has treated stream chironomids as worthwhile imitatees for many years, and drew attention to their importance in a recent article: *Missing the Flight* (*Fly Fishing & Fly Tying*, October 2011).

Look for posts, camp-sheathing, brick or concrete walls, sloping or upright rock surfaces or intentionally placed fly boards or fly slabs – all places where Baetis spinners will be crawling down to lay their eggs, and getting washed off afterwards, to create a regular nightly subsurface feed lane for trout. (Potential imitations are discussed in chapter 13.)

Although nowadays in the southern counties of the UK we get very few caddis hatching, the trout will be watching out for the few that do swim jerkily to the surface to hatch, and a 'pupa' pattern imitating the 'pharate' (shrouded swim-up adult) will often succeed, especially if it has a shiny bead at its head to represent the air used by some species of the insect to buoy themselves. There are still some very good sedge evenings, though, in other parts of the UK, and of course in other countries. The picture that heads this chapter is an example of a recent massive caddis swarm on the middle reaches of the River Usk in Wales.

Go down under for the nymphal drift, and fish nymphs from dusk onwards when all surface activity ceases, through into the night. See also chapters nine and ten for some ideas if you relish an imitative challenge – including trying out silvered Baetis spinner and silvered crawl-down caddis egg layer patterns.

Tie on a mouse pattern, grease up only the front half of it, and tiddle it across a nice deep pool. Where rules permit!

Or go home and get some rest. Then, get up early and fish a really good spinner pattern like the Spinnermalist along the stream edges. Later be ready for the one -third of all dun hatches that happen before 10.30 a.m. – when the average angler starts fishing. The trout will not expect you to be there.

There's a big fish, lives below the road bridge over the upper Itchen at Itchen Stoke. It either feeds two inches off the brickwork on Baetis egg layers that have crawled down it and finally let go, or, if there's a hatch of duns coming down, it moves up into the concentrated feed lane that the current directs, funnelling through the shallow fast water under the central arch. Both positions set you a very hard cast – up under the bridge is very fraught if a loose tippet is to be achieved; and the two inches from the brickwork is almost impossible as well, since again the tippet needs to

An old picture of the bridge at Itchen Stoke

collapse, or the jet of fast water through the arch will whip it away pronto.

Anyway, for several seasons he's been rising when I've been in position below him, just a few times each year. He refused me comprehensively until two years ago. Then he declined my BWO imitations (PhDs) until the Baetis spinners started, and after many inadequate casts to the two inches from the brickwork spot he sucked my untreated Spinnermalist down with a tiny but visible down swirl.

The fish was easily three pounds and firmly on the end of the line, albeit on a size 21 hook. He opened his pink mouth and rushed towards me shaking his head from side to side. I'd been roundly beaten by a much bigger fish that used this tactic on the upper Mataura, so armed with that experience I did not panic too much and stripped in line. As he got to within five feet of my legs, he shot round me in a circle three times, with me spinning to follow him. Then he accelerated downstream for the overhanging willows, going so fast that he tunnelled the water and made the thrumming noise that I thought only mackerel made. I stopped him with side-strain and extreme force at the edge of the willow roots, whereupon he set off upstream towards a long stretch of black swan-deterrent netting. We came to a detente about halfway up that, with him basically head banging, and me giving rod but no line to each thump. I got a very good look at him, and he, angrily, at me. Three pounds of crossness. Then he bit through the tippet (I mean it drew across his teeth under extreme tension, and the severed end was clean cut). Honours about even, I feel.

But the fact was, he was the evening riser, and he was all of the evening rise on all of the river within my sight. If you hadn't been in that position, perhaps because you'd seen nothing move and packed up for the evening … if you hadn't even then seen his little down-swirls, you'd have joined the chorus of complaint instead of measuring yourself against the fish of a lifetime.

A FOOTNOTE ON THE CADDIS: in recent years sedge fishing in the evening has been much reduced as sedge populations have fallen. Caddis numbers are increasing, however (as I write in 2012), and a brief note on fishing the imitations is hopefully going to be more useful than it otherwise might have been.

Although trout do target the hatched caddis fly, especially those laying eggs at the surface, they feed much more avidly on the pharate adult as it swims up to the surface to hatch. In fact frequently the trout you see jumping for caddis has simply shot up after the rising pupa and pursued it into the air as it hatches. It follows that the most appropriate imitation, the one that should be your default first try in a caddis hatch, should be a pattern that imitates the pharate adult – in other words the swim-up pupa rather than the dry sedge – and that this should be fished underwater, letting it sink and drawing it up.

The Bird's Nest in chapter 15 is a very good general pattern, only in this case you would not be scrubbing it with hydrophobic powder so as to cover it with air. Another superb pattern is Gary LaFontaine's Deep Sparkle Pupa – and, if it's a hatch of grannom or of micro-caddis, Stuart Crofts' patterns for each of these, both also in chapter 15.

Obviously if you see fish taking adults at the surface you would go for a dry sedge pattern of the right size and colour to match them, Little Red Sedge, CdC and Elk, or Goddard and Harris's G & H Sedge would be my flies of first resort. They can be profitably twitched and skittered, which adds considerable fun to the proceedings. Thirty five years ago, when I had an evening season ticket on the then developing Bewl Bridge Reservoir in Kent, I fished for ten almost-successive evenings in the windblown waves off the Yacht Club beach, with a fly just the same as the Birds Nest, starting the fast-stripped retrieve as the fly hit the water. The brown trout were hitting swim-up sedge pupae with enthusiasm, and I got a limit every night – sixty fish in ten evenings. It was one of those purple passages you occasionally get in a fishing life, and you never forget either the experience or the lesson. Davy Wotton, later the inventor of SLF dubbings, put me up to it. He was my first fly-tying teacher, and at the time he ran rabbit clearance contracts on the farms surrounding the reservoir, with ferret, dog, gun, and my young son Jim, in constant attendance. He and Geoffrey Bucknall were my formative mentors and, between them, are also responsible for my casting style.

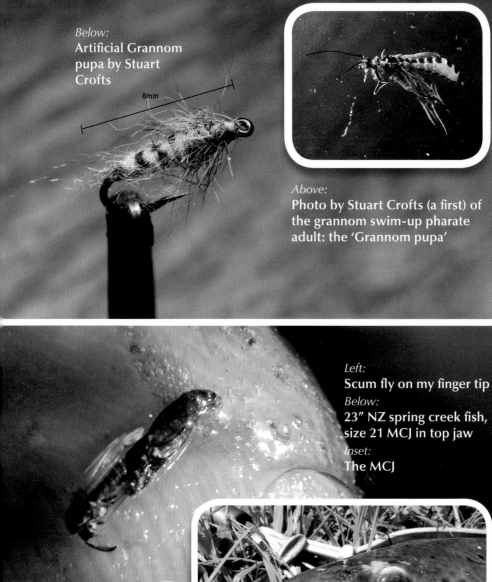

Below:
Artificial Grannom pupa by Stuart Crofts

8mm

Above:
Photo by Stuart Crofts (a first) of the grannom swim-up pharate adult: the 'Grannom pupa'

Left:
Scum fly on my finger tip
Below:
23" NZ spring creek fish, size 21 MCJ in top jaw
Inset:
The MCJ

PUSHING THE ENVELOPE
(Mimicking the hidden secrets of the trout's larder)

THIS DESCRIPTIVE PHRASE, COMING appropriately from advanced flight engineering and extreme human performance, heads a chapter looking at arenas of imitation and presentation in which only a few anglers as yet are working – but those who are, are getting results.

The imitative opportunities we are examining here spring largely from better and more perceptive observation by angler entomologists – particularly those with a strong interest in the behaviour of trout prey.

Illustrated opposite (top) is a prime example. Until a knowledgeable expert autopsied a trout that had been feeding heavily on what he knew were rising pharate (shrouded) adult grannom (the swimming 'pupae'), and photographed the insects, everybody from Halford and Skues to the present day thought that it was a brownish-grey affair with maybe some dark green segments. Nobody realised how bright it really is with black stripes on a chartreuse body and a light orange thorax. The imitation works and is relevant because the pupa is much more eaten by trout than the hatched insect.

The little size 22 dipterid (pictured opposite on my finger) which I collected hatching from its pupa was one of thousands from a huge scum slick on a sweeping willow branch below a large rising (but untemptable) trout. I dug around in my box for a thing I call the 'Midriff Copper John' that a year before, tried in desperation after an hour trying different flies on a nymphing Upper Mataura brown, had got it – 6 lbs 8 oz. This fish went for it too, and so have many big fish ever since. Its photo, and that of the MCJ, are on the opposite page. A serious fish that I'd tried for, for 40 minutes, feeding on something invisible in the film.

The MCJ is a great general imitation of a micro-caddis pupa as well as of hatching small diptera. It is probably a good working approximation of a river midge pupa, and not far off the shape and colour of a reed smut larva. It is best presented on a fully greased leader, so as to sink only a little. It has a black brass (not tungsten – too heavy) bead, size 1.5 mm, at the midriff position on a Tiemco size 21, model 102Y hook, and tapered windings of brown copper wire front and back. I tie it with a brown, tick-marked, squirrel tail to represent a shuck.

It has got me as many big trout as any other single fly since I started using it as an experimental tying in 2002 – in the UK, New Zealand, Iceland, and the Yellowstone region.

River midges are small but far more plentiful than perhaps any other trout food in many rivers including, and especially, chalk streams and spring creeks all over the world. There are hundreds of species (over 400 in the UK). In rivers, most of them are extremely small – size 20 hook and smaller.

They hatch quickly, and typically don't get noticed, or looked for, by anglers in the UK, although they are mightily important in the USA where, lacking a close season for trout, much more winter fly fishing is done. There, whole books are now available concentrating on midge patterns. It's a discipline fly fishers in other countries need to learn from

River midge shucks from the Icelandic Big Laxa
where the midge can be 70% of trophy trout food

as the potential is huge and largely untapped.

Frank Sawyer had a terrific midge pupa tying in the Bow Tie Buzzer, which hung suspended from a bunch of pure white wool. The tippet is threaded through the eye of the hook, and then the wool is tied into the end of the tippet (sufficient to stop it pulling through) and clipped off like a bow tie. Micro-currents make the body swivel and move, even though it is fished dead-drift, and of course on a greased leader. Nowadays we drop down a hook size, or three, from the 14 that Frank used, and we use a curved hook and tie round the bend. The imitative objective is the pupa just touching the meniscus

This River Wylye midge (size 20) touching the film and reflected in the mirror, hatched in a split second

and about to hatch in a heartbeat; and that's exactly what it does. It's a near-forgotten 'not-quite-the-thing-old-chap' pattern that richly deserves rediscovery.

Midge pupae stick around the river bottom before they swim up to hatch, and trout target them down there most of all. The best way of

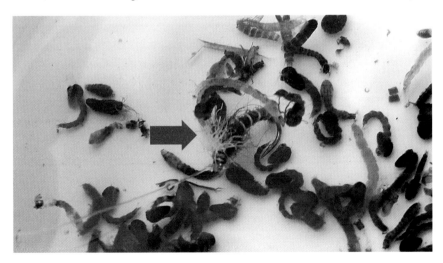

Spot the impostor (the Iceland pattern)

getting a size 20 imitation down there is by trailing it down-tippet from a much larger and heavier pupa dressing. Fishing in company with Stuart Crofts on the midge-dominated Big Laxa River in Iceland in July 2011, I had failed to catch on the top of the water, and decided to get a tiny pupa, copied from a previous trip's stomach sample, down to the bottom in a strong glide where I knew fish fed. The result was immediate and sustained: seven fish from 2 lbs up to 4 lbs in pretty short order. Stuart waded out to throat sample the last of these, and the photo shows that my copy wasn't too far away from the naturals in shape, size, and colour. In the States, one standard tiny pattern, the Zebra Midge, gets down under its own steam by using a silver tungsten bead head. It is tied on a curved silver hook, just made of tying silk in brown, black or red for a thin body, and a silver wire rib.

My size 20 hatching midge pattern

with super-fine grizzly neck hackle as the shuck

The hatching river chironomid is another common target for trout, and in Iceland (where it represents 70% of their July food on some rivers) both Oliver Edwards and I, after seining and examining hatchers, came up with artificials on curved hooks with para hackles to hold them in the film and a sticky-up wing of sparse grey polypropylene fibre. My pattern added a super-fine grizzly neck hackle, straight and not wound, as the shuck. That has got me several good fish in the UK that were obsessed with the hatching midge, as well as in Iceland.

Another 'messy' but massively abundant and nutritious food item for trout of all sizes (including very large ones) is the Simulium larva (reed smut, blackfly). Halford recognised its importance and included a drawing, even though it wasn't the kind of thing he wanted to imitate in the larval form in which it is dominantly available to the fish. It looks like a little caterpillar and moves about on weed and structure by 'looping' like a caterpillar. It moves to the fastest flow and extends two little fans (like those old plastic bug-deflector things you could get for your radiator cap in the days when the polluters had still

Simulium larvae, fatteners of big trout

not wiped out every insect and there were still bugs to deflect from your windscreen). With these fans it collects algae, bacteria, diatoms and silt, and eats them – thus actively cleaning the river. Up to 300,000 can live on a square metre of weed. I have tied visibly accurate simulacra, but never really convinced the trout; the problem is, I think, that the larva seldom drifts, and anchors itself with a silken thread. Trout pluck it from its hold. In a complex procedure it hatches from its specially constructed pupal case (a fully formed fly as pictured opposite), buoyed to the surface swiftly in a bubble of air – a real challenge to imitate, and not one I've yet succeeded in, in spite of experiments with clear glass beads over silver tinsel on tiny hooks. The adult however can be imitated when there is a fall of them after egg laying, even though it is probably the larval form that is most eaten by the trout. Copying adult rather than larva is a bit like the drunken man looking for his lost house keys under a lamp

The Reed Smut (Simulium) with my artificial below
(Photos by Lin Baldock)

post, not because he lost them there, but because that's where the light is.

This little chap (Limniphora – note its size relative to the hairs on the back of my hand) hatches prolifically from the waters of the world wherever the Simulium (blackfly, reed smut) is abundant. It predates

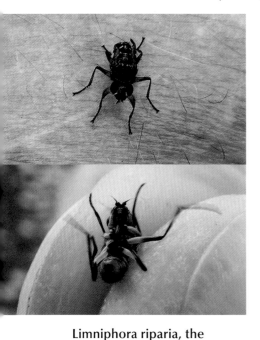

Limniphora riparia, the stiltwalker

trout's view in lower picture

on the Simulium larvae, and also on hatched-out chironomids and other small soft-bodied invertebrates, grabbing them and sucking their juices, dead or alive. Its wings do not extend for a good few minutes after hatching, generally when it has been blown, or floated to its search area in the riparian zone. Trout, including large fish, will appear and feed on the fitfully abundant hatches. Hatched from the surface film, to which it rises in an air bubble having chewed its way out of its distinctive pupal case, it will ride downstream or downwind, sitting up on its six feet like a stilt-walker. In fact the Icelandic for stilt-walker is the name of the artificial I designed to imitate it on the Laxa Adaldal: 'Stulta'.

The Stulta is tied with light khaki-ish pheasant tail fibres, the legs being torn, not cut from the quill so as to leave a foot-like flange on the end. It has a lightly dubbed thorax of khaki hair to match the underside of

Stulta, angler's view and trout's view

the natural. Laxa guides Bjarni Hoskuldsson and Asgeir Steingrimsson copied it immediately and to great effect. Like the Simulium, it also hatches fully-formed in an oxygen bubble, and is equally hard to imitate at that momentary life stage. It got me nineteen decent trout on the Icelandic Laxa in 2012. I mean, over 20 inches.

The next piece of the envelope that's being pushed is that represented by the incredibly abundant, but largely ignored, Agapetus species (A. fuscipes and A. ochripes – duskyfoot and yellowfoot, in the UK). This is known as the 'Little Black Caddis' and it is tiny, being appropriately matched as an adult on a size 22 hook maximum, or size 20 and tied short. It is so small that it has been largely ignored by fly fishermen

Agapetus microcaddis, swim up pupa
(Photo by S Crofts)

until recently. Once hatched, it is not easily available to the trout, being not big enough to be worth them chasing it. However the rising pharate adult pops directly up to the surface, and, staying underwater, swims at a rate of knots perpendicularly to the bank, where it hatches, having found emergent rocks or plants, and cover. It is during this trip, whilst zipping across the current in the slower last inch below the surface, that it is mainly sought and eaten by trout. The picture shows Stuart Crofts' pattern, the ACE or

Agapetus Caddis Emerger, which has been a great success for those who have adopted it and fished it by casting out at a right angle from the bank, ensuring it engages in the surface, and retrieving it nice and fast. The long legs with which it swims are represented by little outriggers.

The Agapetus is the caddis that builds those tiny, stone-igloo-like cases on stones and on pieces of woody debris that are often present in thousands on the stream floor. It actually moves its case around, and grazes on algae from safety, using portholes at both ends of

Agapetus Caddis Emerger
(Fly and photo by S Crofts)

its underneath. The same family, the Glossomatidae, are vastly prolific in the USA as well, where Ralph Cutter, in particular, has drawn attention to its imitative potential.

The last group of prolific but rarely imitated insect life stages that I want to deal with here is the air-silvered, post-crawl-down, post-egg-laying caddis. Many species within the two main caseless families, Hydropsyche and Rhyacophila, the Brachycentrus (grannom) and also the very small Glossosomatidae and the even smaller Hydroptilidae, re-enter the water to lay their eggs. Anyway, all you really need to know is that lots of caddis of widely differing sizes do this. They do it usually by using the grip of their feet to pull their water-repellent selves down through the meniscus at a point where it is weakened, by using emergent structure – posts and rocks are popular, and quite a queue can develop. Some then crawl, and some swim, to their chosen egg laying site.

Bird's nest-style adult caddis egg layer

Just like the small olive (Baetis) crawl-down egg layers dealt with in the next chapter, these sedges acquire a thin covering of air in the process, which they use to breathe while laying their eggs. When they have finished, they drift off downstream and become trout prey. Ralph Cutter's, California School of Fly Fishing (following the dive-based work of Gary LaFontaine and diving dedicatedly themselves), has built a highly successful series of imitations such as the 'Bird's Nest' using natural fluffy-cum-spiky materials like wool, possum, rabbit and wood duck flank. These unweighted caddis-shaped flies are scrubbed with hydrophobic fumed silica dust so as to carry their own covering of air underwater, sunk using an up-tippet split shot, and fished at any depth. They swim so can be usefully given jerky movement.

The same fly hydrophobically coated, under water

If you are, philosophically, an imitative fly fisherman, it is easy to fall into the trap of placing your whole bet on to the appearance of your imitations, and relying on dead-drift presentations of them to fool the trout. I do it all the time. It's a test of my fly-tying skills. But, thereby, I come close to a New Purism; foolishly, because if the right movement is transmitted to the fly even better results can follow. One of the movements that most reliably bring a take is one that mimics the near-escape of the food item from the fish. Sometimes, the exact appearance of the fly is less important than you might think.

In the cold spring of 2012 I had fished all day in the rain and wind over the normally generous wild browns and rainbows of the 'Hallowed Waters' (the Cressbrook and Litton FFC on the Derbyshire Wye). Eight hours for seven small fish. On the trudge back up the gorge of Monsal Dale to the car I passed an angler stripping a streamer – I thought – in a deep waterfall pool I had seen him climb down to a few minutes earlier. We met soon afterwards in the car park. He had caught and released a 4 lb brown trout in that pool. 'What on?' 'Peeping Caddis'. Later in the pub the keeper told me the Peeping Caddis is always his go-to pattern. Now that, I thought to myself, is about as non-imitative as you can get. If there's one thing cased caddis don't ever do, it's shoot across a pool at forty miles an hour. And yet ... if you were a hungry, cold-spring, 4 lb trout and you saw a fat food item getting away from you in open water, might you not grab it? Another lesson re-learnt. When trout are dour, movement matters.

This chapter has been about the potential for catching large wild trout on small rather unprepossessing food items, on which they feed avidly. You might feel that this is just a bridge too far: a niche occupation reserved for specialist trout hunters. That would be true for some of these more recherché imitations, but not for all. I have admitted, for example, my failure to catch fish on visually quite successful simulations of the simulium larva. But the air-coated, sunken, post-egg laying caddis has been widely successful in the USA whilst being virtually untried in the UK and Europe. And the Stulta has been hugely successful recently on the River Laxa in Iceland where it is common. More important for UK and European, as well as for American fly fishermen, are the chironomids. In fact, it would not be too strong a claim to say that successful imitation of small river chironomids can open up a whole new vector of imitative fly fishing for UK fly fishermen who have not yet tried it. Keen anglers are using tiny silver-ribbed slim, dark-bodied curved chironomid larva patterns to target

A chironomid acts its name
(Greek: 'hand-conductor')

winter grayling and spring trout on the limestone rivers of Derbyshire now, following the American lead typified by the accounts of midge fishing in the writings of authors such as John Gierach and Ed Engle.

Yet this is not the first wave of chironomid imitation in the UK. Twenty years and more ago, Tim Benn was experimenting and writing about river midges, and so was John Goddard. Darrel Martin, whose 1994 book *Micropatterns* is immensely useful to those of us who would imitate these small food items, has been a regular visitor to the UK and honoured us with his presence at the Flyfishers' Club in London this year.

On the Big Laxa in August I revisited a very good brown trout that lives by a lava rock in the swift run-off from a rapid in the braided section below Lake Myvatn. This fish had taken my fly in each of the two previous years' visits, and each time dived into the rock unstoppably and smashed the leader. The evening was cursed with a viciously cold northerly wind, but the trout were coming up for flies if you could somehow get them onto the water – and a huge American black foam beetle with rubber legs that had been brought over by Barry and Cathy Beck was doing great execution in spite of the trout almost certainly never having seen an insect that big in their lives. (Same principle as the 40 mile an hour peeping caddis.) Our guide, Gudmundur ('Gummi'), told me that since last year this particular fish had become known to visitors, and had been given the name of Harald. This made me think that he might be on the shy side by this time of the season, but I put the big beetle down his favourite side of the rock anyway and up he came – but I missed seeing his head come up under the water and when the fly disappeared, sucked down in a miniature whirlpool, I struck too soon and pricked him.

Hoping to snatch success from the jaws of failure, as it were, I went back to the same spot the following evening, and put the same giant beetle past his home. This time however, using an old trick learnt from fishing for carp with floating bread crust in which you suspend a small hook baited with a tiny piece of bread flake underneath, I tied a size 20 chironomid pupa imitation onto an 8 in length of 7 lbs breaking strain fluorocarbon and tied that to the bend of the beetle's hook. First cast, the beetle disappeared and Harald, who had taken the pupa, found himself in a do-or-die battle with me. Armed

'Harald's' lie to the left of the underwater rocks and, below, 'Harald' – deceived by a size 20 midge pupa

with my new and unbreakable 8 ft 6 in 5-weight Hardy Sintrix rod, I 'showed him the butt' as the Victorians used to say, and for quite ten minutes he alternately head-butted towards the rock, sometimes hitting it but never gaining its sanctuary, or shot sideways across the current hoping to drown my line and/or, bury me in the weed. I was shouting at him to the effect that, no, he was not going to be allowed to escape this year – and there may have been some other epithets. Anyway, I got him into the net eventually and at that point a distant cheer made itself heard from the road on the other side of the river where, unknown to me, a coach party had stopped to watch the fun. Even better, a group of Icelandic fellow anglers from the Lodge had just parked their car and were walking up the road at the same moment. Harald was 22 inches in length and just under five pounds in weight, and shot off at warp speed to reoccupy his clump of lava rocks.

Stuart Crofts' cranked body, one wing spinner
(idea from Kelly Galloup)

My own 'Spinnermalist'

IMITATION'S LAST FRONTIER

THIS CHAPTER DETAILS ANOTHER imitative opportunity that, so far as I know, no-one has fully solved yet. Of course, there may well be anglers out there who have cracked the code, but aren't sharing their news ... instead, they may be quietly enjoying the fruits. If so, I feel they should honour their responsibilities to the sport and, well ... come out. Meanwhile, the crawl-down, float-up post-egg-laying olive spinner offers huge deceptive potential. Huge because of the numbers of the beasts – four-fifths of all the small upwing nymphs as regularly counted in my own stretch of the Wylye. A potential of which only a few anglers are aware, and which just a very few are working on.

The biggest, as far as I know, unsolved opportunity for fooling trout is this post-underwater-egg-laying Baetis. There are just so many of these olives – in most rivers the most populous of all upwing families – and all completely unseen by the angler when egg laying. Unseen by the angler, but not by the fish.

Because, after crawling down to lay their eggs, and letting go of the post or rock afterwards they are covered by their thin bright silver layer (the *plastron* – Greek for breastplate) of air, coating their entire body, legs and wings and they appear underwater in the trout's direct vision as sparkling silver jewels.

Plastron-silvered female olive (Baetis) egg layer
underwater, with eggs

The plastron of air, particularly the air sandwiched between their wings (which are held together) buoys them up to the surface if they are not eaten on the way there ... and they float along at, and yet under, the meniscus, visible to the trout but not to us. They are trapped, unable to escape, mainly empty of eggs but still affording a nutritious meal and available in sufficient, non-energy-demanding quantities to warrant the trout's close attention.

This is one common reason for the slow porpoising rise of trout to nothing that you can see. 'They're rising', you'll tell your friend or yourself, 'but for the life of me I can't see what they taking.' This familiar phenomenon occurs not just in the evening. The bodies of overnight Baetis egg-layers congregate in side-slicks and on stands of weed, to be disgorged downstream in the morning as well. Or a shower of rain can dislodge thousands of them and send them downstream at any time. The wise angler, like the wise trout, should know this and react to it. But with what, and how?

I certainly (so far at least), have failed to present an appropriate fly in the appropriate place to match this food source.

Little red spinner
(female iron blue)

The fertilised pre-egg laying female is a common sight to fly fishermen and especially to those of us who wade. The reason is that she sees us as an egg-laying opportunity, and will land on our persons and waders with a view to walking down underwater. Her most glamorous manifestation as dramatis persona is as the little red spinner, the female imago of the tiny iron blue, pictured here.

Halford had the insect and its appearance dialled, of course, and he made its imitation into his habitual pseudonym of 'Detached Badger'. But as far as its behaviour went, he just didn't get it. Nor would he have wanted to – what could be a greater anathema to the King of the Dry Fly, than a dry fly that crawled back underwater? The imitation had to float.

Halford and Hall both contributed chapters to the Badminton Library volume, *Fishing: Salmon and Trout*, (5th edition, 1889, and subsequent editions) on dry fly and mayfly fishing respectively, and the olive spinner imitations as shown in Hall's contribution are illustrated here. They were floaters, not sunk spinner imitations, just as Halford's own 'Detached Badger' was. Halford had earlier wrongly maintained that all the Ephemeroptera lay eggs at the surface and fall dying on to it: 'These spinners when dancing up and down, occasionally just touching the surface of the water, are in the act of laying their eggs, which at once sink and adhere to the gravel in the bed of the river, and the spinner, having fulfilled its duty, falls lifeless on the stream.' (*Floating Flies and How to Dress Them*, 1886, pp 76 & 77).

VI. RED SPINNER.

CHALK-STREAM FISHING WITH DRY FLY 343

VI. THE RED SPINNER.

(Fig. vi. p. 340.)

Of all the numberless patterns which have been devised to imitate the gauzy transparency of this fly, I believe this to be the best ; of late years it has been most successfully used in Hampshire, and is known as the ' Detached Badger.'

Body : Detached, made of reddish brown horsehair, and firmly whipped to the hook with strong well-waxed silk.

Legs and Wings : A ' badger hackle' dressed buzz. This hackle is difficult to obtain, and is of a rusty grey in the centre (almost black), with bright shining golden tips.

Hook, o or oo.

H S Hall's plate and description of the 'Detached Badger', Badminton Library chapter

John Goddard and Brian Clarke knew about the crawling down bit as they were researching for *The Trout and the Fly* in the late 1970s. I remember being on the fringes of some of their fishing parties on the Kennet at that time, and helping with the photography – magic times for me as I was a neophyte. Neil Patterson actually lived there, as he does now. John asked him, as a creative fly-tyer, to come up with a (nymph) pattern that would suspend itself just below and in the surface. Neil produced the bent hook Suspender Midge pattern utilising ethafoam balls in little bags made from nylon tights which did the job and went on to become a stillwater standard. This solved the suspension problem, but it wasn't applied to spinners – although maybe it still could be. Neil then moved the suspender ball back to mid-shank to create the Pretty Polly nymph that hung level and straight. Great for nymphs which, contrary to the received wisdom of fly fishing, lie straight and not bent when hatching.

Neil had also been researching, with Frank Sawyer's help, a sunk spinner. This, however, was a deep-sunk spinner (aimed, intelligently, at the river bed feeding lane) and did not address the subsurface spinner presentation.

Neil Patterson says:

Neil Patterson's sunk spinner
tied by himself

'My original pattern that has been written up in many books, used thin red copper wire covered with flattened monofilament for the body. For the wings, I tied a cream badger cock hackle spent, with pheasant tail fibres folded over as a thorax. In effect, a spent spinner spending its last gasping breaths underwater.'

Although Neil later improved it using a silver bead overlaid with clear plastic and silver ribbing, I personally very much liked the original tying, and my attempts using silver beads have not worked for me at all. Spinners tied with silvery materials don't work, or at least not for me, in the rivers I fish. There are several good patterns in non-silvered colours. Pat Fox, Dermot Wilson's keeper on the Itchen, invented an effective fly he called the 'Hatching Spent', with over-long tails, very small hackle, herl body, and no wings at all, to be fished in the film. Stuart Crofts' spinner pattern with the sideways-bent-hook abdomen and single lay-flat wing is terrific. My own Spinnermalist does a great job too (see chapter 12 for the tying). Both these imitations can be fished awash to great effect, but if you treat them to float they will not break through the film at all, but sit defiantly on it – probably for the life of the fly.

It is possible to silver these or similar patterns with air just like the natural, thanks to hydrophobic fumed silica, which you can brush into your fly. But then having necessarily sunk it (for example with a split shot as some of the Americans, led by the highly perceptive Ralph Cutter, do), how the hell do you get it to sit there, just under the meniscus? Ralph doesn't – he makes them 'fall up' by imparting upward movement from an initial sunk cast. The search goes on ...

An experimental sunk spinner (?) pattern

tied by Frank Sawyer and given to Tony Wells

If tumbled in a riffle, or in bankside or weed-induced turbulence, these float-up spinners will lose the covering of air but still remain sub-surface and unseen to us. I have a very strong suspicion that the success in fast rocky rainfed rivers of the classic 'northern' spider patterns is due to their success in imitating the float up Baetis spinner. I believe they could usefully migrate south to the chalk streams. When I talk to the 'Sheffield School' about this, both Stuart Crofts and Paul Gaskell (of the Wild Trout Trust) tell me that they use a fly plied just under the surface by drawing it up and frequently recasting. Stuart uses spiders. Paul uses 'hairy' beadheads on an ultra long French leader. Timothy Benn tells me that the approved southern chalk stream technique is to twitch

The RS2 created by Rim Chung

your spinner pattern just after it lands so as to slide it just under the surface. That's pretty much what I do – I degrease my Spinnermalist with fuller's earth, and tweak it under if it won't fish awash.

I have a suspicion that in the States the very successful RS2 nymph invented by Rim Chung may be taken on occasion for a float-up Baetis spinner, too. It is predominantly tied in silver and grey, commonly sunk by the use of a small split shot, and uses materials that tend to carry air below the surface, including the webby base-fibres of saddle hackle feathers for the upright wing.

The unsolved problem is, I feel, more one of presentation rather than one of fly design. Something like the stillwater anglers' 'washing-line' approach for holding the operative fly just below the surface is required. In fact that, or something similar, might well be the answer. Or back to the Suspender idea. It's a problem looking for a creative solution: a really important solution, such that could unlock a great deal of so-far unachievable deception.

FOOTNOTE 1: Tony Hayter, who is writing the definitive book on Skues, tells me that around the turn of the century Skues had been experimenting with some Scottish river (Tweed and Tummel) sunk flies which had vertical wings. Skues was puzzled, and eventually quite distressed by their considerable success, particularly when the fish were rising to what he took to be black gnats, and smutting. So distressed – he didn't know what the trout took them for – that he stopped using them. He had a very good day indeed with these vertical-wing sunk flies at Abbotts Barton in 1904 (before he got into the development of what he later published as his nymphs after working on them with Martin Mosely (one of the leaders in aquatic entomology at the Natural History Museum). I am daring to suggest that these patterns used early on in experiments by Skues did not in fact imitate nymphs, but were good representations of float-up, post-egg-laying olive spinners with their wings still 'glued' together by the plastron. We'll never know; but Tony doesn't disagree with it as a slightly less than wild hypothesis – and the picture makes one think it might well be right.

Skues says he never saw olives crawling down underwater, but

Egg laying Baetis under water
with wings upright and glued together by the plastron of air

acknowledged that the Rev. E A Eaton had. Isn't that weird? Never – in 46 years of fishing up to the publication of *The Way of a Trout with a Fly*? After asking myself this rhetorical question I realised why – Skues almost never waded. Baetis never mistook him for useful in-stream structure.

FOOTNOTE 2: Roy Christie also has a crank-shanked spinner tied to represent the great red spinner of the Usk and northern rainfed rivers, published on the Internet. Oliver Edwards has told me that whilst the dun (the autumn dun, Ecdyonurus dispar) is not very available to trout, the spinner is, and is a very worthwhile objective for imitation. The false march brown (Ecdyonurus venosus) is the same, in that its nymph crawls out to hatch rather than emerging at the surface – but the spinner returns to lay eggs at the surface and falls spent, and hence the imitation of that is useful. I believe the same is true of many of the clinger mayflies in the United States.

Keep the fish upstream of you
(Photo by Owain Mealing)

PLAYING AND NETTING BIG TROUT

MY ONLY TRAINING IN this arena has been by large trout. And arena is the right word. We are talking about a gladiatorial fight in which there are only two contenders (and, hopefully, no crowd). I, Retiarius, with my net; he, Secutor, with his scaly armour. It was years before I started catching trout of any great size. I went thirteen years between my first and my second two-pounder on the Wylye. But then I got better at it and also started going abroad as well for much larger fish. In any average year of the last twenty, I'll have landed and photographed a few dozen fish of between two and six pounds. There have been a sprinkling of much bigger trout too, but they aren't the ones that train you; they're too big, too scary, and too infrequent.

I'm tempted to say: 'How long have you got?' A chap could write a book about playing big trout. But perhaps because it's such an instantaneous, stuff-of-the-moment thing, a short list of dos and don'ts will serve better than a long enumeration of all the things a trout can do to you, and how you should respond to each.

I have taken a lot of video of my friends playing big fish in recent years (Owain Mealing in NZ, Nick Measham, Oliver Edwards and Stuart Crofts in Iceland) and that body of evidence is added to my own more visceral memories to inform what I have to say here. Also, Owain has taken a lot of autoshoot photographs of me playing fish, and I have been able to plunder that store to help illustrate some points.

The main thing to do with any big fish is to keep it upstream of you.

Obviously that's pretty much impossible if it knows the trick of running straight at you with its mouth open shaking its head; or if it knows how to run downstream past you and then turn at right angles across the current and drown your line so that it breaks you. With these stratagems you know you have an experienced fish and the odds in your favour have already halved. Get the rod as high as you can, as bent as you can, and strip line as fast as you can to get it, and keep it, above the water. Nobody can stay in touch with the fish that sprints towards you the moment it's hooked, although the closer you get to him, and the shorter the line in consequence, the better you're fixed.

But mainly, the bad news of being hooked, the unwelcome realisation of being tethered, dawns more slowly – and if you don't aggravate things by sudden movements or by horsing the fish, you may be able to achieve some tiring before things get crucial. I was once able to net and release a 20 in wild brownie on the Wylye, with Gordon Mackie who had just written an article about not playing trout too hard looking on, and he said that he didn't really think the fish knew it had been hooked. Anyway, that's the objective, if you can achieve it, for the first few moments at least. (Gordon was my predecessor-but-one as President of the Wilton Fly Fishing Club; he writes every month for *Fly Fishing & Fly Tying* magazine, and his book *Fly Leaves and Waterside Sketches* [1998] is a damn good read.)

If there aren't any upstream snags to keep the fish away from, while still holding him fairly firmly, let him take a little line in an upstream direction so as to avoid giving him the impression that all progress upstream is impossible.

If he starts to run downstream, immediately apply side strain to turn him around into the current again and frustrate his rush. You can afford to do this with considerable force, although not snatchily, using the full shock absorbency of the rod right down to its butt. In fact, all the time use side strain to impose your will on the fish and make sure that he stays upstream of you. For heaven's sake don't use rods that don't have enough backbone to do this. I use a 5-weight the whole time and I can't think of a single reason why I would want to go any lighter if big trout were anywhere in prospect. As for Tenkara – don't make me laugh.

Minor downstream gains on his part can be put right by you, again using side strain – if you hold him hard enough at an angle with his head into the current, he virtually has to move upstream back above you again. But this is a delicate business, and once he is downstream of you he has the constant option to use his body as a plane against the current and exert more force than you might want to try and overcome.

If that happens, in the absence of downstream refuges for him, you

Turning a fish from a downstream rush with side strain
(Photo by Owain Mealing)

will need to follow. In the worst cases it may be better for you to get out of the river if you are wading and run down the bank so as to get below him again.

On the whole, if you start to see your backing you have lost three quarters of your chance of landing the fish. Either he knows of a holt that you don't know about that he will be in within seconds, or he will drown your line and break you. In any case he has gained much more control over the situation than you want him to have.

You will often see pictures of people fighting fish with the rod held way up high. This is entirely appropriate for bonefish and for any situation with trout in which you need to keep your line clear of the water. Specifically it's the right thing to do when a fish has run downstream, or when there are many stands of weed or other similar refuges that you want to keep him above. But bear in mind that he has all his swimming strength available to him in this configuration – tail power, wiggle power, planing against the current power, and pectoral fin power. Whereas, if he is upstream of you and you are exerting side strain successfully, he has only got tail power in full measure.

The default fighting position that maintains your control to the highest degree is a short line and side strain. When this is what you have got, you can switch that side strain around from one side of the trout to the other (the more easily if you are wading) so as to tire him without him being able to gain ground or trump you.

Be careful of keeping him too high in the water if you don't need to, in case he decides to have a total thrash and throws the hook. And if he jumps, of course you know what to do because you have read the book like me: drop the rod and give him line but in my view not too much. Every jump of a big fish is a memory to treasure in your photographic memory, not least because it raises the distinct possibility that it may be the only photograph you get.

I gave too much line when it jumped, to a fish that I had stalked for over an hour on the Waitangitaona that was well over eight pounds. I had nearly drowned crossing the river to get into position below it. It was under an overhanging willow just downstream from a sunken log, and when I stopped it getting into that by giving it the butt it jumped over six feet into the branches of the tree. But it broke me by crashing back onto the line.

Of all the hard-fighting trout in the world, probably the fish of the big Laxa in Iceland are the most exciting to tangle with. Oliver Edwards calls them 'flat-rodders', because however gentle and evanescent was the sipping rise that you floated your tiny dry fly over, the next second the fish is ten yards away and your rod is flat, with no hope of getting it up and absorbing the rush. Generally speaking, the next thing is that everything goes slack and the leader comes back abraded to a break on the lava rocks, or the tippet cut through by being dragged across the trout's teeth, or the hook opened out.

Unfortunately this experience gives you very little opportunity to learn. All you can do is to try something different next time. The best idea seems to be to set the reel drag fairly (but not completely) loose and raise the rod immediately the fish runs – then clamp down on the reel and try to stop it quickly. This all has to be done in a split second or you are lost. And it takes considerable determination to do it, as it runs counter to all your instincts and experience – it is in my view a far more difficult thing to achieve than for a trout fishermen not to strike a salmon when it takes. But it does work, and my rueful photographs of broken leaders, cut-through tippets and opened hooks have gradually declined in number as I look through my Iceland photographs.

In fact in many cases when you lose a fish it is impossible to tell what you should have done otherwise than what you did. The main thing to do is to cultivate the thought that after all, honours turned out even between two superb contestants. You beat the fish in terms of deception and he beat you in terms of escape. Whatever you do, don't get depressed about it. You are doing this because you enjoy it, so smile.

When it comes to getting the fish into the net, it is even more important that whenever possible he is upstream of you. The fish needs to go into the net headfirst or you run the risk of chasing it once more into panicked flight in bringing the net up from behind. And if the fish is turned into the net head first from upstream, going with the current, the chances of a last-minute gyration and escape on his part are minimised. If you can possibly avoid it, don't drag the fish upstream into the net which puts everything, especially the hook hold, under maximum strain.

Next left turn and he's in the net

Downstream, and head first

Head up is preferable, and already you will have been making a judgement, based on the extent to which you are now able to get his head up in the fight, as to his readiness for netting. I don't use scoop nets myself partly on account of weakened wrists and a debilitated back which inhibits my bending – I use an extending handle net. There is a better reason though. In the pictures, you will see me with the rod in a hoop at the full extent of my rod arm whilst the net is at the full extent of my net arm at 180° to the former. That way the full shock absorbency of the rod is still in play, and an earlier netting is enabled, with the fish less exhausted. Scoop nets are for fish that are tired out, unless the angler is a real toreador.

It remains to unhook the fish, take any photographs quickly, and make sure it is revived fully before releasing it. I like to thank the fish. This is not because I think the trout understands. It is simply because it seems to reinforce the appropriate attitude of mind in me. If it did understand, it would give me the finger.

A great fish to a horned caddis on one of South Island's west coast spring creeks
(This photo and those on the previous page by Owain Mealing)

FOOTNOTE: Just in case I should fall foul of my own strictures about angling skills being forgotten and then reinvented and claimed as his own by the next upcoming author, let me share with you the fact that virtually the same instructions on playing and landing big fish (in this case Thames salmon) were given by Thomas Barker in his book, *The Art of Angling* in 1651:

> 'You must be sure you have your line of twenty six yards in length that you may have your convenient time to turn him; but if you turn him you are very like to have the fish with small tackles; the danger is all in the running out both of salmon and trout, you must forecast to turn the fish as you do a wild horse, either upon the right or left hand, and wind up your line as you find occasion in guiding your fish to the shore, having a good large landing hook to take him up.'

A 6 lb trout returned
(Photo by Owain Mealing)

Top: **F M Halford and Wm Senior at Manor Water, St Cross (River Itchen)**
Above: **G E M Skues posing for the camera**

PURISM HAS GOT US FACING THE WRONG WAY

'Those of us who will not in any circumstances cast except over rising fish are sometimes called ultra purists and those who occasionally will try to tempt a fish in position but not actually rising are termed purists ... and I would urge every dry fly fisher to follow the example of these purists and ultra purists'
(*The Dry Fly Man's Handbook*, p69) F.M. HALFORD

'Moreover in the fish I killed there were only three winged flies among swarms of nymphs, so why hammer nymphing fish with floaters?'
(*Flyfishers' Club Journal*, Summer 1937) G.E.M. SKUES

IF I HAD A wish about Halford, it would be that he had not taken an ethical stance upon fishing totally dry, and upon fishing only to trout that are seen to be rising to hatched duns. On just about everything else he wrote in such a way as to be helpful, entertaining and informative to fly fishermen. His writing was based on information derived from his experience, his friends, and from his reading. His drawings of nymphs, for example were groundbreaking, and accurate, even down to the reed smut larva and pupa. He wrote extensively on the subject of avoiding drag and of the futility of the straight-line cast. He recognised the importance of concealment, and I illustrate this overleaf with a superbly illustrative photograph of his creeping approach to a fish.

He recognised the difference between a fish that was rising to hatched duns (and hence in his view an ethically appropriate target for the dry fly), and other fish that were bulging, nymphing, tailing, taking emergers, eating floating snails or chasing fry. He simply refused to imitate any

Halford stalking a trout

of these subsurface foods, and pointedly recommended that if these otherwise-behaving fish were to be addressed, they should be addressed with a fly that was fished dry. Yes, dry. And the fish's rise had to be 'bona fide', to the dun only and not to the nymph. Nose bitten off to spite face. Baby thrown out with bathwater. Argument started in empty room. Why have we fly fishers filled that room for him?

There is considerable circumstantial evidence that, in terms of fishing technique, perceived ethics, and of general inflexibility, he differed from his great friend Marryat – but was held back by Marryat from proclaiming the 'narrow path and straight way' of dry fly fishing according to Halford until after the death of that great guru. You can see F M H's perfectly formed prejudice in favour of the dry fly and against all other methods, emerging from its shuck in the chapter that he wrote in 1889 for the *Badminton Library,* and in his second book, *Dry-Fly Fishing in Theory and Practice,* in the same year. In both of these he describes an emerger imitation tied without wings (and originated by Marryat), but insists that it should be fished floating, even if, with deigning dispensation, 'semi-dry'. He also recommends two winged patterns for sub-surface feeding trout and suggests that these should be fished floating, but toppled over with one wing in the surface, 'semi-dry' – in perfect imitation of a cripple.

From a Photograph by A.S. Kent, Esq.

Detached Badger at Work.

F M H – kind, but unyielding

This was his position in 1888–89, and it only changed by becoming more uncompromising.

So Halford was in no way ignorant of the way trout feed on sub-surface foods. He simply laid down the law in tablets of stone that the imitation of these foods was unethical and was, in effect, not to be practised by gentlemen. And then he added to this by his pharisaical approach to codifying and listing the dry fly patterns which he clearly intended to be the only flies meaningfully to be used on the chalkstreams; for all time. A few survive.

Nobody could query Halford's right to write only about dry fly fishing, or to fish in the way that he felt was ethically correct, but in proselytising his apostles and a numerous and influential subset of future fly fishermen, one cannot but feel that he spoiled the sporting, intuitive, and imitative practise of fly fishing. And spoiled it for generations – from then until now – and still to come. His followers became even more 'halieutically correct' and their arguments in the Great Nymph Debate entrammelled the ageing Skues in fishing-meaningless arguments about whether rising nymphs wriggle or are inert. Sir Joseph Ball succeeded in turning a good-natured debate into a Judge Jeffreys' courtroom. You can almost hear the Halfordians singing, like the Tennessee creationists against Darwinism in *Inherit the Wind* (a rather similar courtroom drama): 'It was good enough for Brady, and it's good enough for me!'

If I had a further wish about Halford, it would be that he and his disciples had not destroyed with retrospective spin the wonderful and accurate imitative and presentational work that the earlier fly fishing writers had laid down as a base for our learning.

As we saw in chapter three and shall see in chapter 19, this most impressive (looked at with unprejudiced eyes) corpus was rubbished as being all about wet fly downstream fly fishing, when in fact it was nothing of the kind. It was about imitating the hatched-out fly. And the upstream dry fly purists have led us ordinary folk – poor credulous, want-to-believe-it fly fishers – into fishing our dry flies the wrong way round without thinking about it, whenever the wind is in our faces.

A sketch by Skues' close friend Dr E A Barton

If I had a wish about Skues, it'd be that he had had less of a chip on his shoulder, and was less shy in company (as opposed to in writing). (Dr E A Barton's sketch at left says it all.)

It wasn't just Skues who challenged Halford. Nor was Skues, by a long chalk, the first to challenge him. William Senior, editor of *The Field,* and R B Marston, editor of the *Fishing Gazette,* expressed their reservations in their reviews of his first book (*Floating Flies and How to Dress Them,* 1886) from their positions as close colleagues and friends. But a more serious challenge to Halford following the publication of *Dry Fly Entomology* in 1897 came from Charles E Walker (soon to become a highly involved collaborator with him on the 'Natural Fly Subcommittee' of the Flyfishers' Club), who, in 1898, published his own book, *Old Flies in New Dresses*. In that book Walker recommended tying imitations of many terrestrial dipterids, caterpillars (he flatly contradicted Halford's statement that they are unimportant as a trout food), the alder fly, and three underwater food items, the Corixa, the shrimp, and ... the nymph. With tying instructions – twelve years ahead of Skues and seventeen ahead of Mottram.

Walker's book, *Old Flies in New Dresses*, was caught in the undertow of Halford's Dry Fly Revolution and submerged, never to appear again – or be discussed in 'polite company'. By 1920, when, in *Salmon & Trout Magazine*, P Morgan Watkins recommended books for a 'dry fly fisherman's library', it wasn't even mentioned, although a year later J W Hills in *A History of Fly Fishing for Trout* did give it one approving reference.

Walker was gone from the Natural Fly Subcommittee (formed in 1901) by 1903, and by 1908 Halford was the only member left. Two pages of the book of the *Proceedings of the NFS* following the entry for 1902 have been cut out and the entry for 1903 follows on fresh pages over FMH's signature. (Possibly, therefore, with different content from what had previously been minuted – or possibly a glass of claret was spilt). There is an unminuted gap in the *Proceedings* from March 1903 to May 1908, and the book comes to an end in 1910, although it's clear from subsequent reports in the journal of the club that the work of collecting naturals via keen club members was

FRESH-WATER SHRIMP   113

and *debris* brought up, the Shrimps will be found among the contents of the net. I should strongly advise any one possessing a trout stream which is not inhabited by the Fresh-water Shrimp to introduce them, for they are, as I have pointed out, one of the very best forms of trout food. I have been very successful with the imitation shrimp on waters which contain the fresh-water shrimp.

This imitation has also met with general condemnation of an even more decided character than that of the Corixa. In neither case, however, have any reasons been given for the condemnation.

As undoubtedly some of the hackle flies used wet must be very like a shrimp, and if the imitation shrimp is condemned, so also should these hackle flies.

LARVÆ OF WATER-INSECTS, which have the power of swimming in the water, are best imitated by making a very taper body, with a large head. They are many of them small, and these should not be tied on a hook larger than No. 1, new size. There are, however, many larvæ

I

114   *OLD FLIES IN NEW DRESSES*

which are larger, but not many of these swim about much in the water. Some are brownish-yellow, and some nearly black. Some should have a tail made of two or three strands of hackle the same colour as the body. Some have appendages on the sides of the body, and in the imitations of these the hackle must be tied in at the tail, carried up over the body, and a couple of turns given at the shoulder. They may be made in various shades, from brownish-yellow to black. I have not yet had time to work out any proper scheme of imitations, but only write this as a suggestion.

Shrimp and nymph imitations proposed by C E Walker, in *Old Flies in New Dresses*

energetically continued under Martin Mosely well into the 1920s. It's hard to know whether Conspiracy Theory or Sod's Law provide the appropriate interpretative logic here, but there's more than a whiff of unseen emotions, actions, and politics.

But Skues was made of stronger stuff than Walker. When, in 1911 (as told by Skues in a 1946 letter to Otto von Kienbusch – but possibly in 1910) Halford took him on one side privately in the Flyfishers' Club and told him roundly that his use of subsurface flies would never work and he would merely scare fish with them, Skues asked him quite simply what good it was for him to tell him that he couldn't do something that he did frequently and successfully. Each was equally unbending and persistent in a lengthy exchange. (Halford had, however, according to his fishing diary, successfully used the nymph on five un-confessed occasions during 1908 and 1909 at normally dry-fly-only Mottisfont ... Ahem. Do as I say, not as I do.)

Both men were upset by this argument for the rest of their lives, which in Skues' case was four decades. Tony Hayter speculates that they never spoke again, and that Halford may never have set foot in the club again. Certainly his last transactions with the main vehicle of his Flyfishers' Club involvement, the Natural Fly Subcommittee, seem to have come to a rather abrupt end after 1910 with Martin Mosely taking over the running of it. Skues' brother, C A M Skues, was Club Secretary at the time, and would have been there every day, possibly to F M H's embarrassment. It was he who, after his brother's death, reported G E M S's lifelong perturbation.

The thing was, whereas with C E Walker a very wide disparity of published credo was merely technical; in the case of Skues, who at this time had just published his first book, the counter-revolutionary *Minor Tactics of the Chalk Stream*, it was personal.

Halford was the appointed 'collector and collator of natural fly' for the Flyfishers' Club, and Skues was 'collector and collator of fly-tying materials for the creation of artificials'. The two men were, however, treading separate and increasingly divergent paths, especially when it came to imitation. F M H had in 1897 (*Dry Fly Entomology*) nailed his colours to the mast by dictating the final and definitive list of 100 best chalk stream patterns. Skues' ideas were, however, typically fluid and malleable and would be characterised by his enquiring, widely collaborative, and inventive mind for another half century.

It is understandable that dry fly fishing got to be the preferred, and then the fashionable, method on the chalk streams. It was genuinely thought by many to be the most practical and effective way of catching reasonable numbers of (mainly stocked) trout, consistent with preserving expensive resources and not over-exploiting scarce yards of fishing on the one hand, and having a good time on the other.

Stocking itself was viewed as quite okay, mainly because the lessons later drawn from the damage it did to wonderful wild fisheries (Ramsbury, the Bourne, and Abbotts Barton were the highest profile disasters) had not yet been learnt. As we have seen, dry fly fishing is the method of choice for stock fish that have been fed all their lives from above and are now turned out and hungry.

The imitation of the chalkstream-prolific upwinged flies, proclaimed by Halford, became fashionable, and imitation of other much-consumed trout food items both aquatic and terrestrial (things that until recently had been cheerfully stuck on a hook and fished as live bait) became unfashionable, then derided, then frowned on – even if fished as a dry fly as C E Walker recommended – and then banned.

But like all new religions, the Dry Fly went too far. The Thou Shalt Nots got above themselves.

FOOTNOTE 1: Seen by looking, as it were, in the rear view mirror of our current vehicle, the attitudinal positions struck by the Victorians, and the saluting obedience of their disciples back down the road behind us, is hard to understand.

We live in a world in which it is quite okay at the highest levels in society, apparently, to sublimate all sense of ethics and moral values to financial gain – and in one where spin trumps real achievement and also obliterates fact.

Nowadays it is of relatively much less value to be thought honourable, or to be a gentleman, than it was at the time that Halford was working on and writing about the Dry Fly Code.

That was a time of modest heroism such as that displayed by Capt. Scott of the Antarctic (and also by the 'other ranks' in his team). It was a time of great (and real) nationalism, what we would now call jingoism, and a respect for one's social superiors that had not yet been smashed by the Great War let alone by World War II; nor yet been much invaded by American ideas of open democracy.

The middle classes had been created and enriched by Victorian commercial success right across the industrial and consumer spectrum, and their members were upwardly mobile and highly aspirational – to be gentlemen. This new spending-power fuelled the growth of fly fishing in its comet tail, and freed up the great Victorian ideas men to think – general naturalists like Darwin, entomologists like the Reverend A E Eaton ... and Halford.

That was the economic sweet spot which, incidentally, had created the Hyam/Halford business fortune, based on the national advertising, mass production, and highly successful mass sales of aspirational clothing. (We shall not speak of the imperial, and indeed local, British sweated labour involved.)

His own branch of the family had a great big factory in Leeds and a very large shop on Oxford Street. Their nationally-distributed catalogue, *The Gentleman's Illustrated Album of Fashion,* was an institution in the 1850s and 1860s, before switching to heavy newspaper advertising for self-measured mail order, or for visiting one of the their many provincial outlets. I don't expect that most of his fly fishing colleagues even knew that, but I bet that as a lawyer and an inveterate investigator, Skues did. Skues by contrast had to work for his living until he was over 80.

This goes a long way to explain the grip exerted on people by Halford's positioning of 'not perfectly dry' as 'not expected of a gentleman'. Aspiration to be seen as a gentleman was very powerful juju.

It also explains the reluctance of Skues to write openly about the successful experiments he quite clearly had made, but not confessed to, with more deeply sunk nymphs. He commonly used 'Integer Vitae' as a nom de plume when writing of his friend 'the Novice,' who was always in trouble for various angling transgressions. This suggested that by contrast he, Skues, was a man of integrity – and 'Integer Vitae' would also have carried with it to his audience of those times, familiar with the writings of Horace, the second half of the quotation: *scelerisque purus* meaning pure

When did you last see your father ... use a nymph?

of all villainy. His friend might do knavish things, but not he. Oh no. He did confess that they fished together with bread-flies for publicly-fed fish off a bridge and ... 'our tickets were not renewed'.

But not with deep nymphs. Hell no.

I am not saying that Halford wasn't a spin doctor – he absolutely was – I am simply trying to explain the willing suspension of disbelief which greeted the behavioural and ethical content of his writings. And I do think that the cult of the celebrity was as rampant then as it is now, albeit based on more solid achievements than seem now to be required.

'When did you last see your father ... use a nymph?'

FOOTNOTE 2: Here are two pictures of the same 'Egyptian Goose' pattern originated by Marryat for the mayfly emerging nymph, each published with exactly the same materials and tying instructions. The first (right) is, as referred to earlier, published by Halford in the chapter that he wrote in 1889 for the Badminton Library (5th Edition), *May-Fly Fishing*, and described as 'a hackle fly ... to be fished floating, but not too dry as it is intended to imitate the subimago when only partially withdrawn from its shuck, but not altogether clear of it.'

So far so good, but it is clearly shown to be tied so heavily hackled that there would be zero chance of its sinking, even partially.

The second picture (left) is taken from George A B Dewar's *The Book of the Dry Fly* (1897), and shows the same pattern as tied by Farlows to Marryat's instructions, described as 'Nymphae Marryat'. The hackles are insubstantial, the tails are angled downwards, and it is clearly designed to fish awash.

These two images provide us with a rare opportunity to compare the then-burgeoning must-be-dry Halford approach with that of the soon to be discarded, whatever-it-takes-to-imitate-it, philosophy of the now departed

Marryat. Nothing could be more illustrative of their divergence, or of Halford's unswerving determination to keep the angler's fly dry for him.

Prior to their amicable parting of the ways on mandatory dryness, Halford and Marryat had collaborated on developing nymphs. Halford in *The Dry Fly Man's Handbook* (1913, p 126) says 'years and years ago Marryat and I dressed most effective patterns to represent the nymphs of duns and mayflies by tying in a few fibres of black feather at the head ....' There then followed their (well, Halford's) reasons for discontinuing their use, including breach of ethics, and too many fish lost and rendered shy. The two friends also shared an innovative shrimp pattern tied with a gutta percha/soft moulded latex body, which they swore to keep to themselves, and even excluded from their fly boxes.

This nymphing period was between 1879, when they first met, and 1883 (which Skues later established as an end-date by reference to Marryat's gift of some nymph patterns to his friend, the Rev. E Nicolls). That is the same period as that established for Marryat's portmanteau of flies, which does contain a good few nymphs tied, as was everything in it, on eyed hooks and so post-1879 (see Footnote 2 to chapter 19).

So in 1879, and for a year or three, for Halford your fly could be a nymph if rules allowed it and the fish were nymphing. Then in 1883 Marryat originated the new double split-wing tying method and taught it to Hall, Halford, Sanctuary and the commercial fly-tyer Holland, who was brought down from Manchester to Salisbury – and Halford became fixated and by 1889, pretty obsessive, but actually in the meantime the others didn't. Or to nothing like the same extent. Halford secretly went back to the nymph in 1908–09, but subsequently became even more dry fly obsessed and confronted Skues in the 1911 stand-off. The culture clash was set to run and run.

Opposite:
The man who finally legitimised the nymph with the help of Skues
Frank Sawyer fishing more stealthily than either Skues or Halford
(Photo by kind permission of Nick Sawyer)

**Boy fishing – detail from the lower left of a wall painting
of St Christopher, Church of St Mary the Virgin, Layer
Marney, Essex**
*in my view this is nicer than the Frontispiece of the Treatyse of
1496, and probably slightly earlier*
(Picture from Fish & Fishermen In Medieval Church Wall Paintings
by Frederick Buller, Medlar Press 2009)

READING OUTSIDE THE BOX

A fresh look at the history of fly fishing before we got put in the box

There has been a tendency for us to ignore the earlier writers on fly fishing, partly because they have been dismissed as having been rather crude wet fly fishermen. I plead guilty myself, asking for many such earlier acts of omission to be taken into consideration, and I now recant. I said in chapter three that I would be calling these earlier writers as witnesses, and this chapter contains their testimony.

I ask the court, and that's you the reader, to rid your mind of any prior inferences you may have been led to draw from second-hand reportage about their work, and from all hearsay. I'm asking you to put them, and them alone in the witness box – but yourself to join me in reading their material strictly from outside the conceptual box that we have found ourselves to have been confined in on the way through this book.

Although I have had a very pleasant scamper through the main sources myself, I make no pretence of being a scholar in this field, and I have been well advised by those who are (Andrew Herd, Paul Schullery, Richard Ward, and Tony Hayter in particular). In addition, through David Beazley I have been able to make reference to the work of Jack Heddon, who was a leading scholar on the development of angling history and literature. Jack never got the chance to author the book that he deserved to write.

But the truth is, fly fishermen were no less dry fly men before Halford than after him. Actually, more so, since imitative use of the nymph was not on the radar until 1910, and just about all imitation was of floating flies. Wet flies came later. The fact is, from Berners to Halford they all fished floating flies, and fished them as dry as they could.

The earlier dry fly men, for nearly four centuries, had just as much fun, albeit greater skill levels were required to work with their tackle's limitations, and will have found the sport just as satisfying. The early writers' instructions are all about concealment, observation, the imitation of the fly's behaviour as well as of its appearance, visual concentration, targeting the rising fish, and quick striking. The same things were important to them as are important to us. For them too, though sadly not for us, it will also have been a pre-serpent, pre-apple Garden of Eden, free of the knowledge of Halfordian 'Right and Wrong'.

Post-Halford, anglers have either spent too much time worrying about doing something wrong (moral turpitude if you weren't perfectly dry), or smugly and piously confident of doing everything right. That said, Halford did help people to deal with the difficulties of fishing the dry fly. He put it on the map, too. But he also put it inside a box.

In this chapter, we are going to look at – and enjoy – the evidence for a long period of dry fly fishing prior to its adoption in the new cocked-fly, upstream form in the middle-to-late 19th century.

We can be a little bit disinterested in who precisely should claim the encomium of having first invented the cocked split-wing dry fly. It may have been David Foster from Ashbourne in Derbyshire and it may have been in 1833, or it may have been James Ogden in 1839 or thereabouts. Both were, at the time in question, competing tackle dealers in Cheltenham with Derbyshire bases. It looks in fact more likely to have been invented by William Shipley Snr, an angler on the Derbyshire River Dove as early as the 1780s, whose notes were written up as a book, *A True Treatise on the Art of Fly-Fishing* (1838), by William Shipley and Edward Fitzgibbon. It was certainly very well in advance of Halford's appearance on the scene, and he never claimed any credit for the invention – he codified its use.

The split-wing cocked dry fly was a pretty good innovation, and it was heavily marketed, but it did not of itself change the world.

We should be more interested in reinstating the reputation of the earlier and concurrent designers and fishers of the downwind, swept-wing dry fly – and in making it clear that they fished it as a floating hatched fly imitation. The past can make a contribution to the present. What is Tenkara if not a yearning for a simpler past?

It's hard to tell where the generalised disapprobation by purists of the earlier swept-wing fly designs became inaccurate defamation of them as being wet flies. This spin is something that Tony Hayter, the respected author of *F M Halford and the Dry Fly Revolution,* has confirmed to me as being mainly oral and mainly post-Halford, but in writing it was led by J W Hills. It was foisted on an angling audience that hadn't looked at the evidence and didn't care to since they were enthusiastic adherents to the 'Modern Development of the Dry Fly'. Peter Lapsley in his article, *Anglers All*, in *Fly Fishing & Fly Tying* magazine (February 2011) says that Halford's heavy marketing of the dry fly was so all-pervasive that it can be blamed for killing off the use and development of regional flies, and this is all part of the same set of influences on our (insufficiently critical) perceptions.

J W Hills simply could not allow himself to interpret the words of these early authors as referring to fishing dry (*A History of Fly Fishing for Trout*, 1921, chapter VIII). He keeps on saying: 'But this is not the dry fly' about the patterns and presentations recommended by these early writers, when it patently was. He maintains that flies were never dressed to float until the cocked dry flies of Ogdens and Fosters were marketed in the middle 1800s. That was wishful thinking inspired by Halfordianism. He said that it wasn't until the (real) dry fly was developed that you could watch for and see the trout and its rise, cast over it with a fly you could see on the water, and be sportingly taken or rejected in full view. (But, of course, you always could have done – that was the whole fun of it.)

This was the basis on which he maintained the modern development of the dry fly had changed the world: 'in all the long history of fly fishing there has been no change so great as its introduction', an overstatement of its advantages and perversely inconsistent with his otherwise clear appraisal of the historical facts and literature. For Hills, the only purpose of the past had been to get to the present, the sunlit uplands established by the dry fly revolution. But as we have seen, the past had inherent worth, and some of that worth had now been lost, and was now being dismissed.

Jack Heddon may never have got to write his book, but he did write (in the *Fly Dressers' Guild Newsletter*, June 1980): 'Probably the most widely held misconception in the entire field of angling is that the floating fly or dry fly is a modern development and that the sunk, or wet-fly, dates back to the very origins of fly fishing.' He goes on to state, in a later article, that the original method of fly fishing was dry, and that wet fly fishing was a much later development, to which he could find only a very few early references in the 17th and 18th centuries, mostly relating to special situations like stillwaters or slow rivers. Wet fly fishing was not described separately from dry until *A Book on Angling* by Francis Francis appeared in 1867.

The testimony for floating flies

Our main witnesses are: Leonard Mascall (1590), Gervase Markham (1614), Thomas Barker (1651), Robert Venables (1662), Charles Cotton (1676), James Chetham (1681), John Gay (1720), Richard & Charles Bowlker (1747–1826), George Scotcher (circa 1810), Thomas Best (1787–1846), Alfred Ronalds (1836), and William Blacker (1842).

It helps, when reviewing these words from the past, to visualise their authors fishing in their frock coats, leggings, and tricorn hats. One can crystallise that vision with a study of angling prints of the period so beautifully portrayed in David Beazley's definitive book from 2010, *Images of Angling,* which I cannot recommend too highly. Wearing one's hat was apparently de rigueur. It must have frightened a million trout in the early 19th century when the stove-pipe top hat came in – they wore it all century long, and it added six inches of shiny blackness to their height (see the Pollard print 'Fly Fishing' from my living room wall). (The italics in the following quotations are mine, and show these flies were floating, fished dry.)

Fly Fishing by J Pollard
in scary stove pipe hats

Leonard Mascall, in *A Book of Fishing with Hook and Line* published in 1590 said:

> 'The ruddy fly, in the beginning of May is a good fly to angle *with aloft on the water.*'

And he said to use cork:

> '... thus they are made upon the hooks, *lapt about with some corke* like each fly afore mentioned.'

This was to make them float.

Gervase Markham in 1614, in a chapter entitled *The Art of Angling,* in his book *The Second Book of the English Husbandman,* proposed again the twelve flies of *The Treatyse* and about the first of them said:

> '... and suitable, *fixed upon a fine piece of corke,* and folded so cunningly about the hooke, that nothing may be perceived at the point and beard [barb] only.'

Again, to float the fly. He also said to lay live captured flies in front of you and use your art to imitate their shape and colour. (These were hatched flies.)

Thomas Barker, in *The Art of Angling* in 1651, was the first Englishman to write explicitly of winding a hackle round the body of a fly.

Robert Venables, in *The Experienced Angler* of 1662, said that artificial flies should be fished like naturals – 'upon or above the water'. And he was the first, as we shall see, to recommend clipping a fly's hackles over the shank so as to create a dun that will float upside down and conceal the hook.

In 1676 in *The Compleat Angler,* Charles Cotton wrote about hackling a fly:

> 'For we sometimes barb (cut) the hackle feather short all over, sometimes barb it only a little, and sometimes barb it close underneath, leaving the whole length of the feather on the top or back of the fly, *which makes it swim better* and, as occasion serves, kills very great fish.' ('barb'='barber' as in cut hair)

This is floating-fly fishing.

James Chetham also used cork for some of his fly bodies (*The Angler's Vade Mecum,* 1681) – and cork had been used by then for at least 90 years. He also wrote:

> 'All fish take the fly, sometimes best *at the top of the water,* at another time much better a little under the superfices of the water. Therefore, if they will not rise at the top, try them a little under.'

And it is clear that this is an idea that runs against the general practice of fishing on the top: 'otherwise your fly is to swim on the top'. (This was Jack Heddon's point.)

In his 1760 edition of Walton and Cotton's *The Compleat Angler,* Sir John Hawkins uses plates with some of the first good illustrations of flies that were clearly intended to imitate hatched flies on the surface: a Palmer

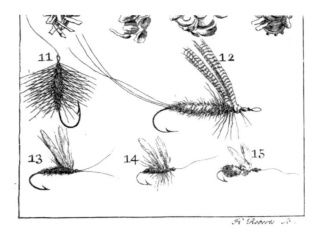

or caterpillar; a Green Drake or mayfly; a Dun Cut or olive; a Hawthorn; and an Ant Fly (numbers 11 and 15 respectively in the collective plate, shown above, from the 1775, 3rd edition).

In George Scotcher's *The Fly Fisher's Legacy,* published circa 1810, he gives instructions for catching smutting fish, saying that you must have a light cast and a small fly, and must place it on the water in the direction in which the fish is cruising, *so that it floats.* Scotcher's book was described by Jack Heddon as being the first angling book devoted entirely to fly fishing. (It is rare – a copy was sold for £55,000 in 2006.)

These were floaters. This was clear use and publication of dun imitations fished dry. Going back to the picture of the hydrophobic duckling in chapter seven – flies don't have to be proud of the surface to be dry and to float. There is no waterproof fly that does not dent, and bend around it, the meniscus.

Thomas Best, in *A Concise Treatise on the Art of Angling* (thirteen editions from 1787 to 1846) recommends the starling feather over the mallard as being more water-repellent:

> 'Observe, that in many instances hereafter that you will meet with, where the mallard's feather is set down for the wings of an artificial fly, that the starling will be preferable, because it is of a finer grain, *and will not imbibe the water so much.*'

Richard Bowlker (soon to be edited – and followed – by his son Charles), in many editions of *The Art of Angling,* from 1747 to 1826, marked the start of modern fly-dressing. All of his flies were intended to float, and he fished to individual fish, casting a yard above the fish and 'letting the fly move gently towards him, by which means he will show it more naturally.' Charles almost completely rewrote the book for the 2nd edition of 1774 and of the 'Palmer-worms' wrote '... that are to be made artificially, and *to be used upon the Surface of the Water*, after the same manner as the Artificial Fly.' The generalist palmer, in other words, should float, no less than the specific artificial fly pattern should.

Robert Salter, in *The Modern Angler* (1811), recommended many good fly-dressings, all for surface flies, and instructions that each fly should be fished so as to '*float alike on the surface*'.

It is clear from all these testimonies from the 1600s and the 1700s that floating flies were used and recommended right through both centuries. By the early 1800s, developments were underway which would lead to the development of the classic dry fly, although the earlier downwind designs were still going to be dominant for another eighty years at least.

Materials were important, not just for their colour and texture for visual imitation of the naturals' appearance, but also for their hydrophobic, water-resistant properties, so that your artificials would float better. See the scans below from Thomas Best's book *The Art of Angling* (1810), in which he praises the downy under-combings of hog's fur for resisting getting wet. And later admonishes the fly-tyer not to forget to add that, and the equally water-repellent bear hair, to his dubbing mixes. In this he followed Sir John Hawkins who contributed well-known and useful footnotes to Walton and Cotton's *Compleat Angler*.

HOG'S DOWN,

COMBED from the roots of the bristles of *black*, *red*, *whitish*, and *sandy*-coloured hogs; the white down you may have dyed to any colour you like. It is excellent dubbing, because it will stand the water and shines well. To be a competent judge of the real colour of any dubbi... when you make flies that are not palmers, dub with silk that resembles the colour most predominent in the fly; and in making your flies, remember to mix bear's hair and hog's down, with your other dubbing, because they repel the water; make your flies always in hot sun-shiny weather, for your waxed silk will then draw

How floating flies were fished

What we lack is a contemporary book that sets out with total clarity how these early hatched fly imitators fished. We don't really know to what extent they used one fly or more, (for example, anchoring a point fly in the surface, and dibbling a dry hatched fly pattern up-leader on a dropper) and/or, continually lifting off, 'spreading' (whirling rod and line to dry the fly) and re-casting. The two-fly dibbling technique was certainly widely used, and recommended by Ronalds, with the point fly being often a 'palmer worm' which he saw, even then, as imitating the emerger form. A quarter of a century earlier, Thomas Best (1810) wrote:

> 'A young angler should never use more than one fly on the stretcher at first, but when he can throw out pretty well, he may add to the stretcher one or more droppers, observing always to let them be one yard asunder.'

But by the time of Ronalds, it is clear that leading fly fishers involved in the early development of the upstream technique and the split-wing dry fly were fishing just one fly.

With respect to their tackle, we have instructions for making it and for tying the flies; the detailed fishing techniques are not so clearly described – but described they are.

We can gain some insights into the way these flies were fished way back in 1613 by the following excerpt from the poet John Dennys:

> For the Chub and Trout.
> See where another (angler) hides himselfe as slye,
> As did Acteon or the fearfull deere;
> Behind a withy, and with a watchfull eye,
> Attends the bit within the water cleare,
> *And on the top thereof* doth move his flye,
> With skilfull hand as if he living were. (*One floating fly*)
>
> His rod or cane made dark for being seen,
> His line well twisted is, and wrought so cleane,
> That being strong, yet doth it shew but small.
> His hook not great, nor little, but between,
> That *light upon the watry brim may fall.*

This was written when Izaak Walton was in his teens.

Like Dennys, John Worlidge in his amazing encyclopaedia of husbandry, *Systema Agriculturae*, (1675) wrote of the necessity for dark clothing ...

> Treafure that Mortals enjoy) and Pleafure, go hand in hand in this Exercife. What can be more faid of it, than that the moft Ingenious moft ufe it?
> When you have any leafure days or hours from your ordinary Profeffion or Imployment, you cannot better fpend them than in this innocent Exercife; wherein obferve that your Apparel be not of any bright or frightning Colour, left that drive the Fifh out of your reach, or make them timerous. ...
> That you bait the place you intend to Angle in, with fuch things the Fifh you aim at generally af-

And he also says to wade, and to fish upstream ...

> will bite in any Wind. Keep your felf as far from the Water-fide as you can, and fifh down the ftream. In a fwift ftream where the bottom is hard, and not too deep, if you go into the middle of it and caft your Fly up againft the Stream, the Trout that lies upon the Fin in fuch ftrong Currents, and difcerns you not, being behind him, prefently takes your Bait.
> In *March*, *April*, and *September*, and all the Winter-months, it is beft Fifhing in a clear, ferene, and

It wasn't all bank fishing either.

Some anglers liked to fish the fly upstream, as we saw in chapter three, and some, like Worlidge, waded in midstream so as to make an unseen presentation from directly behind the trout. Ronalds, much later (1836), suggests rubber waders. William Lauson, in his footnotes to John Dennys' *Secrets of Angling* published in 1652, was the first to mention the need to learn to *cast* the fly:

> '... which must counterfeit the May flie, which is bred of the cod-bait, and is called the water-flie: you must change his colour every moneth ...'
>
> (*Second ever mention of nymphs, first mention of May fly as a general term – one floating fly.*)

Charles Cotton, in *The Compleat Angler: Part Two* (1676) adjures Viator to fish 'Fine and Far Off', Which he says is the 'first and principal rule for trout angling'(within two rod lengths, that was).

Cotton refers all the time to the hook and the fly *in the singular*. He also recommends fishing downwind. Not downstream.

'You … are to endeavour, as much as you can, to have the wind evermore at your back, and always to be sure to stand as far off the bank, as your length will give you leave when you throw to the contrary side; though when the wind will not permit you so to do, and that you are constrained to angle on the same side where you stand, you must then stand on the very brink of the river, and cast your fly at the utmost length of your rod and line, up or down the river as the gale serves.'

On the second day of the dialogue he chooses a day of upstream wind on which to recommend fishing still deep water upstream. And Viator catches 'three brace of trouts and three graylings'. So it is pretty clear that Cotton was well convinced of the advantages both of fishing downwind, and fishing upstream.

Nicholas Cox, in *The Gentleman's Recreation* (1686) gives these full instructions for trout fishing with the fly:

'The next direction is how to angle with a fly for a trout. In the first place let the Angler fit himself with a Hazle of one piece or two fit conveniently together, light and pliable. The lower part of his Line next the Fly must be of three or four hair links, but if he can attain as aforesaid; to angle with a single Hair, he shall meet with more profit and pleasure. Before he begin to angle, having the wind on his back, let him try how far he can cast his Line, or what length his Fly, and *let him be careful that the Fly fall first on the Water*; for if any of the Line light upon the Water, he had better to have stood still than to have thrown at all. He must always cast down the Stream, with the Wind behind and the Sun before him: it is a great advantage to have either Sun or Moon before him.' *(One floating fly)*

Thomas Best also quotes the poet Thomson's *Summer*:

There throw, nice judging, the delusive fly,
And as you lead it round in artful curve,
With eye attentive mark the springing game;
Straight as above the surface of the flood
They wanton rise, or urged by hunger leap,
Then fix with gentle twitch the barbed hook; *(One floating fly)*

The poet John Gay, in *Rural Sports* (1720) wrote:

'Upon the rippling surface, let it glide,
With natural motions from thy hand supplied,
Against the stream, now let its feathers gently play,
Now in the rapid eddy, float away.' *(One floating fly)*

Best wrote as follows before the end of the 1700s:

'... when you see the fish rise, throw your fly over him and drop it gently over the place where he rose; and if it is a proper fly for the season, and you cast it with a nicety the fish is your own.' *(One floating fly)*

He went on to say:

'... the lighter your flies fall on the water the better; this you will not accomplish by strength, but by practice, always raising your rod by degrees, after you have made your cast.' *(Possibly two or more flies)*

'When you angle in slow-running rivers, or still places, with an artificial fly, cast it across the water and let it sink a little in the water, and then draw it gently over to you again, letting the current carry it slowly down: this is the best way for slow waters; but for quick ones your fly must always swim on the top, under the continual inspection of your eyes, which ought, for this kind of angling, to be as sharp as the basilisk's.' *(One floating fly)*

Skues said of this passage in a letter to the *Flyfishers' Club Journal* in 1927: 'Surely this is the floating fly definitely enough.'

The unknown author of *The North Country Angler* (four editions between 1786 and 1817) often fished with two flies, the point fly sunk two or three inches to imitate a swim-up nymph, and the dropper just touching the surface. Scotcher, circa 1810, used one fly only.

As I have mentioned, these early writers' instructions are about

FRONTISPIECE.

A

CONCISE TREATISE

ON THE

ART OF ANGLING.

Confirmed by actual Experience,

AND

MINUTE OBSERVATIONS,

Exempt from Redundancies, and Superfluities, which
tend more to perplex, than instruct,

WITH

The proper Methods for Breeding and Feeding Fish,
and of making Fish-ponds, Stews, &c.

With Several Arcana never before made Public.

TO WHICH IS ADDED

THE COMPLEAT FLY-FISHER,

The Game-Laws relative to Angling, and Prognostics of the
Weather, independent of the Barometer.

Now let the Fisherman his toils prepare,
And arm himself with ev'ry watry snare;
His hooks, his lines peruse with careful eye,
Increase his tackle, and his rod retye.   GAY.

THE SECOND EDITION, CORRECTED AND ENLARGED,
BY THOMAS BEST, GENT.

LONDON:
Printed for C. STALKER, Stationer's Court, Ludgate Street,
and may be had at all Booksellers and Fishing Tackle Shops
in Town and Country.

Thomas Best, 2nd Edition, 1789 frontispiece

a gentleman nets his lady's fish. Fly is perhaps implied by the illustrations beneath

concealment, observation, the imitation of the fly's behaviour as well as of
its appearance, visual concentration, targeting the rising fish, and quick
striking. The angler was often advised to impart appropriate movement
to the fly.

The word swim, in 'swim on the top' above, and 'makes it swim better'
in the Charles Cotton quote on (p221) may seem to indicate partial
immersion, but it doesn't. I did think originally that this meant swim
like I swim myself, i.e. 90% to 100% underwater. But then, reading on

in Thomas Best's book, I discovered the five instances in which he quite clearly described different species of hatched dun floating down on the water's surface with these words: '… as it swims down the water, its wings stand upright on its back; its tail forked, and of the same colour of its wings'. He also uses the word 'swim' to describe caddisflies and the yellow Sally stonefly floating on the water's surface.

This makes it crystal clear: there is no question but the word 'swim' meant, as late as 1810, sitting up above the surface perched on the meniscus, rather than being partially immersed in it.

As the poet John Dennys put it in 1613:

> '… for heavy things downe to the bottome fall,
> and light do swim, and seldome sink at all.'

Robert Venables, in 1662, suggested that flies should be tied to float with the point of the hook upwards (the first, and very early manifestation of the USD Dun):

> 'If I turn the feathers round the hook, then I clip away the feathers that are on the back of the hook that so (if it be possible) the point of the hook may be forced by the feathers (left on the inside of the hook) to swim upwards; and by this means I conceive that the stream will carry your Flies wings in the posture of one flying …'

George Bainbridge in his *Fly Fisher's Guide* (1816), who, like Ronalds but slightly before him, illustrated natural flies and their imitations, wrote:

> 'When a trout is observed to rise of his own accord, the flies must not be thrown directly over him, but about a yard higher in the stream, so that they may float down to his view, without the fear of agitating the water.'

Sir Humphrey Davy in *Salmonia* (1828) wrote, 'Now I shall throw a drake a foot above him. It floats down, and he has taken it. A fine fish.'

Ten years later, in 1838, Shipley and Fitzgibbon wrote from their Derbyshire base:

> 'Let your flies float gently down the water. We distinctly recommend frequent casting, the quick repetition of casting whisks the water out of your flies and line, and consequently keeps them drier and lighter than if they were left to float a longer time on the water.'

This advice was repeated by G P R Pulman in 1851 in *The Vade Mecum of Fly Fishing for Trout*, and by the Rev. James Martin in *The Anglers Guide* in 1854.

In my view, and in those of my mentors, these quotations provide sufficient evidence to show that right through the 1600s, 1700s, and the early 1800s, at least on the part of the top practitioners and writers, imitation of the hatched fly was considered desirable, normal, verging on de rigueur and, if their readers followed their instructions, possible, with flies that floated. By necessary design these flies faced the angler in terms of orientation, as he normally fished with the wind behind him, and hence matched the orientation of the hatched flies that were on the water, those duns being many times more abundant than they are now.

Of course, plenty of anglers did fish downstream wet flies, and indeed spider patterns, and many probably did so all the time; others would be opportunists, and fish floating or sunk flies as conditions and the way fish were feeding dictated. Most, imitating the hatched dun as they were, will have cast across for a short drift over the fish, and lifted off to recast – or dibbled downwind.

FOOTNOTE 1: The flies that were described by the many earlier authors, from Berners in 1496 through to Ronalds in 1839, prior to the arrival of the cocked dry fly, were (as Hills showed in his long ninth chapter list, and as Skues later modified) adult hatched flies. They were obviously not intended to be imitated underwater. This is the same conclusion Andrew Herd came to in his definitive book *The Fly* (now revised and expanded as *The History of Fly Fishing*).

In his book, however, Andrew draws attention to the period of about two generations at the start of the 1800s when silk lines and gut casts were replacing horsehair. Anglers rushed to the use of the new materials, no less than we to carbon fibre – you could cast further, and reach that distant riser by the far bank. And they were mass-produced too. But they made the fly sink. So actually it is true that by 1850 many people were, perforce, using wet, flies that were originally designed to be fished dry – and up until then, had been. Richard Ward of Bakewell, who has built and fished with 15 ft to 18 ft, 17th century-style rods and horsehair lines, says horsehair sinks as fast as silk, but they never let it get wet; whereas with the new shorter greenheart and cane rods popularised by George Ogden (his was the 'Multum in Parvo' 8 footer), plus silk lines, gut casts, and much longer casting, flies were dragged under.

FOOTNOTE 2: I have been privileged to look at, handle, and take photographs of the enormous portmanteau of flies that G S Marryat left behind him on his death in 1896, now back in the possession of the Flyfishers' Club. These flies (all on eyed hooks), were reviewed by Skues in two detailed articles in the *Flyfisher's Journal* in 1923 and it is easy to agree with his conclusions that they were tied, mainly by Marryat and his friend Tom Sanctuary, between 1879 when eyed hooks became available, and the end of 1882 when he invented the new double-wing-slip-from-matched-wings technique. Which he and H S Hall then adopted and popularised thenceforward among the cognoscenti. From that point on the flies in the portmanteau seem not to have been used, and it is believed that Marryat relied upon his friends and George Holland the fly-dresser for the flies that he actually used over the next dozen years, and that these were stored separately. (The flies in the portmanteau are therefore rather like an interesting small section of a scientific polar ice core, telling us what was going on in a defined slice of time.)

What is interesting about the generality of the portmanteau flies is that they are tied in the style of the old downwind dry flies. Their wings are two slips from the same wing feather tied-in with their curved faces inwards so as to curve outwards from each other. What you get with this, is that the wing tips 'point' in different directions, one forwards and one backwards, 'cross-billed' – but presenting an effective imitation of the dun's wings.

A fly from Marryat's portmanteau I'd be happy to fish with

(Copyright reserved: The Flyfishers' Club)

Although many of the hooks are very slightly bigger than were soon to be recommended by Halford (in *Floating Flies and How to Dress Them*, on which he and Marryat collaborated closely), they are lighter in the wire than Hall's and Halford's, of a generally appropriate size to imitate chalkstream duns, and the flies were very much more lightly-dressed particularly in the hackle than Halford's would be when he published.

Skues says that many of them are more appropriate to being fished wet – and from his point of view forty years into the paired double wing slip revolution you can see how he would think that. But in fact I believe they represent the very acme – the highest point of development of the earlier tying method for floating flies.

Glance back at the happy hydrophobic duckling pictured in chapter seven. Note

A page of olive dun patterns from Marryat's portmanteau
(Copyright reserved: The Flyfishers' Club)

you don't have to be proud of the surface to be dry and floating. His feathers bend with, and do not pierce, the meniscus. Sharp, unbending hackles would sink him. With soft hackles a fly can swim as he is swimming, and as the Ancients describe.

Terry Griffiths, in his review of them for the *Flyfishers Journal* (Summer 2009), offers the opinion that they do indeed mark a transitional stage, draws attention to the fact that the hackle was wrapped behind the upright wing to bolster it, and 'would create a footprint in the surface film, or otherwise be fished wet in what we nowadays call an emerger style, a most killing manner of presentation'. Marryat is known from the reports of his contemporaries to have fished avidly, dry or wet, as appropriate to the weather and the hatch.

The idea that Marryat's post-portmanteau flies were stored and used separately (and thus that the portmanteau flies are indeed a 'polar ice core') has been given added credence by the energetic research of Simon J Ward. He has discovered an early, advanced-design fly box with spring loaded, windowed compartments containing 158 very small dry flies tied in Marryat's style, which was held by Marryat's descendants in South Africa and is now in Simon's safe keeping. (His findings are published in two Internet articles).

There can be no doubt about the provenance and the very strong probability is that this was the fly box, and these were the flies, that Marryat went on to use after the portmanteau was laid aside with its old style dry flies. The portmanteau flies therefore probably do represent the epitome of the dry fly as tied and used before 1883, when Marryat, Halford, H S Hall (the eyed hook developer), and George Holland (the fly-dressing entrepreneur), collaborated to change the tying methodology to produce, and set as standard, the double split-wing, sharp collar hackled floater.

FOOTNOTE 3: For more information about the books discussed in this chapter and where to access them please see the introduction to the Bilbliography on p 257.

FOOTNOTE 4: I sat next to Jack Heddon at the twice-yearly Flyfishers' Club rummage sale many years ago. I had inspected the lots, he hadn't. A nice 7 ft cane rod came up, and he started bidding. I hissed, 'Don't buy it, it's bent.'

Jack said he didn't care about its provenance, and bought it.

FOOTNOTE 5: Skues did sometimes rather like people to think that the Ancients fished wet. In *The Way of a Trout with a Fly* (1921 – p 148) he wrote, 'For generations, wet-fly fishing was the only fly fishing' – this in a long argumentation in favour of nymphing. That was as much spin in retaliation as Halfordians were spinning in attack. He had read all the sources as carefully as anyone.

Skues went into the detail of the dating of the introduction of the cocked dry fly very thoroughly in 1934 in two articles and a letter in *Salmon & Trout Magazine*, and placed it firmly in the 1850s (Pulman, Foster, Ogden) on the basis of extremely thorough research, but said:

> '... though probably there had previously been, as there was for long after, a more or less extensive use of the dry, and even the dried, fly not specially built to cock and float.'

Skues did however doubt in the same letter whether many of the early flies were capable of floating, agreeing with Hills, and saying, 'So that I should not think even the palmers were dressed to float.' I very seldom disagree with him, but I firmly oppose his view on this, and I believe the literature review in this chapter shows beyond all doubt that the older angler-writers' flies were indeed dressed to float and imitate the hatched fly.

Skues, like everyone else post-Dry Fly Revolution, failed to appreciate that in earlier times it wasn't the design and build of the fly that ensured its floating dry, but the behaviour and skill of the angler.

FOOTNOTE 6: The two lovely primitive watercolours overleaf are by the Rev. H Veitch, who was a founder member of the Wilton Fly Fishing Club. They are on display

Date, March 1872. Place, River Exe Below Bickleigh Bridge.

An Artistic & Imaginative Friend thus depicts his Brother of the Angle

Harsh March Reality
(Copyright reserved: the Wilton Fly Fishing Club)

Date, Place, and Artist, Identical.

This is the Angler's View of the Matter.

Rose Tinted Spectacles
(Copyright reserved: the Wilton Fly Fishing Club)

in the club room and tell us something about the way fly fishing was done in the transitional period between the old way and the new way. The date is 1872, well after George Pullman had advocated the use in the West Country of the upstream dry fly – and the location is in the West Country on the river Exe. Both in the dreadful reality of a March storm and in the halcyon day of the 'Angler's View of the Matter', he is fishing upstream, but under an eyeglass it can be seen that the fly is of the swept-wing downwind variety, and definitely not tied with cocked wings and a collar hackle.

In fact under the magnifying glass two flies are visible, one being on a dropper. You can't see the reel, but the line goes through rod rings and so it seems certain that there was one. The rod is somewhere between 12 ft and 15 ft in length. The angler would appear to be wearing waist-high waders. In the halcyon day, angler's imagination picture, the large trout is being led downstream and headfirst into the net making full use of the shock absorbing power of the rod, which is exactly what I suggested in chapter 17. You can see what I mean about published angling truths being forgotten and reinvented time and time again.

(Photographs of Tenkara flies by kind permission of Daniel Galhardo – www.tenkarausa.com)

FULL CIRCLE
WITH TENKARA?

THOSE OF MY READERS who have any knowledge of Tenkara, the very simple Japanese mountain stream technique with fixed line and one fly, will have recognised quite clearly in the preceding chapter that an exactly analogous method of fly fishing was in use in Britain from (at least) the 1500s through to the 1800s.

We have seen how new tackle and fly developments accompanied by what I can only describe as managed attitudinal change achieved the so-called Dry Fly Revolution at the cost of almost completely sublimating the earlier technique and, more importantly, consigning the associated skills to what many people chose to view as a small side channel of the main stream.

It is more than a little weird to see the modern, state-of-the-art UK fly fishing world being led back in full circle to those only-just-lost simplicities and skills by this thing called Tenkara that comes to us from undocumented, oral-tradition Japanese practices via the highly web-documented, enthusiastic descriptions of new American aficionados. Our own, much stronger, more highly developed and copiously documented fly fishing tradition had effectively been suffocated. Nature abhors a vacuum.

It was only the prolonged isolation of Japan, and more particularly of its mountainous backwaters, that ensured the survival of Tenkara. Of course, similar methods were practised all over the world until quite recently, for example in Slovenia and Macedonia. But somehow Tenkara has caught the imagination of the New Age angler in Japan and the United States (and increasingly in the UK) and focused attention on the way back to simplicity of tackle and the development of the angler's skills.

The last century of development has put a stronger emphasis on gear rather than on technique: Tenkara reverses that trend and puts stronger emphasis on technique rather than gear. This is especially true of approaching fish close-to; of concentrating on presentation rather than on fly pattern; and of clever manipulation of the fly to imitate the living insect rather than dead drift – just exactly what we looked at in the last chapter.

It will be pretty evident to you by now that I am in favour of change, and of new things, and of experimentation – and by the same token not in favour of unthinking perseverance with ways of fishing which owe their survival more to social 'fit', to inertia, and to constant repetition by self-appointed authorities than to efficacy. It's not a question of old and new – as I have pointed out, many of the old ways were particularly good and effective, and the new ones not necessarily better – it's a question of seeing things clearly in the context of what actually happens out there on, and in, the water.

What we need to do is to take the brilliant new things that science has given us, such as carbon fibre rods, reliably floating lines, extraordinarily effective floatants, strong lightweight hooks, advanced fly design, and amazing fly-tying materials and feed the use of them back into the basic principles of hunting fish, regardless of tradition, prejudice, cant, and fashion. Regardless, also, of the angler-perceived, retailer-encouraged need to have the mountainous armoury of kit that most of us have acquired. And use the advantages that polarised glasses and camouflaged breathable waterproofs have given us to help us see fish and get closer to them.

We have the ability to fit our fishing much more precisely than ever before to the demands of the water we wish to fish in, and the fish we want to deceive. Simple minimalist techniques like Tenkara will be appropriate for waters where the fish are smaller, and where there is less trouble for us to keep them out of when hooked (rocks, roots, weed masses, etc.). A more powerful rod and a reel with a good drag will be necessary when bigger fish are included in our target, and when there will be a need to shorten and lengthen line so as to gain and maintain control. A modern plastic casting line will be necessary when casting distance is of the essence, and that brings with it the need for special loose-tippet casting skills.

Casting with a tapered plastic line and dead-drifting the fly accentuates the need for fly floatation – and aggravates, and accelerates drag. When currents have to be crossed to reach fish without drag, the advantage of the long Tenkara rod comes into its own, and additionally brings with it an ability to enliven the fly with movement.

Chalk streams, with their complement of trout over 2 lbs, are not going to be an appropriate arena for Tenkara (apart from grayling fishing). Smaller upland and rain-fed rivers and streams will be perfectly suited to the fixed line approach – and this is where Tenkara has especially caught on in the UK as well as in America. In the Rockies no less leaders of opinion and practice than John Gierach and Ed Engle have tried and enjoyed Tenkara on the fabled St Vrain.

Here, Stuart Crofts is an enthusiastic adopter of Tenkara. He tells me that he has not fished with a conventional rod for two years. He carries three rods of lengths from 8 ft to 15 ft in a quiver on his back, and a minimal amount of supportive tackle. With various combinations of light leaders of different designs he can address every angling situation for which Tenkara is a good solution. In his part of the world, in and around Yorkshire, that covers most fly fishing situations.

He says that if you approach an upland stream characterised by pockets and runs, and fish blind with a conventional rod and line, dead drifting and doing your best to avoid drag, you will probably hook a fish in one in four pockets. But, he says, what you do with the Tenkara rig is to cast quickly and repeatedly into each pocket multiple times, flicking your hand back at the last moment so that the fly lands first and the leader doesn't touch the water – then you lift off immediately before re-presenting the fly and kissing the water with it again. You will do this five or six times and then let it drift. This way, he says, you will get a fish from every single pocket. It's a teasing, interest-enlivening, fish-bewitching technique, far different from the conventional approach. Repeated teasing presentations may also bring the trout's eyes from wary-lookout long-focus mode into close-focus feeding mode, in which more distant objects (i.e. you) become fuzzy.

A very similar technique for 'working up an appetite' in the fish, by 'shadow casting', until the fish imagines there's a hatch getting started, is described by Norman McLean in the first chapter of *A River Runs Through It* (1976) – and this forms an iconic scene in the film as well, with Brad Pitt playing the errant brother, Paul. The film certainly made fly fishing come alive for America: perhaps not crazy to speculate that that single scene has provided some of the fertile ground on which the Tenkara seed has grown.

The fly, Stuart says, is your slave (and you are not its slave, as you can so easily feel you are when fishing conventionally). You can lift it, skip it, drag it forwards, drag it backwards, and bounce it up and down making little rings. You can, of course, change it as well although the Japanese take pride in using 'one pattern in one thousand ways'. But their little yamame trout are particularly happy to be attracted by attractor patterns, exact imitation of specific insects is apparently lost on them (or at least unnecessary). It is no good using a Tenkara rod in combination with the Dry Fly Revolution mentality. You are going to be fishing the fly as a living insect.

Fishing the Dry Fly as a Living Insect is in fact the title of a very useful and clearly written American book by Leonard M Wright Jr published forty years ago. Wright saw that up until the Dry Fly Revolution it was the angler that was responsible for making the fly behave like a living insect but that, after Halford and his insistence on dead drift:

> 'For the first time in fishing history, the imitation fly was truly on its own: it now had to dupe the trout solely on the basis of its size, shape, and colour.'

Listing several life stages of different flies that commonly attract trout by their movement on the surface, he says:

> 'Halford simply wasn't interested. He was a portrait painter, not a newsreel cameraman.'

Stuart Crofts has something helpful to say about playing fish on a Tenkara rig. The objective is not to tire the fish out, but to fool it into giving up, and to try and avoid it understanding that it has been hooked and is being corralled. Playing a fish with Tenkara has been likened to exercising an untrained horse on a lead rein, where getting into any kind of tug-of-war will see you dragged across the paddock flat on your face. You need to influence it, direct it, bend it away from positions in which it can add the force of the current to its own strength. In principle this is not different from using side strain as I have indicated in chapter 17 – but there we are trying to tire out and vanquish a large fish whereas in the Tenkara situation we are trying to get a smaller fish into the net without its being too stressed either physically or 'emotionally'.

Polish competition anglers in the World Fly Fishing Championships astonished other national teams by their ability to lull hooked fish into a state of acceptance by simply not pulling on them, just keeping the line tight to the hook and then leading them gently downstream to the net.

When this was adopted as a strategy by our own team it resulted in four out of five being landed instead of two out of five.

A technique that has been widely adopted by the competitive fishing fraternity is the use of extremely long leaders – in some cases no fly line is used at all, just an extremely long leader tied onto the backing. This is a fairly extreme manifestation of what is sometimes known as 'leader-to-hand'. Although there are several people promoting its use for general fishing, it does not yet seem to have attained any great level of popularity or general use.

To be successful with it, you do have to fit yourself out with exactly the right rod – and the good ones are expensive. Then you have to learn to cast something that has very little weight. This means either going for a fairly heavy level leader with just enough weight to bend the rod, or alternatively relying on the weight of tungsten-beaded nymphs to unleash the rod's spring like a gaucho throwing his bolas. In neither case is it a satisfying and artistic way of getting your fly to the fish, and it can be extremely tiring.

I have myself used a long leader (twice as long as the rod) consistently for the last dozen years, and I was an early convert to the long leader approach following two experiences. The first was fishing the fast, deep, Tongariro River together with John Goddard, with heavy nymphs that had to get down to deep-lying fish – that experience showed me that it could be done. The second was learning from a group of extremely talented French anglers who came over to fish the River Wylye as our guests a dozen years ago – they used leaders fifteen feet long, very fine nylon and absolutely tiny painted lead nymphs. Then I found that long leaders utilising poly-leaders as butts with long soft tippets could be made to extend and yet collapse and so avoid drag in dry fly fishing. So I'm a convert, and I was an early one. I do however usually have quite a bit of fly line outside the tip ring, whereas these new leader-to-hand experts wouldn't dream of it.

Frankly, given that at 15 ft long your leader is never going to let your fly line come anywhere near a target fish, I fail to see the logic in giving up the castability provided by having a fly line in order to gain what seems to me to be a non-existent advantage in having leader all the way back to the reel; and having to thrash at the casting of it so much as to exhaust your arm.

I also, in common with friends who have been trying this technique recently, fail to see any great point in having to acquire a new and different rod so as to cast these 'ooo weight' leaders. When, by just using a 15 ft to 18 ft leader on the end of your fly line, you can continue to use your favourite rod with which you have built up all your existing familiarity and skill.

I enjoy casting and get a lot of satisfaction from making a fly line and leader combination do exactly what I want (okay, I suppose I mean 'more or less' what I want). I specifically do not want to tire myself out trying to extend something with no integral weight, nor do I want to be unable to cast effectively into a wind. And if I cannot transmit sufficient energy into the bit of kit connecting me to the tippet and fly, I cannot perform the dump cast or the bounce-back cast that I have taught myself to use to avoid drag.

So I'm a devotee of long leaders, but not of line-free leader-to-hand. And I'm up for Tenkara, though I haven't yet had the training. But I don't entirely see why you can't have the good bits of an imported technique without the less good bits.

If Tenkara is not an adoptive religion (and we have had enough of those, thank you) then I don't understand why, other than for aesthetic and preferential reasons, you should not have a lightweight ring on the end of each section of your telescopic Tenkara rod and a lightweight reel fitting. And so benefit from the greater rod length whilst not having to give up the ability to play a bigger fish if you are blessed with hooking one.

I am looking for serendipitous convergence between the two approaches.

A further advantage of Tenkara is that it makes it possible, and indeed preferable, to fish with the wind rather than against it. So in yet another way, using the technique brings us closer to what we have seen our ancestors doing in chapters 3 and 19. This actual use of a ringed long rod and downwind fly is pictured in the 1872 watercolours in chapter 19.

A last bit of deep thought on Tenkara. To the extent that we get ourselves back towards the methods of our forbears, and thereby much closer to the fish, we need to be paying proportionately more attention to their not spotting the rod – and we shall not be able to hold it still so as to keep them from spooking.

Now there is quite an intermittent history of heron-coloured rods. I had one myself when that great innovator, Geoffrey Bucknall, was in business in Lewisham and I fished with him on his lakes at Sundridge on the River Darent in the 1970s. We cast so far in those days that it didn't make a difference, and the idea died the death.

Two generations earlier however, Skues had a Farlows greenheart rod painted heron grey-blue. It was also matt and didn't flash. He refers in *The Way of a Trout with a Fly* (p 30) to 'its extreme invisibility to the trout'. He wrote: 'Again and again I have held it over a trout lying under my bank, and have waved it to and fro until I showed myself, and it certainly seemed as though it were a colour to which the trout was almost insensible.'

So my Tenkara rod, when I get one, will have rings and a reel fitting, and be heron grey.

FOOTNOTE: The repeated teasing presentation idea seems to have been mooted first in print by H G McClelland in *The Trout Fly Dresser's Cabinet of Devices* (1899) and then taken up in America by George M LaBranche.

From Angling in Japan, M. Matuzaki, 1940

IF TWO MEMBERS OF A FLY-FISHING CLUB ARE CAUGHT USING NATURAL BAIT;
THE GENTLEMAN WITH THE LARGEST WORM SHOULD APOLOGISE FIRST.

'If two members of a fly-fishing club are caught using natural bait,
the gentleman with the largest worm should apologise first.'

This cartoon by G E Studdy (circa 1910) hangs in the Flyfishers' Club in
London and embodies the importance of correct behaviour at all times

A PHILOSOPHY
OF FLY FISHING
OUTSIDE THE BOX

'Scholars have long known that fishing eventually turns men into philosophers. Unfortunately, it is almost impossible to buy decent tackle on a philosophers salary.'

Patrick F McManus of the Wilton Fly Fishing Club

IT IS GREAT TO enjoy a sport in which you can make mistakes all the time and continually learn from them without the penalty being too great and without too many people looking at you whilst you are doing it. Generally speaking, it's only yourself you have to live with if you mess it up. This means you have more permission to do so (i.e. mess it up) than you would have if you were fishing for an audience or in a competition. That makes it more pleasurable unless those latter circumstances turn you on. If they do, you are a different kind of fisherman than me. For me, the only meaningful competition is versus the fish.

I go fishing because I enjoy it – but it also has a philosophical, almost religious side. Now I am not religious, and the main reason for this is that I cannot accept that what you should believe, what you should do and how you should do it is governed by some deity-generated (or, worse still, other-person-generated) set of rules with which you are either compliant or non-compliant. For me, the whole point in living your life is to work it out for yourself and having done so, to be able to live with yourself.

You have to be your own person, you form your attitudes for yourself, you decide what to do and what not to do for yourself. You are allowed to go and get help in developing yourself, but you have to seek personal development and choose it. Being spoon-fed with it isn't going to get you there. Extraneous gods and religion and canons just make you worth less – not worthless, but worth less. It is not a side issue that all of this applies to fishing as well as to life in general. You might think, for example, that the issue of catch and release versus killing trout is a moral issue. You either should, or you shouldn't kill fish. You either should, or you shouldn't release fish. One or the other is wrong. One or the other is right. To me this is not a moral issue. It is in fact a mistake, in my view, to make it too much of an issue at all.

To be a good angler, you need to be able to make an informed (and if you insist, morally correct) decision on the future of each fish as you get it to the point where it is helpless in your hands and you have power over it. You are free to do what you want. You decide. And it is a separate and subsequent decision to those involved in catching it in the first place.

Kill it and eat it if that's what you want to do. Kill it and eat it if it is a fertile (non-triploid) stockie – a quick test is bent fins and short or over-worn fins – or else it may mess up your wild gene pool. Most wild populations will sustain a low level of harvest, and too many caught and released fish in a fishery may mean too many shy fish, and a few 'collateral', angler-induced deaths.

There is nothing to prevent you having a general rule of conduct, and nothing to prevent you having a preference for deciding one way or the other. There is nothing to prevent you trying to persuade other anglers to take one route or the other. Nothing to prevent you making decisions which may help trout in general, and not just this one you have in front of you. But it really ought to be, in my view, a decision, and not a non-decision. In the Wilton Fly Fishing Club, we do not have a no-kill rule, but the only fish that get killed each year are interloper stockies. Our decisions are consistent, but they are real and not forced.

Recognizing that most of the time we are not spending our lives worrying about the definition of the Seven Deadly Sins and trying to avoid them ... we are nonetheless working our way through a mishmash of judgements, attitude formations, and behavioural decisions at a very everyday ordinary level and this is no different with fishing.

Hence I am not, by predilection, in the F M Halford camp. I do not believe that there is a single set of right ways to do things, and that this has been, or could be, codified for me. I find the idea that I don't need to think about things, simply refer to the code and do what it says, pretty stupid.

Now don't get me wrong, I am not arguing against clubs and fisheries having rules. For the benefit of the fish and hence of the members, there do have to be rules, and I am not preaching anarchy or setting myself up as, or encouraging you to be, some kind of scofflaw or outlaw. 'No nymphs before July 15' for me means precisely that, because it is a rule and I respect it. I find that easier, because it protects wild trout from excessive fishing pressure and repeated hookings. Let's not follow any false logic that says the trout aren't eating nymphs in the first half of the season – they eat far more of them then, simply because many times more nymphs are available then. In the second half of the season the nymphs have mostly hatched.

For me and I think for many others, fishing is more sporting if it is made up of lots of real decisions, and if those decisions follow speculations and past lessons learnt – if, that is, they result from a thoroughgoing campaign of trying to understand trout and fly. It isn't like golf. It is actually not capable of being done perfectly, if that isn't too crazy a thought. Even your tackle selections and constructions cannot end in perfection. There are just too many degrees of freedom in the behaviour and the response of trout to different presentations for there ever to be a single perfect way of delivering the fly, or a single perfect fly, or a single perfect strike or netting of the fish.

And of course the one thing that makes fly fishing for trout more sporting is when the fish you are trying to catch is a wild one. And it isn't a matter of size. David Beazley says that he doesn't want to fish for anything that isn't wild, and he doesn't want to catch anything that is. We were born only three days apart, but he's more mature than I am.

The wildness of the target fish by itself doesn't seem to maximise the sportingness of what you are doing. Whatever the historic exploits of Zane Grey and Ernest Hemingway, if the main reason why you catch a whacking great wild fish in the sea is because some sea-captain drove you out to the right spot in his boat, found the fish with a Fish Lo-K-Tor, and teased the fish up either with chum or with feather teasers, as far as I'm concerned you can keep it. The fishing I mean, not the fish. There are continuums here, not just of size, but also of wildness of the fish, and of how much you did it yourself or got spoonfed. As I said in chapter 11, any amount by which a fish's ability to be on the qui vive, to spot you, evade you or rumble your deceit is reduced, other than by your own success in hunting him, lessens the sportingness of what you are doing. But it doesn't necessarily reduce the fun, and you shouldn't hesitate to take a guide when it's clear you're going to need one – I don't. And being guided is always a major opportunity to learn how to find fish and fish better.

Veering off in a slightly different direction ... just in the same way as you are not worth much if all your attitudes are made for you and all your decisions are, too, you are also worth less if you do not have the means to enjoy and to learn from your memories. In a very real sense, you are your memories. Without them, you have as it were, minimized your window.

I relish my memories. It's one reason why I write. Of course, you get forgetful, but I find that diaries and pictures bring them back to life – like hot water on pot noodles only with more appetising results. Fuzzy, unaided memories may be better for some people but they are harder to bring to mind and learn from, mainly because one tends to remember the best bits and forget the problem areas. You remember the fish you caught but you mainly don't remember the fish you didn't catch, or why you didn't catch them. And those are the ones you learn from.

Without clear memories, not only am I without the full colour of the experience, but I lack the ability to learn from what I did or failed to do. You can be allowed to take note of the number and size of fish that you catch. But in addition you should count the fish you scare, fail to hook, and fail to land; permission to count fish has to be earned. Being an unthinking, non-learning fish-counter can also tend to make you worth less – more especially, worth less to your fishing friends.

Fishing friends, non-competitive friends that is, can help you to get it right and to become a better fisherman. They can help you to enjoy your memories, to fix them in your brain, and to learn from them. In a very practical sense, they can spot fish for you and put you into them – and you can do the same for them and please two people instead of just one. And on the whole you are nothing much if you are always alone. A good fisherman can bring interest, warmth, pleasure, stimulation, understanding and maybe even development to others. What is the point, if he doesn't? So fish with, and talk with, friends.

One of the things that makes fly fishing good is the way in which it takes you back to feelings that you may have last experienced in your childhood, when not just fishing but life itself was one long chain of not-entirely-planned happenings. This was the main learning curve of your life, some of it joyful and some less so.

I am sometimes tempted to use the term 'learning curve' when writing about fishing but I'm not sure of the existence of a permanent upward trend. I guess it is true that as you learn certain things (as for example in learning better knots), you do not in fact forget them and you do tend to incorporate them into the way in which you fish – so in that sense there is a learning curve and it does go upwards. The access to *savoir faire* about things like knots is incremental. But other mistakes that you make and therefore lessons that you might learn do not seem to be quite so additive. There are many mistakes that an angler makes which are easy to make again. Fly in the tree behind you is probably the classic. Well it is in my case.

An important issue is whether we allow these to frustrate us, or whether we take the view that they are just keeping us permanently young, in that youthful experimental and discovery mode, keeping our brains exercised and keeping the excitement in our lives. How dull it would be if we always got it completely right, every time we did something in fishing. Remember G E M Skues' old story about Canon Theodore Castwell. 'Hell!' he said. 'Yes, Hell,' said St Peter, as the umpteenth trout rose to his fly. Keep saying this stuff to yourself instead of swearing. I am youthful. I am experimental. I am learning. I am a child again.

And there is something attractive in learning, and in developing skills in an unstructured way. This is why many 'how to do it' angling books are soon left behind by most anglers – simply because they are essentially boring to somebody who has learned the basics. I suppose this is evidence of an upward trend to the learning curve, but I'm not sure how long the upward trend continues, after the fundamental methodologies and skills have been learnt. It is also a reason why all new fishing books have to struggle to get ahead of the rest, and most fail. Why so many have re-invented stuff that has been worked through long before.

Most anglers, even when experienced, still need constantly to improve, and hence to learn, and they still have an impetus to buy books that they think might help them. We are all familiar with the hindsight that goes with buying a book because you thought you might learn something from it, and then not really coming away from it any better equipped than we were before. But if learning is the reason why we are buying a book, it is going to have to help us think about fishing and fish, not just tell us how to do things.

It is better to teach a man to fish than to give a man a fish ... but it is even better to teach a man to think about how to fish. A book needs to lead us to insights and to our own experimentation and courses of incremental learning. It needs to give us ways of understanding what is going on which can be tailored to our own particular water and to our own particular fish

**Small wild trout, happy
domesticated man**

– but also be carried with us into new circumstances such as might crop up when we move to a new water or go on a fishing holiday. It needs to tell us as much about making mistakes as it does about doing it right.

Prescriptive, didactic books aren't all that much help to any angler who wants to progress and get better. Because the fishing that I most enjoy is not that which is practised to a formula, I don't really find myself sitting terribly well with any of the more authoritative and encyclopaedic angling authors. The books I feel I learn from are those by the thinkers.

Stories are good. Stories contain mistakes and surprises, and the best ones are usually remarkable for this. I always thought that they totally spoiled James Bond in the films when they stopped him making the mistakes that Fleming originally had him making in the books. With stories, you can see how people get to make mistakes, get it wrong, fail to catch fish, and hence either learn to do a better job yourself ... or at the very least enjoy the schadenfreude.

I'd like to be able to tell stories like Hemingway, Haig-Brown or Gierach. And I'd like to be able to think about fly fishing as penetratingly as Mottram, Skues, Marinaro, Sawyer, Proper, LaFontaine, or Leeson. But as long as I can keep thinking for myself, I'll be happy.

One story I like is a true one – I know, because I was there.

A group of members were having a final nightcap in the Flyfishers' Club after the end of the annual rummage sale. The auction had followed an excellent dinner, and the assembled company had launched into fishing war stories. One particular member told the tale of his greatest trout, and turning to David Beazley said, 'What's the biggest trout you've ever caught David?'

There was a short pause and a moment of anticipation before David replied, 'I'm not sure I remember. What's the tallest woman you've ever made love to?'

The art of self-management
Stephen Beville shows how getting in a zizz beats getting in a tizz

H M Bateman's cartoon, the frontispiece of R D Peck's book, *Fly-fishing for Duffers*

THE DUFFER—THE MAN WITHOUT SKILL OF HAND, WITHOUT GOOD EYESIGHT AND NO LONGER YOUNG—THE MAN WHO REALLY OUGHT TO FISH!

CAUDAL FIN

I HAVE IN MY library a book entitled *Fly-fishing for Duffers*. It was once owned by G E M Skues, which is maybe slightly ironical. Judging from its pristine state, I don't think he read it a lot – but it is nice that he had it. The author, R D Peck, writing in 1934, already at that time draws attention to the enormous number of books about fly fishing, almost all being books for the advanced: 'None of them dealt with the duffer, the man without skill of hand, without good eyesight and no longer young – the man who really ought to fish!'

Now, I readily admit that *this* book is not obviously a book for the duffer, either. Lots of it is pretty damned technical. It strays all over the place, from the history of fly fishing development to the detail of fly behaviour. And it draws a lot of often heretical conclusions about how best to design flies and how best to present them to fish.

And yet I should like to think that there are things about this book that may be helpful to fly fishermen in all stages of development. I hope it will be helpful to the advanced angler and the duffer alike, and helpful in two main ways.

Firstly, I hope that readers by following my argumentation will be stimulated to think for themselves about what we do when we fish the fly, rather than uncritically to accept the hand-me-down received wisdoms of the fishing world. I want you to send away to auction all the didactic, here's-the-right-way-to-do-it books that you own, just as I have done, and keep only the ones that embody thinking, learning, and experience and encourage those things in you. Including, hopefully, this one.

Secondly, this book bears a message to the duffer which is pretty consistent throughout, to the effect that – thanks to the preference of trout for flies that have got themselves into a mess when hatching – imprecise, oversized and half-sunk flies will get you success in spite of everything that has been written about precise imitation by people who have looked only at the emerged insect.

You absolutely don't have to be an entomologist in the taxonomical sense, able instantly to recognise and classify flies by their Latin names. Instead you have to have enough curiosity and interest to identify broad classes of aquatic insects and their behaviour. And if you are a lousy caster judged against the standards set by demonstrators at fly fairs, and your tippet falls in a heap instead of extending in a straight line, you will also catch more fish than they do.

But there is one positive thread which runs right the way through this book which I should like you to account as important – and which is equally relevant to the beginner and to the advanced angler alike. In letting ourselves drift into the conceptual box that we find it so hard to think outside, we have partly been seduced there by the ever-advancing technology of flies and tackle: seduced into thinking that they can do our job for us. As in all parts of human life, the incessant and indeed very welcome developments of technology have taken the drudgery, but also the skills, away from many of the things that we need to get done and also from things that that we take pleasure in doing, like fly fishing. This book suggests that we may have allowed those skills, and our ability to think about what we are doing, to be too much eroded for our own good.

Just about every development in flies and fly tackle, and many of the developments in technique over the last two centuries, have ended up with the angler's success depending more and more on the fly and on the tackle, and less and less on the angler. This process didn't start with the Dry Fly Revolution since the invention and mass production of silk lines and cane rods came earlier. But the new flies – my goodness, such good imitations were they – that all the angler had to do was to get them to the fish and the fish must take, so we were told or so we assumed as we lapped up the new writings. Better lines, better leaders, better flies, better rods, and better reels – yes, and false casting and floatants and the double-haul and non-wind-dependency – all made more effective fly fishing possible. And these were all hugely beneficial developments, they really were. But when we used them (such is human nature and the angler's hunger to catch fish) – when we used them to address fish at greater distances, we also forgot half of what our predecessors knew and, effectively, we distanced ourselves from the trout rather than making use of these advances to get us closer. Do we not frequently use our Polaroids to spot fish from further away rather than to watch fish more intensively at closer quarters? How many fish do we fail to catch because actually the fly that we cast to them is just too far away for us to see clearly what happened to it?

I just love technology, and it's good to use it, but sometimes I think it's lucky you can't shoot trout with a rifle.

Thus the pressure came on the tackle to deliver results that were harder and harder to achieve, and the sharpest focus of that pressure was on the fly. Tackle developments, the way we have used them, have actually made it increasingly less possible to see, evaluate and imitate the behaviour of the fly the fish is eating, and also harder to interpret the behaviour of the fish. The effectiveness of the fly in deceiving fish has come to be almost entirely dependent on its appearance, in other words on its colour, construction, and the exactness of its imitation (to our eyes) of the natural. It has to do all of the job of selling itself. This distancing of ourselves from our prey is not dissimilar in principle from the way in which organisations use technology to distance themselves from their customers by making use of remote call centres and by channelling all customer attempts to secure information and help to IT-driven, Internet-based, non-human relationships. These organisations think they are making gains in efficiency, but in fact, they are losing customers. Of course, anglers aren't going to do that precisely. The fish is real enough, and the connection, when and if it is made, is real enough too. But the slippery slope of self-delusion, to the effect that it must be better because it is cleverer, is exactly the same and we have slipped a little way down it. We could do with re-establishing a closer relationship with our customer. Closer to what our forbears had. So don't get sucked 'n' suckered too far down the must-have-tech route when getting good basic gear and concentrating on the fish in front of you would bring you more success and more satisfaction.

Advanced fly fishing will yet come to be defined in terms of improved presentation in its broadest sense – improved imitation by virtue of the angler better representing what a trout actually sees through his eyes and wants to eat, and offering it to the fish in ways that do a better job of mimicking the appearance and behaviour of his food.

There are many fly designs which succeed in this, some of my favourite dries are included in chapter 12, and nymphs in chapter 13. They include some complicated constructions but also some very simple ones. But if your time, patience, and curiosity are limited and you just want to get on and enjoy your fishing, then buy yourself a supply of Parachute Adams, Beacon Beige, F-Fly, Elk Hair Caddis, a good spinner pattern, Gold Ribbed Hare's Ear dry and nymph, and Pheasant Tail Nymphs with and without bead heads, in sizes 14 to 18. Find a feeding trout, and after doing your best to diagnose what he is feeding on and how, go and cast the likeliest fly at him loosely and without drag.

SELECT BIBLIOGRAPHY

MOST OF THE POST-1900 books are readily available from specialist booksellers. Many of the earlier and rarer works can also be accessed through – and downloaded from – websites such as Google Books and www.archive.org. John Denny is a good place to start, as he is the sort of straightforward poet it's easy to like and he takes you back a long way into the past, but Best, Cox, Blacker, Bowlker, Davy, Dewar, Francis, Hi-Regan, Mosely, Pritt, Ronalds, Salter, Stewart, Theakston, Venables, Walker, Walton, Younger and some of Halford's books are accessible in this way for a laptop browse.

Print-on-demand reprints of many of these can also be bought, but be aware that these may be incomplete and will certainly lack the colour plates that are such a beautiful feature of many early angling books. For a little more money there are the facsimile reprints published by the Flyfisher's Classic Library and the Easton Press. These are attractively bound, well illustrated, and usually have the advantage of extra material in the form of a scholarly introduction or essay by someone who ought to know what he is talking about.

If you have trouble finding any of these, talk to a specialist dealer (my publisher, Paul Morgan, would be a good start). Booksellers are happy to advise on the availability of out-of-print books – partly because they love to share their knowledge – but mostly in the hope that one day you will decide to treat yourself to one of their expensive antiquarian treasures!

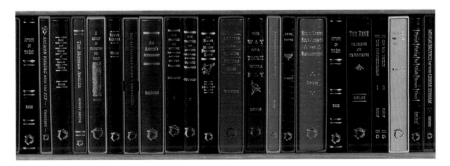

Allan, P. B. M., *Trout Heresy*, Philip Allan, London (1936).

Anon, *The North Country Angler*, Richardson, London (1786).

Arbona, Fred L. Jr., *Mayflies, the Angler and the Trout*,
    Winchester Press, New Jersey (1980).

Bainbridge, George, *The Fly Fisher's Guide*, Harris, Liverpool (1816).

Barker, Thomas, *The Art of Angling*, London (1651).

Beazley, David, *Images of Angling: An Illustrated Review of Three Centuries of Angling Prints*, Creel Press, Haslemere (2010).

Berners, Juliana (attributed), *The Treatyse of Fysshynge with an Angle*
    from *The Book of St Albans* (1496).

Best, Thomas, *A Concise Treatise on the Art of Angling*, London (1787).

Blacker, William, *The Art of Fly-Making*, published by the author, London (1842).

Bowlker, Richard and Charles, *The Art of Angling*, Birmingham (1774).

Chetham, James, *The Angler's Vade Mecum*, Thos. Bassett, London (1681)

Cholmondeley-Pennell, Harry, *The Badminton Library, Fishing: Salmon and Trout*,
    Longmans, Green, London (1889 fifth edition).

Cotton, Charles, *Instructions How to Angle for a Trout or Grayling in a Clear Stream*, in
    Izaak Walton's *The Complete Angler: Second Part*, (1676 fifth edition).

Cox, Nicholas, *The Gentleman's Recreation. Part Four: Fishing*, London (1674).

Cutter, Ralph, *Fish Food: A Fly Fisher's Guide to Bugs and Bait*,
    Stackpole Books, Mechanicsburg PA (2003).

Daniel, George, *Dynamic Nymphing*, Stackpole Books, Mechanicsburg PA (2012).

Davy, Sir Humphrey, *Salmonia or Days of Fly Fishing*, Murray, London (1828).

Dennys, John, *Secrets of Angling*, London (1613).

Dewar, George A. B., *The Book Of The Dry Fly*, Lawrence & Bullen, London (1897).

Dunne, J. J., *How and Where to Fish in Ireland, by 'Hi-Regan,'*
    Sampson Low, London (1904 eighth edition).

Dunne, J. W., *Sunshine and the Dry Fly*, Black, London, (1924).

Edye, Huish, *The Angler and the Trout*, Black, London (1941).

Edwards, Oliver, *Oliver Edwards' Flytyer's Masterclass*, Merlin Unwin, Ludlow (1994).

Engle, Ed, *Fishing Small Flies*, Stackpole Books, Mechanicsburg PA (2004).

Fitzgibbon, Edward, *A Handbook of Angling*, Longman, London (1847).

Foster, David, *The Scientific Angler*, Bemrose, London & Derby (1882).

Frake, Allan & Hayes, Peter, *The Millennium Fly Abundance Survey* (2000).

Francis, Francis, *A Book on Angling*, Longmans, London (1867).

Gierach, John, *Good Flies*, Lyons Press, New York (2000).

Gierach, John, *Another Lousy Day in Paradise*, Simon & Schuster, New York (1996).

Gingrich, Arnold, *The Fishing in Print*, Winchester Press, New York (1974).

Goddard, John, *Trout Fly Recognition*, Black, London (1966).

Goddard, John & Clarke, Brian, *The Trout and the Fly*, Benn, London (1980).

Grey, Sir Edward, *Fly Fishing*, Dent, London (1899).

Halford, Frederic M., *Floating Flies and How to Dress Them*, Sampson Low, London (1886).

Halford, Frederic M., *May-fly Fishing*, A chapter in *The Badminton Library, Fishing: Salmon and Trout*, Longmans, Green, London (1889 fifth edition).

Halford, Frederic M., *Dry-Fly Fishing in Theory and Practice*, Sampson Low, London (1889).

Halford, Frederic M., *Modern Development of the Dry Fly*, Routledge, London (1910).

Halford, Frederic M., *The Dry Fly Man's Handbook*, Routledge, London (1913).

Hall, H. S., *Chalk-Stream Fishing with the Dry Fly*, A chapter in *The Badminton Library, Fishing: Salmon and Trout*, Longmans, Green, London (1885).

Harding, Col. E. W., *The Fly Fisher and the Trout's Point of View*, Seeley Service, London (1931).

Harrop, René *Learning from the Water*, Stackpole Books, Mechanicsburg PA (2010).

Harvey, George, *Techniques of Trout Fishing and Fly Tying*, Pennsylvania Fish Commission, Harrisburg PA (1976).

Hayter, Tony. *F M Halford and the Dry Fly Revolution*, Hale, London (2002).

Heddon, Jack, *Scotcher Notes*, Honey Dun Press, London (1975).

Herd, Dr Andrew N., *The Fly*, Medlar Press, Ellesmere (2001).

Herd, Dr Andrew N., *The History of Fly Fishing*, Medlar Press, Ellesmere (2011).

Hewitt, Edward Ringwood, *A Trout and Salmon Fisherman for Seventy Five Years*, Scribner's, New York (1948).

Hills, John Waller, *A History of Fly Fishing for Trout*, Philip Allan, London (1921).

Hills, John Waller, *A Summer on the Test*, Philip Allan, London (1924).

Hills, John Waller, *River Keeper*, Geoffrey Bles, London (1934).

Humphreys, Joe, *Joe Humphreys's Trout Tactics*, Stackpole Books, Mechanicsburg PA (1981).

Jackson, John, *The Practical Fly-Fisher: More Particularly for Grayling or Umber*, Farlow, London & Swallow, Leeds (1854).

Judy, John, *Slack Line Strategies for Fly Fishing*, Stackpole Books, Mechanicsburg PA (1994).

Kissane, Joseph, *Drag Free Drift: Leader Design and Presentation Techniques for Fly Fishing*, Stackpole Books, Mechanicsburg PA (2001).

LaFontaine, Gary, *The Dry Fly: New Angles*, Greycliff, Helena, MT (1990).

Lawton, Terry, *Marryat: Prince of Fly Fishers. The Life and Times of George Selwyn Marryat*, Medlar Press, Ellesmere (2010).

Lawton, Terry, *Nymph Fishing: A History of the Art and Practice*, Swan Hill Press, Shrewsbury (2005).

Leeson, Ted & Schollmeyer, Jim, *The Fly Tier's Benchside Reference*,
    Amato, Portland OR (1998).

Marinaro, Vincent, *In the Ring of the Rise*, Crown, New York (1976).

Marinaro, Vincent, *A Modern Dry-fly Code*, Putnam's, New York (1950).

Markham, Gervase, *The Second Book of the English Husbandman*, London (1614).

Martin, Darrell, *Fly-Tying Methods*, Nick Lyons, New York (1987).

Martin, Darrell, *Micropatterns*, Lyons & Burford, New York (1994).

Martin, Darrell, *The Fly-Fisher's Craft: The Art and History*,
    Lyons Press, Guilford CT (2006).

Martin, James, *The Angler's Guide*, Cox, London (1854).

Mascall, Leonard, *A Booke of Fishing with Hooke and Line*, London (1590).

Mosely, Martin E., *The Dry-Fly Fisherman's Entomology*, Routledge, London (1921).

Mosely, Martin E., *Insect Life and the Management of a Trout Fishery*,
    Routledge, London (1926).

Mottram, James C., *Fly-Fishing: Some New Arts and Mysteries*, Field & Queen, London (1915).

Mottram, James C., *Thoughts on Angling*, Herbert Jenkins, London (1948).

Patterson, Neil, *Chalkstream Chronicle: Living Out the Flyfisher's Fantasy*, Merlin
    Unwin, Ludlow (1995).

Peck, R. D., *Fly Fishing for Duffers*, Black, London (1934).

Proper, Datus, *What the Trout Said: About the Design of Trout Flies and other Mysteries*,
    Knopf, New York (1982).

Ogden, James, *Ogden on Fly Tying*, John Norman, Cheltenham (1879).

Overfield, T. Donald, *G. E. M Skues: The Way of a Man with a Trout*,
    Ernest Benn, London (1977).

Pritt, Thomas E., *North Country Flies*, Sampson Low, London (1886). Originally
    published as *Yorkshire Trout Flies*, Goodall & Suddick, Leeds (1885).

Pulman, George P. R., *Vade Mecum of Fly-Fishing for Trout*, Wills, Axminster (1841).

Ritz, Charles, *A Fly Fisher's Life: The Art and Mechanics of Fly Fishing*,
    Max Reinhardt, London (1959).

Robson, Kenneth, editor, *The Essential G. E. M. Skues*, Black, London (1998).

Ronalds Alfred, *The Fly-Fisher's Entomology*, Longman, London (1836).

Salter, Robert, *The Modern Angler*, Salter, Oswestry, (1811).

Sandford, Chris, *Flytyers' Flies: The Flies that Catch Fish*, Medlar Press, Ellesmere (2009).

Sawyer, Frank, *Nymphs and the Trout*, Stanley Paul, London (1958).

Schollmeyer, Jim & Leeson, Ted, *Tying Emergers*, Amato, Portland, OR (2004).

Schullery, Paul, *American Fly Fishing: A History*, Nick Lyons, New York (1987).

Schullery, Paul, *Fly-Fishing Secrets Of The Ancients: A Celebration of Five Centuries of
    Lore and Wisdom*, University of New Mexico Press (2009).

Schullery, Paul, *The Rise: Streamside Observations on Trout, Flies, and Fly Fishing,* Stackpole Books, Mechanicsburg PA (2006).

Schwiebert, Ernest, *Trout,* Dutton, New York (1978).

Scotcher, George, *The Fly Fisher's Legacy,* Chepstow (circa 1810).

Shipley, William, *A True Treatise On the Art of Fly-fishing, Trolling, etc.,* Edited by Edward Fitzgibbon, Simpkin, London (1838).

Skues, G. E. M., *Minor Tactics of the Chalk Stream and Kindred Studies,* Black, London (1910).

Skues, G. E. M., *The Way Of a Trout with a Fly,* Black, London (1921).

Skues, G. E. M., *Side-lines, Side-lights, and Reflections: Fugitive Papers of a Chalk-Stream Angler,* Black, London (1932).

Skues, G. E. M., *Nymph Fishing for Chalk Stream Trout,* Black, London (1939).

Skues, G. E. M., *Silk, Fur and Feather,* The Fishing Gazette, Beckenham (1950).

Stewart, William C., *The Practical Angler: Or The Art of Trout Fishing, More Particularly Applied to Clear Water,* Black, Edinburgh (1857).

Swisher, Doug & Richards, Carl, *Selective Trout,* Crown, New York (1971).

Swisher, Doug & Richards, Carl, *Emergers,* Lyons & Burford, New York (1991).

Taverner, John, *Certaine Experiments Concerning Fishe and Fruite,* London (1600).

Theakston, Michael, *British Angling Flies,* Simpkin, London & Harrison, Ripon (1862). Originally published as *A List Of Flies That Are Taken By Trout, Grayling And Smelt, In The Streams Of Ripon,* Harrison, Ripon (1853).

Thomassen, Arlen, *Bugwater: A fly fisher's look through the seasons at bugs in their aquatic habitat and the fish that eat them,* Stackpole Books, Mechanicsburg PA (2010).

Turing, H. D., *Trout Problems,* Black, London (1948).

Venables, Robert, *The Experienced Angler,* Marriot, London (1662).

Voss Bark, Conrad, *A History of Fly Fishing,* Merlin Unwin, Ludlow (1992).

Walbran, Francis M., *Grayling and How to Catch Them,* The Angler, Scarborough (1895).

Walker, Charles E., *Old Flies in New Dresses,* Lawrence & Bullen, London (1898).

Walker, C. F., *The Angling Letters of G. E. M. Skues,* Black, London (1956).

Walker, C. F., *The Complete Fly-Fisher,* Herbert Jenkins, London (1963).

Walton, Izaak, *The Compleat Angler,* Marriot, London (1653).

Ward, Francis, *Marvels of Fish Life: As Revealed by the Camera,* Cassell, London (1911).

Ward, Francis, *Animal Life Underwater,* Cassell, London (1919).

West, Leonard, *The Natural Trout Fly and its Imitation: Being an Angler's Record of Insects seen at the Waterside and the Method of Making their Imitations,* published by the author, St. Helens (1912).

Williams, A. Courtney, *A Dictionary of Trout Flies: And of Flies for Sea-Trout and Grayling,* Black, London (1949).

Worlidge, John, *Systema Agriculturae: The Mystery of Husbandry Discovered*, Johnson, London (1669).

Wright, Leonard M, Jr, *Fishing the Dry Fly as a Living Insect*, Dutton, New York (1972).

Younger, John, *On River Angling for Salmon and Trout, More Particularly as Practiced on the Tweed and its Tributaries*, Blackwood, Edinburgh (1840).

REFERENCES FROM JOURNALS, WEBSITES AND OTHER SOURCES

Barton, E. A., *The Loaded Nymph*, Flyfishers' Club Journal, Autumn 1929.

Beazley, David, *The Saga of the 'Snecky Limerick,'*
Flyfishers' Club Journal, Summer/Winter 1995.

Benn, Timothy, *Missing the Flight*, Fly Fishing & Fly Tying, October 2011.

Christie, Roy, (*Reversed parachute flies*), website: *www.reversedparachutes.com.*

Eaton, Rev. A. E., *Revisional Monograph of Recent Ephemeridae or Mayflies*, 1883.

Eaton, Rev. A. E., *Note of Baetis rhodani imagos crawling underwater*,
Entomological Society Notes, 1865.

Griffiths, Terry, *The 'Portmanteau' of George Selwyn Marryat*,
Flyfishers' Club Journal, Summer 2009.

Hall, H. S., *The Birth of the Dry Fly, Parts 1 & 2*, The Fishing Gazette, March 1883.

Heddon, Jack, *Two articles on dry and wet fly fishing*,
Fly Dressers Guild Newsletter, 1980.

Herd, Dr Andrew N., *A Fly Fishing History*, website: www.flyfishinghistory.com.

Kimmins, D. E., *Under-water Emergence of the Sub-imago of Heptagenia Lateralis*, The Entomologist, August 1941.

Marryat, George S., (*Newly invented double split-wing tying method*),
Private Letter to H. S. Hall, November 1882 in Ward, Simon J., (see below).

Mosely, Martin E., *The Ephemerid Nymph at its Last Moult*,
Flyfishers' Club Journal, 1939-40.

Mottram, James C., *A Right and Left at Humbugs*,
Flyfishers' Club Journal, Autumn 1915.

Sanctuary, Dr Thomas, (*Letter about duck preen gland*), The Fishing Gazette, 1924.

Schullery, Paul, *History and Mr Gordon*, in The American Fly Fisher,
Volume 28 No 1, Winter 2002.

Skues, G. E. M., (as Seaforth & Soforth in H. S. Hall's obituary), (*Dating of Marryat's Portmanteau and its flies and hooks*), Salmon & Trout Magazine, June 1934.

Skues, G. E. M., (as Seaforth & Soforth), *The Portmanteau; or 'George Selwyn Marryat – his Book,'* Flyfishers' Club Journal, sequential issues 1923.

Ward, Richard, website, (*Dry fly only rule started on Derbyshire Wye*), website: www.dryflyexpert.blogspot.com.

Ward, Simon J., *George Selwyn Marryat Remembered,* website: www.catchtheimage.com.

Wild Trout Trust, *Wild Trout Survival Guide,* website: www.wildtrout.org.

Additional Thanks

Paul Morgan of Coch-y-Bonddu Books and I have known each other for a very long time, regularly seeing each other at shows on his sporting books stand, and chatting at Grayling Society Symposia, Wild Trout Trust events and so on. We have never fished together, something you could put down to what the scientists would call spatial and temporal separation – and that's a shame. We do however pretty much know where each of us is coming from. When I told him about this book and asked him if he would be interested in publishing it, I was just delighted when he agreed – and even more pleased as the project moved forward.

What I didn't know was that I would be given the unstinting services of two such brilliant and insightful people as Paul Curtis the managing editor of this book, and Pete MacKenzie its designer. It would be fair to say that they have both leapt to appreciate both the general drift of the book and its many nuances, and together with Paul Morgan have hugely contributed to its fruition in the great shape you find it in. None of them changed it very much (for which I am supremely grateful) but they certainly improved it terrifically and I'm even more thankful for that.

ABOUT THE AUTHOR

I was originally an archaeologist, ancient historian, ancient linguist and (very bad) philosopher who studied in Jerusalem, Jordan, and Oxford. Reading Literae Humaniores (Greats) I was welcomed as a scholar to St Edmund Hall by our Visitor, Harold Macmillan, the British Prime Minister. In his much-parodied patrician accents he declamed: 'Ah, my boy, nothing that you learn here will be of any use whatsoever to you in future life ... except this: you will always be able to tell when someone is talking rot.' He was right.

I then spent 35 years in management, first in Unilever and then in WPP Group, the global marketing services conglomerate. I specialised in Marketing and Marketing Research, and spent nine years as Chairman of a subsidiary before retiring in 1998.

Since then I have been doing pro bono work for local and national ecological organisations, focussing on rivers, invertebrates, fish and other wildlife. This has included setting up the National Fly Abundance Survey with the Environment Agency and the Salmon and Trout Association, and a long running campaign with the Wiltshire Fishery Association and others to reduce chalk aquifer abstraction, as well as work on other issues including diffuse pollution.

I was involved with the EA and Natural England in setting up the Sites of Special Scientific Interest and the European Special Areas of Conservation on the Rivers Wylye and Till. Together with colleagues I have spent a lot of time on restoration work, covering seven miles of the former and three miles of the latter, directing diggers, banging in stakes and weaving willow to re-energise the river and encourage it to re-naturalise itself after suffering at the hand of man. Much of this seems to have worked.

I have written a few articles for *Fly Fishing And Fly Tying* magazine and for *Salmo Trutta*, the iconic publication of the Wild Trout Trust, where I am on the Executive Board.

I have fished in some of the 'before you die' places around the world and currently I go hunting big trout in Iceland and New Zealand every year. I have spent 30 years on the trout streams of England, chalk and limestone spring creeks, and made a dozen long visits to similar spring creeks in New Zealand, getting feedback from trout.

For recreation, I fish, photograph wildlife and support my wife Di in competitive carriage driving. We have two grown-up children and one granddaughter, six dogs, two cats, three horses, and a fair number of fish.

INDEX

A

Abbotts Barton 194, 211
ACE 183
Adams 29, 105, 135, 137–8, 256
Agapetus 183
Airflo polyleaders 78
Airflo Ridge line 123
Allan, P B M 167
Angler Monitoring Initiative 133, 168
Anthropomorphising 108
Anton, River 151, 155
Anusol 94–95
Arbona, Fred L Jr. 28, 45, 65, 102, 153
Avon, River 33, 97, 114, 171

B

Bainbridge, George 229
Bakewell 59, 123, 230
Ball, Sir Joseph 208
Barker, Thomas 48, 203, 220–1
Barrett, Cosmo 59
Barrett's Bane 59
Barrett's Professor 59
Barton, Dr E A 194, 208, 211
Bateman, H M 252
Beacon Beige 256
Beaverkill, River 45
Beazley, David 15, 217, 220, 247, 250
Beck, Barry and Cathy 186
Bennett, Dr Cyril 15, 34, 36, 132, 171
Berners, Dame Juliana 12, 217, 230

Best, Thomas 48, 53, 220, 222–4,
    226–9, 233, 257
Bewl Bridge Reservoir 175
Bird's Nest 175, 184
Black-cadder 149–150
Blacker, William 15, 40, 45, 48, 220, 257
Blythe, River 101
Bond, James 250
Bourne, River 85, 87, 131, 211
Bow-tie Buzzer 172
Bowlker, Richard and Charles 42, 48–
    9, 51–2, 90, 220, 222, 233, 257
Brachycentrus 164, 184
Brook Dun 30, 61
Bucknall, Geoffrey 175, 242

C

Carshalton Dodge 56
CdC 9, 27, 32, 92, 97, 146–9, 151–2, 175
CdC and Elk 175
Chetham 48, 220–1
Christie, Roy 155, 195
Chung, Rim 193
Clarke, Brian 105, 121–2, 191
Collins, Dave 15, 166
Coot.com 150
Copperknob 161
Cotton, Charles 48, 81, 220–1, 223,
    226, 228
Cox, Nicholas 226, 257
Cressbrook and Litton FFC 185

Crofts, Stuart 15, 36, 39, 79–80, 124,
    148, 160, 170, 175–6, 180, 183,
    188, 192–3, 197, 239–40
Crowe, John 100
Cutter, Ralph 37, 86–7, 100–1, 105,
    184, 193

D

Daniel, George 236
Darent, River 242
Darwinism 208
Dave's Bug Flote 92, 152
Davy, Sir Humphrey 175, 229, 257
Deep Sparkle Pupa 175
Dennys, John 118–119, 224–225, 229
Derbyshire 27, 38, 54, 58–9, 62, 70,
    106, 112–13, 123, 133, 148, 150,
    161, 171, 185, 218, 229
Detached Badger 190–1
Devi-ant 154
Dewar, George A B 213, 257
DNA analysis 130
Dovedale 54
Driffield Angler 59
Dry Fly Man's Handbook 33, 205, 214
Dunne, J J (Hi-Regan) 91

E

Eaton, Rev A E 195, 212
Eden, River 46, 162, 218
Edwards, Oliver 25, 79–80, 161, 180,
    195, 197, 200
Egyptian Goose 213
Engle 186, 239
Environment Agency 127, 132–3, 167,
    171, 264

Evans, James 59

F

F-Fly 256
Farlows 213, 242
Field 208
Fish Lo-K-Tor 247
Fishing Gazette 59, 96–7, 208
Fitzgibbon 218, 229
Flyfishers' Club 15, 99, 186, 208, 210,
    231–3, 244, 250
Flyfishers' Club Journal 28, 59, 109,
    205, 227
Foster, David 59, 218, 235
Fox, Pat 192
Frake, Dr Allan 167
Francis, Francis 87, 109, 220, 233, 257
Frome, River 96, 114
Funneldun 105

G

Galhardo, Daniel 236
Galloup, Kelly 188
Gam 'R Us 162
Gaskell, Paul 193
Gawesworth, Simon 78
Gay, John 48, 220, 227
Gentleman's Illustrated Album of
    Fashion 212
Gierach, John 20, 105, 186, 239, 250
Gingrich, Arnold 54
Gink 92
GISSO 7, 48, 101
Goddard, John 105, 121–2, 175, 186,
    191, 241
Great Red Spinner 195

Greenwell's Glory 135
Grey, Sir Edward 68
Grey Duster 135, 137–8
Grey, Zane 247
Griffiths, Terry 232
Gudmundur 186

H

Haig-Brown, Roderick L 250
Halford, Frederic M H 8, 12, 17–18,
      27–30, 33, 35, 45, 49, 53, 56, 66,
      79, 90, 95–6, 99, 101, 104, 149,
      165, 177, 180, 190–1, 204214,
      217–19, 231, 233, 240, 246, 257
Hall H S 27, 58, 95, 191, 214, 231, 233,
      264
Hallam, Clive 15, 105, 136–7, 148
Harding, Col E W 102
Hardy Sintrix 187
Harrop, René 124–125
Harvey, George W. 78, 87, 100
Hawkins, Sir John 221, 223
Hayestuck 10, 27, 32, 146–7, 151, 155
Hayter, Tony 15, 18, 30, 79–80, 96–7,
      194, 210, 217, 219
Heddon, Jack 15, 52, 217, 219, 221–2, 233
Hemingway, Ernest 247, 250
Hendrickson 103
Henry's Fork 57–8, 61, 124
Herd, Dr Andrew 15, 25, 52, 101, 109,
      217, 230
Hewitt, Edward Ringwood 21
Hi-Regan 91, 257
Hills, J W 49, 54–5, 117, 171, 209, 219,
      230, 235
Holland, George 214, 231, 233
Horsfall-Turner, Eric 86

Hoskuldsson, Bjarni 182
Humphreys, Joe 78
Hyam 212
Hydropsyche 184

I

Images of Angling 220
Impey, Andrew 30, 115–16
Itchen, River 2, 19, 28, 30–1, 36, 38–
      39, 58, 74, 96, 115, 129–30, 133,
      153, 160, 173, 192, 204
Itchen Nymph 160

J

Jackson, John 59
Judy, John 79, 163

K

Kell, James 103–4
Kimmins, D E 37, 45
Kissane, Joseph A 78
Kite's Imperial 135–36
Klinkhamer 58, 152
KmC 27, 32, 83–4, 93, 148

L

LaFontaine, Gary 45, 99, 101, 103–5,
      123, 136–7, 141, 175, 184, 250
Lambroughton, David 163
Laming, Percy 99–100
Lapsley, Peter 2, 15, 19, 219
Last Chance 124
Laxa, River 43, 112, 178, 180, 182–3,
      185–6, 200

Leckford Professor 59
Leeson, Ted 25, 116, 250
Leeson & Schollmeyer 25
Little Red Sedge 175
Lobachevsky 135, 137
Lunn, William James 117, 149, 171

M

Macedonia 55, 237
Mackie, Gordon 133, 198
Mackintosh, Alexander 59
Madison, River 117, 163
Marinaro, Vincent 27, 68, 83, 98–9,
    101–3, 143, 152, 250
Markham, Gervase 48, 220–1
Marryat, George Selwyn 17, 27, 33, 79,
    95, 165, 206, 213–14, 231–3
Marston, R B 208
Martin, Darrel 186
Martin, James 230
Mascall, Leonard 48, 220
Mason hard monofilament 78
Masters, Lindsay 151
Mataura, River 44, 161, 174, 177
Maxima 78, 100
MCJ 159, 162, 176–7
McManus, Patrick F 245
Mealing, Owain 15, 42, 118, 151, 196–7,
    199, 202–3
Measham, Nick 197
Michigan 45
Midriff Copper John 159, 177
Milligan, Spike 21
Monsal Dale 106, 185
Mosely, Martin E 45, 194, 210, 257
Mottram, Dr James C 35–6, 101, 165,
    209, 250

Mucilin 91
Muskrax 10, 143–145

N

Nadder, River 97
Natural Fly Subcommittee 208–10
Natural History Museum 194
Nemoura 50
New Zealand 20, 38, 44, 62, 68, 87,
    114–15, 121, 123, 149, 161, 178, 264
Nicolls, Rev E 214
North Country Angler 165, 227
Nymphae Marryat 213

O

Ogden, James 59, 218, 230, 235
'Ookey Rat 151, 172
Orange Quill 135, 137

P

Palmer-worms 223
Parachute Adams 29, 105, 137–8, 256
Paraloop 139, 143
Patagonia 161
Patrick, Chris 114–15
Patterson, Neil 105, 162, 191–2
Peck, R D 252–3
Peeping Caddis 161, 164, 185
Pollard, J 220
Pretty Polly 192
Pritt 59, 257
Proper, Datus C 20, 89, 99, 101, 103,
    143, 152, 250
Pulman, George P R 230, 235

R

Reversed PhD 143
Reversed Kiss my Cul 148
Ritz, Charles 2, 76
Riverfly Partnership 36
Ronalds, Alfred 48–50, 58, 91, 101–2,
    107–9, 220, 224–5, 229–30, 233,
    257
Royal Wulff 105, 135–136
RS2 193

S

Saint Vrain River 239
Salmon & Trout Magazine 209, 235
Salmon and Trout Association 132, 264
Salter, Robert 52, 223, 257
Sanctuary, Dr Thomas 27, 96–7, 214,
    231
Sawyer, Frank 34, 36–7, 79, 95, 156,
    159, 172, 179, 192–3, 214, 250
Sawyer, Nick 15, 34, 156, 214
Schollmeyer, Jim 25
Schullery, Paul 15, 25, 52, 55, 65, 86,
    101, 105, 217
Schwarzenegger 75, 79
Schwiebert, Ernest 55
Scotcher, George 48, 220, 222, 227
Scott of the Antarctic 211
Senior, William 204, 208
Services Dry Fly Fishing
    Association 79
Sexyloops 155
Sheffield School 193
Shipley, William 59, 218, 229
Simmons, Adrian 126
Sites Of Special Scientific Interest 133

Skues, C A M 210
Skues, G E M 17–18, 28, 35, 39, 48,
    59, 64–6, 68, 72, 87, 101, 104,
    109, 117, 165, 177, 194–5, 204–5,
    208–10, 212, 214, 227, 230–1, 233,
    235, 242, 249–50, 253
Slovenia 237
Special Areas Of Conservation 133
Spinnermalist 149, 173–4, 188, 192–3
Steingrimsson, Asgeir 182
Stephens, Taff 94
Stewart, W C 52, 105, 257
Stiltwalker 182
Studdy, G E 244
Stulta 182, 185
Sturgeon, Nigel 57, 108
Sundridge 242
Swisher and Richards 27

T

Tambour, Wolfgang 159
Taverner, Eric 25
Taverner, John 40
Teeny, Jim 79, 123
Tenkara 13, 81, 198, 218, 236–40,
    242–3
Test, River 36, 54, 58, 97, 129–30, 167,
    171
Theakston, Michael 59, 257
Thomson, James (poet) 226
Tiemco 92, 139, 178
Tongariro River 161, 241
Torrentis sampling net 124
Trout Hunter Lodge 124
Tummel 194
Tups Indispensable 135
Turle knot 95

Turle, Major W G 95
Tweed, River 194
Tyjas, Pete 124

U

USD PhD 142–3
Usk, River 42–4, 60, 112, 151, 162, 166,
    172, 195

V

Veitch, Rev H 233
Velikanov, Andrej 108–9
Venables, Colonel Robert 48, 52, 54,
    105, 220–1, 229, 233, 257
Vines, Major Sidney 95–6
von Kienbusch, Otto 210
Voss Bark, Conrad 52

W

Waitangitaona, River 200
Walker, C F 86
Walker, Charles E 208–11, 257
Walker, Dick 114
Walton, Izaak 221, 223, 225, 257
Wandle, River 56
Ward, Dr Francis 87, 109
Ward, Richard 15, 123, 217, 230, 232
Ward, Simon J. 232
Water Framework Directive 171
Waters, Jeremy 67–8, 87, 94, 185
Watkins, P Morgan 209
Wells, Tony 15, 79, 193
Wey, River 171
Wharfe, River 36
Wickham's Fancy 135, 137

Wild Trout Survival Guide 128
Wild Trout Trust 23, 84, 128–9, 131,
    193, 264
Williams, Courtney 15, 33
Wilson, Dermot 192
Wilton Fly Fishing Club 22, 68, 94,
    126, 198, 233–4, 245–6
Windebank, Jamie 126
World Fly Fishing Championships 240
Worlidge, John 225
Wotton, Davy 175
Wright, Leonard M, Jr 55, 240
Wye, River (Derbyshire) 58–9, 62, 70,
    106, 112–13, 123, 150, 171, 185
Wylye, River 46, 94, 97, 110–11,
    114–16, 126, 129–30, 133, 150,
    179, 189, 197–8, 241, 264

Y

Yamame trout 240
Yellow Breeches 103
Yellow Sally 229
Yellowstone, River 45, 124, 178
Younger, John 35, 42, 165, 257

Z

Zebra Midge 180